Making Sense of Iranian Society, Culture, and Business

Hamid Yeganeh

Making Sense of Iranian Society, Culture, and Business

First published in 2015 by
Business Expert Press, LLC
222 East 46th Street, New York, NY 10017
www.businessexpertpress.com

ISBN-13: 978-1-60649-598-8 (paperback)
ISBN-13: 978-1-60649-599-5 (e-book)

Business Expert Press International Business Collection

Collection ISSN: 1948-2752 (print)
Collection ISSN: 1948-2760 (electronic)

Cover and interior design by Exeter Premedia Services Private Ltd., Chennai, India

First edition: 2015

10 9 8 7 6 5 4 3 2 1

Printed in the United States of America.

Abstract

Iran represents a large and emerging economy with a strategic location extending from the Persian Gulf to Central Asia, a huge consumer market, tremendous natural resources, and numerous petrochemical and manufacturing industries, which require heavy investment and development. Understanding the Iranian business environment requires a holistic approach as in Iran society, culture, religion, economy, politics, and family are intimately intertwined. For this reason, the book adopts a broad scope and relies on a wide range of academic and professional resources to bring insights into the Iranian context. It tries to bridge theory and practice by offering a reasonable blend of academic perspective and practical expertise. It aims at offering an analytical, readable, quite comprehensive, and supposedly impartial account. This book consists of 14 chapters organized in two parts. Part 1 touches upon the broader social and historical conditions and moves progressively from the physical geography and current issues to sociopolitical system and geopolitical environment. Part 2 is devoted to more practical topics including Iran's national culture, negotiation and communication styles, economic system, energy market, nonoil sectors, business environment, and consumer behavior. While the chapters are interrelated, they stand fairly distinct from each other and offer the convenience of being consulted separately.

This book is a valuable reference for business managers, investors, analysts, policy makers, scholars, students, expatriates, travelers, and all those who are concerned with the Iranian affairs.

Keywords

Central Asia, emerging markets, international business, international management, Iran, Iranian culture, Iranian economy, Middle East, Persian Gulf

Contents

Introduction

After the Islamic Revolution of 1979, Iran underwent profound socio-political changes, took a radical ideological and revolutionary discourse, distanced itself from the international community, and ultimately slid in isolation and disregard. The image of Iran as portrayed by the Western media, and even as displayed by the Islamic Republic outlets, is tinted with radical frenzy. The word Iran often triggers multiple connotations of authoritarian rule, Islamic law, theocracy, war, conflict, instability, and antagonism. These associations and impressions may be factual, but they are naïve and partial narratives that do not tell the whole story. Beyond the myopic image of the media, under the heavy veil of isolation, and behind the revolutionary discourse of ruling clerics, there is a vibrant culture, a sizeable economy, and a buoyant population. Despite the decades of international sanctions, Iran is still the 19th largest economy of the world and is recognized as one of the most stable and influential countries of the Middle East. The country represents a large regional economy with a strategic location in the Persian Gulf and Central Asia, a huge consumer market, tremendous natural resources, and numerous industries that require hefty investment and development. Iran is rather a complex and puzzling country with a diverse population and a peculiar, ancient, and boisterous history. Iran is located in the Middle East but lies at the crossroads of Asian civilizations. It is overwhelmingly Muslim but differs from many other Muslim countries. It has been torn and split between the West and the East but has never been colonialized. Iran is the distinct land of Aryans among the Arabs, Indians, Turks, and Europeans. It is a multifaceted, sophisticated, and paradoxical nation.

This book is designed to provide a better understanding of Iran; its society, culture, and business altogether. Understanding the country requires a holistic approach as in Iran religion, society, culture, economy, politics, and family are intimately intertwined. For this reason, the book adopts a broad scope and relies on a wide range of academic and professional resources to bring insights into the Iranian context. It tries to bridge theory and practice by offering a reasonable blend of academic perspective and practical expertise. It aims at offering an analytical, readable, relatively comprehensive, and supposedly impartial account. This book can be considered as a valuable reference for business managers, political analysts, policy makers, scholars, students, and all those who are concerned with the Iranian affairs.

The present volume consists of 14 chapters organized in two parts. Part 1 touches upon the broader social and historical conditions and moves progressively from the physical geography and current issues to sociopolitical system and geopolitical environment. Part 2 is devoted to more practical topics including national culture, negotiation and communication styles, economic system, energy market, nonoil sectors, business environment, and consumer behavior. While the chapters are interrelated, they stand relatively distinct from each other and offer the convenience of being consulted separately.

PART 1

Making Sense of Iranian Society

CHAPTER 1

Iran and Iranians

Physical Geography

Iran or Persia is located in southwest Asia. As shown in Figure 1.1, Iran shares land and sea borders with 15 countries; land borders with seven countries namely Armenia (35 km), Azerbaijan (611 km), Turkmenistan (992 km), Turkey (499 km), Iraq (1,458 km), Afghanistan (936 km), and Pakistan (909 km); and sea borders with eight countries including Kuwait, Saudi Arabia, Bahrain, Qatar, the United Arab Emirates, and Oman in the Persian Gulf and Kazakhstan and Russia in the Caspian Sea.[1] With an area of 1,648,000 square kilometers, Iran is ranked 16th in size among the countries of the world. Iran is highly diverse, especially in topography and climate. It comprises 14 percent arable land, 8 percent forest, 55 percent nonarable pastures, and 23 percent desert. Iran is one of the most mountainous countries of the world and hence major cities, including the capital, Tehran, are located in the foothills. The country has two main mountain chains surrounding the central Iranian plateau. Lowland areas are mainly along the Caspian coast, in Khuzestan Province, and along the coast of the Persian Gulf.[2] The largest mountain chain is Zagros that stretches from the border with Armenia in the northwest to the Persian Gulf and has several peaks over 4,000 meters high. The Alborz Mountains in the north and northwest run along the south shore of the Caspian Sea. The Mount Damavand with a height of 5,671 meters is located in the center of the Alborz chain. The two mountain chains meet at Tabriz, beside Lake Orumiyeh in the Iranian portion of Azerbaijan.[3] The Iranian Plateau is located in between these two mountain chains and covers over 50 percent of the country. Toward the east of the Iranian plateau there are two large inhabitable deserts called Dasht-e Kavir and Dasht-e Lut. The cultivable area of the central plateau is estimated to be about 31 percent of the total area.

Figure 1.1 The physical map of Iran

Source: Ezilon maps.[4]

At the lowest elevations, the land is mainly dry, but as elevation rises, surfaces of sand and gravelly soil gradually merge into fertile soil on the hillsides. Between 1990 and 2010, the cultivable area of the central plateau has become dryer. The Alborz and Zagros mountains have deeply affected the socioeconomic conditions of the country since they surround agricultural plateaus and urban settlements. Historically, the plateaus have been isolated from each other and organized, independent urban settlements are found there. The mountains also impede easy access to the Persian Gulf and the Caspian Sea and for centuries have acted as physical barriers protecting the Iranian heartland from the raiding Turkish hordes of the north and the Arabs of the south.[5]

Natural Environment

The country is rich in mineral deposits; in particular petroleum and natural gas and also coal, chromium, copper, iron ore, lead, manganese, and zinc. Despite this natural generosity, disasters and especially earthquakes frequently occur in Iran. Tehran has at least five or six significant fault lines, and experts believe the city is at risk of major earthquakes.[6] Iran is also frequently prone to drought, floods, dust storms, and sandstorms. The most productive agricultural land is located close to the Caspian Sea and makes up about 5.5 percent of the country's total land area.[7] Over the course of the past two decades (1970–2010), there has been rapid urbanization and vehicle emissions and industrial operations have resulted in poor air quality in major cities. Tehran and other large cities are vastly polluted and pose major health risks to their inhabitants. According to the World Health Organization—four Iranian cities namely Ahvaz, Kermanshah, Sanandaj, and Yasouj—were ranked among the world's most polluted cities in 2010.[8]

Most of the country, especially the eastern deserts, suffers from lack of water resources and receives little rainfall. The exceptions are the higher mountain valleys of the Alborz, Zagros, and the Caspian coastal plains that receive heavy precipitations.[9] The Alborz and Zagros mountains act as natural barriers and make the Iranian plateau very dry particularly in the central and southeastern part of the country. There are no major rivers in the country and the only navigable river is Rud Karun, which is 830 kilometers long. Other rivers include Sefid Rud (1,000 km), Karkheh (700 km), and Zayandeh Rud (400 km). The largest inland body of water is Lake Orumiyeh, which is salty and shallow and is located in northwestern Iran. In the recent years (2002–2015), Lake Orumiyeh has lost large amounts of water, and according to experts at Iran's environmental agency, the lake contains only 5 percent of the amount of water it did just 20 years ago.[10] There are also several connected salt lakes in the province of Sistan-Baluchestan. During the past three decades (1980–2010), industrial and urban wastewater runoff has severely contaminated rivers and coastal waters in the Persian Gulf and the Caspian Sea.[11] Since ancient times, the problem of water supply has led Iranians to design efficient techniques for harnessing limited water resources. For instance, some 3,000 years ago the Persians invented the *qanat* or underground aqueducts that brought water from highlands to the surface at lower levels by gravity.[12] Dams have always played an important role in harnessing Iran's precious water reserves.[13] Historically, the lack of water resources has had a very deep effect on the Iranian society. For instance, in the Persian language the word *water* (*aab*) and its derivatives such as *aabad* are used as synonyms for development, growth, and prosperity. The shortage of water supply is recognized as a major factor that has hampered the agriculture, and by extension, the socioeconomic development. Moreover, due to lack of major rivers, transportation across the country has been traditionally very slow and difficult. A combination of smart irrigation systems, canals, dams, and traditional architecture has allowed Iranians to settle in the arid central and southwestern parts.[14]

Thanks to its diverse topography, the country has variable climates. In the mountainous northwest, winter is extremely cold and snowy, spring and fall are mild, and summer is dry and hot. During winter, temperature of minus 22°F (minus 30°C) is recorded in the northwest and minus 4°F (minus 22°C) is experienced in central provinces. By contrast, in the south, winter is relatively mild and the summer is extremely hot reaching 131°F (55°C) in Khuzestan province. Overall, Iran has a continental climate with hot summers, cold to mild winters, and abundant sunshine. More than 2,000 plant species are found in Iran. The vegetation varies across the country according to topography, water, and soil mixture. Roughly one-tenth of Iran is covered by forest, which is mainly concentrated in the Caspian region and Zagros foothills. In mountainous regions, a wide range of vegetation is found such as oak, elm, maple, hackberry, walnut, pear, and pistachio trees. In addition, juniper, almond, cotoneaster, and wild fruit trees grow on the dry plateau. Willow, poplar, and plane trees grow in the ravines and thorny bushes cover most of the plains. Oases may have different kinds of vegetation such as vines and tamarisk, date palm, myrtle, oleander, acacia, willow, elm, plum, and mulberry trees. In marshes and plains, pasture grass is abundant during spring season. Wildlife of Iran is relatively diverse and consists of many species such as leopards, bears, hyenas, gazelles, rabbits, wolves, jackals, panthers, foxes, stork, eagles, and falcons. Main domestic animals include sheep, goats, cows, horses, donkeys, and camels. Due to massive urbanization, the population of some of wild species has substantially decreased. The Persian leopard is the largest of all the subspecies of leopards in the world and lives in the Alborz and Zagros mountains. A wide variety of reptiles, toads, frogs, tortoises, lizards, salamanders, racers, rat snakes, snakes, and vipers are found in Steppes and deserts. Among birds, seagulls, ducks, and geese live close to the Caspian Sea and the Persian Gulf shores. About 200 varieties of fish live in the Persian Gulf and Caspian Sea. The Caspian Sturgeon is commercially very important and is used in the production of Iranian caviar.

Demographic Trends

Iran's population is estimated to be 80,840,713.[15] While the entire Middle East excluding Iran and Turkey has a population of 128.8 million people, the sheer size of Iran's population can be seen as an important strategic factor in geopolitics and business matters. Motivated by religious reasons, shortly after the Islamic Revolution (1979) the government abolished family planning programs. In the 1980s, it was believed that children are a gift from God and that contraception should be discouraged.[16] Moreover, during the war with Iraq (1980–1988), Iranian political leaders endorsed the population growth as a matter of comparative advantage. The rising casualty of the war was another reason that encouraged many middle-aged couples to procreate more children.[17] Consequently, the population of Iran grew at an average annual rate of 3.9 percent between 1977 and 1986, one of the most rapid rates of population growth in the world at the time.[18] Faced with the grave social consequences of the population growth, the government was obliged to adopt new family planning programs and subsequently, fertility declined dramatically after 1988.[19] In the recent years (2000–2015), the population growth has declined sharply and Iran now has the slowest birthrate among all the Middle Eastern countries including Lebanon and Israel.[20] In some Iranian provinces, the fertility has fallen below the replacement rate.[21] There are many factors that explain this declining trend. In addition to government policies, it should be noted that Iran is a modernizing and urbanizing society. Over the course of the past 15 years (2000–2014), Iranians have changed their attitudes toward marriage and children, and subsequently the age of marriage has increased significantly.[22] According to a report by Iran's National Organization for Civil Registration, 48 percent of women and 46 percent of men were at the marrying age but had not married in 2012.[23] More recently (2010–2015), the rapid pace of modernization and urbanization has made children less of a benefit and more of an economic burden for their parents.[24] As the young people are increasingly in school, they tend to delay their marriage. In addition, it seems that Iranians are becoming more comfortable with the contraceptives and vasectomies.[25] Thus, the decline in fertility rates may be attributed to a combination of factors such as inflation, unemployment, lack of affordable housing, success of the government family planning programs, legitimizing birth control, cultural and social modernization forces, and higher levels of education and urbanization.

Facing the sharp drop in fertility rates from more than six children per woman in 1985 to less than two in 2013, the country's Ministries of Health and Medical Education are considering policies to promote the population growth. In 2013, Iran's parliament has suggested a ban on vasectomies as the country seeks to boost its birthrate. At any rate, Iran is still a young country and almost 70 percent of its population is under the age of 35 but as illustrated in Figure 1.2, Iran's age structure

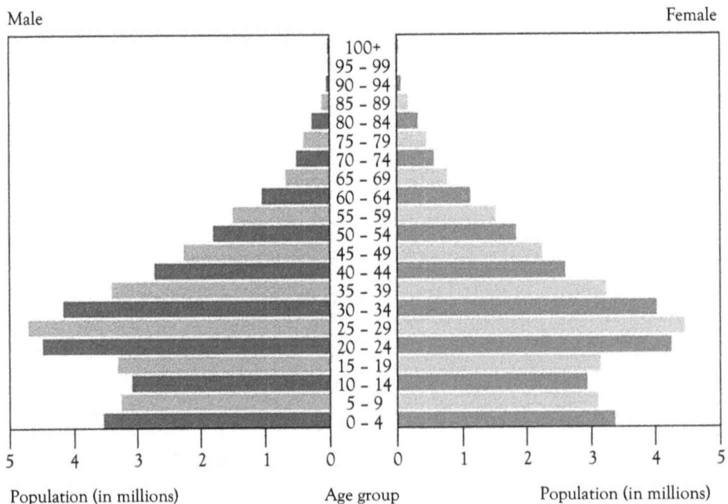

Figure 1.2 Iran's age structure as of August 2014

Source: CIA World Factbook.

is showing signs of maturity. It is estimated that fertility rate will remain at 1.7 children per woman over the course of the next decade.[26] While Iranian population is estimated to grow, the growth rate is projected to be among the lowest in the Middle East.[27]

These two demographic waves, first a sharp rise and then a sharp decline in the birthrates, are transforming Iran to a modern and sophisticated society that is strikingly different from neighboring countries like Pakistan and Iraq. One may speculate that as Iran's population is becoming mature, the working-age population will grow larger relative to children. This may create opportunities for the population to accumulate saving, to educate, and eventually to move toward a knowledge-based economy characterized by more technical industries and higher living standards. Under these circumstances, economic development could take place quickly and result in a society marked by cosmopolitan, educated, and secular middle-class citizens.[28]

Settlement and Urban Geography

Iran is far from being a monolithic country. Iranians are rather divided along cultural, ethnic, and linguistic lines. Amazingly, the topography and the water supply determine the regions fit for human habitation, the character of the people, and their types of dwellings. Most of Iran's population is concentrated across the north as well as in the western parts where farming is promising.[29] Historically, the huge mountains, the narrow rivers, and the empty deserts have resulted in insular settlements and formation of distinct ethnicities and dialects across the country. During the 20th century, as a result of a rapid modernization, major networks of roads were constructed and different regions and provinces were interconnected. Subsequently, the Pahlavi Land Reforms during the 1960s resulted in substantial urbanization and massive migration from villages to large cities. The migration to Tehran was accelerated shortly after the Islamic Revolution because of the weakening economic conditions in the rural areas and small towns.[30] In addition, there were many Iranian refugees from the Iran–Iraq War and Afghans fleeing the Soviet assault on their country who migrated to Tehran in the 1980s and the 1990s.[31] As a result of these waves of migration, the urban proportion of the population increased from 27 percent to 60 percent between 1950 and 2002.[32] In the 21 years from 1976 to 1996, the number of cities with a population of over 100,000 increased from 23 to 59.[33] According to the United Nations reports, 80 percent of Iran's population will be urban by 2030.[34]

Tehran and other big cities have always attracted most of the resources and investments, and consequently, the gap between big and small cities has been growing steadily.[35] A traveler can see considerable differences between urban and rural regions. While urban regions are marked by modernized commercial and industrial centers, rural regions have remained mainly poor and underdeveloped. High concentration of investment in several big cities, especially in Tehran, continues to attract many rural inhabitants from diverse ethnical backgrounds. New migrants generally become submerged in the Persian or Tehrani culture and dialect and quickly adopt urban lifestyle.[36] In general, the Iranian urban inhabitants have smaller families, are more educated, and are less religious. Iranian cities are not managed independently; therefore, urbanization is a huge financial and managerial burden for the Iranian government. Large cities tackle an increasing number of issues such as appropriate infrastructure, housing, transport, sewage, water supply, education, health, security, and recreation services. Overall, the process of urbanization in Iran has led to an overconcentration of administrative, economic, social, political, and cultural activities in Tehran and also a few large cities.

The country is subdivided into 31 provinces (*ostan*), which constitute major administrative units and are run by appointed governors (*ostandar*). Tehran, the capital of Iran, lies at the southern side of the Alborz Mountains, in north-central Iran, and less than 150 kilometers south of the Caspian Sea. Tehran is a rather young city that became the capital at the end of the 18th century, and its importance drastically increased under the Pahlavi and the Islamic Republic with their highly centralized administrative and economic systems.[37] Tehran has become the center of government institutions, industries, businesses, universities, hospitals, and political power. Tehran's population has quadrupled from 1956 to 1996. An estimated 16.5 percent of Iran's population lives in Tehran and more than 70 percent of the economic and financial resources are concentrated in this city.[38] If the greater metropolitan area is included, the population of Tehran reaches 11 million.[39] In Tehran, the physical slope of the land is an accurate measure of socioeconomic status as the rich reside in the higher northern parts while the poor live in the lower southern suburbs. As one moves from lower parts of the southern Tehran to the higher northern neighborhoods, the infrastructure, the roads, and even the air quality are progressively improved. The residents of southern Tehran are generally poorer and less educated, have larger households, and are more religious.[40] A large portion of Tehranis are employed by the government agencies and work in the public sector. Many others work in manufacturing industries or in small firms and businesses.[41] Since the 1970s, heavy traffic has been a major problem in Tehran causing air pollution and long delays. Motor vehicle emissions are estimated to cause about 70 percent of the air pollution and smog. More recently (2010–2014), due to international sanctions, the substandard fuel and older vehicles have contributed to the exacerbation of air pollution in Tehran and many other Iranian cities. Most of the year, the levels of pollutants are significantly above those recognized as safe by health standards making Tehran one of the most polluted cities in the world.[42] It is believed that air pollution is a major cause of coronary artery diseases and different types of cancers in Tehran.

In addition to Tehran, other big cities include Mashhad, Esfahan, Tabriz, Shiraz, Karaj, and Bandar Abbas (See Table 1.1). Mashhad is the second largest city and is located 850 kilometers northeast of Tehran near the border of Turkmenistan. Mashhad is considered to be a holy pilgrimage site for Shia Muslims. Recent statistics (2010) evaluate its population to be over two million. Esfahan is an important city and is located about 350 kilometers south of Tehran. Esfahan is famous for classic architecture and is also home to major industries, including steel, armaments, medicine, and textiles.[43] Tabriz is located in the northwest corner of Iran, near the borders of Azerbaijan and Armenia. Tabriz is the center of the East Azerbaijan Province, has a population of over 1.5 million, and is ranked as the fifth most populated and second largest commercial city. Thanks to its location as a western gateway of Iran, Tabriz has played an important role in Iran's socioeconomic development. Karaj is the capital of Alborz Province and is situated 20 kilometers west of Tehran. Shiraz is 935 kilometers south of Tehran and is especially famous for art, architecture, and poetry.[44] Shiraz has a very mild and pleasant climate. Bandar Abbas is the major port in southern Iran at the Strait of Hormuz in the Persian Gulf. Rail,

Table 1.1 The list of the largest cities in Iran by population in 2012

1	Tehran	7,153,309	16	Azadshahr	514,102
2	Mashhad	2,307,177	17	Arak	503,647
3	Esfahan	1,547,164	18	Yazd	477,905
4	Karaj	1,448,075	19	Ardabil	410,753
5	Tabriz	1,424,641	20	Abadan	370,180
6	Shiraz	1,249,942	21	Zanjan	357,471
7	Qom	900,000	22	Bandar Abbas	352,173
8	Ahvaz	841,145	23	Sanandaj	349,176
9	Kahriz	766,706	24	Qazvin	333,635
10	Kermanshah	621,100	25	Khorramshahr	330,606
11	Rasht	594,590	26	Khorramabad	329,825
12	Kerman	577,514	27	Khomeyni Shahr	277,334
13	Orumiyeh	577,307	28	Kashan	272,359
14	Zahedan	551,980	29	Sari	255,396
15	Hamadan	528,256	30	Borujerd	251,958

Source: Based on the Statistical Center of Iran.[45]

air, and land routes connect Bandar Abbas with other cities. According to the Statistical Center of Iran,[46] in 2012, Iran had six cities with a population over one million, 61 cities between 100,000 and one million, and 125 cities between 10,000 and 100,000. Over the course of the past decade (2004–2013), the government policies have resulted in an astonishing increase in the cost of living in urban areas. It is interesting to know that relative to income, housing costs for Iranian urban residents are among the highest in the world.[47]

Ethnic and Linguistic Groups

Iran has one of the world's most diverse ethnolinguistic groups gathered in one country. The main ethnic and linguistic groups consist of Persian (56 percent), Turk (Azeri) (24 percent), Gilaki (8 percent), Kurd (8 percent), Lur, Baluch, Arab, and Turkaman. (See Table 1.2). The ethnic and linguistic minorities account for half of the Iranian population and as shown in Figure 1.3, they reside generally far from the center and close to Iran's borders.[48] This diversity is surprising, because unlike many of its

Figure 1.3 The distribution of ethnic, linguistic, and religious groups

Source: University of Perry-Castañeda Library Map Collection, 2005.

neighbors, Iran has a long history as a state. Indeed, other neighboring countries such as Turkey, Pakistan, and Iraq are ethnolinguistically more homogenous than Iran. Despite this ethnolinguistic diversity, Iran enjoys a significant national identity perhaps because of its history and religious homogeneity. Around 90 percent of Iranian population is Shia Muslim, and this may explain the unity of the country over time.

Persians are considered the main descendants of Iran's tradition and history and have a dominant position in Iran's politics, culture, education, and economy.[49] According to Iran's constitution, the official language of the country is Persian (Farsi), which is an Indo-European language and is taught and practiced in all schools from the first grade across the country. Many other languages are also spoken in Iran including Azeri, Kurdish, and Baluchi. All government business and public instruction is conducted in Persian (Farsi), and the state-run radio and television broadcasts are mainly in Persian but they offer limited programs in local languages. Over the past decades (1960–2010) the modernization programs of Pahlavi era followed by revolutionary agenda of the Islamic Republic have contributed to the prevalence of Persian language among other Iranian ethnolinguistic minorities even in small towns and villages.[50] Many young migrants who arrive in Tehran or large urban centers adopt Persian to boost their social status and achieve professional success.[51]

The Old Persian language came to Iran around 1500 BC, evolved into Middle Persian, and after the Arab-Islamic conquest, changed to New Persian.[52] The Arab-Islamic conquest introduced a large number of Arabic words into Persian and subsequently the Arabic script replaced the old alphabet, but the makeup of the language was largely preserved. This linguistic difference makes Iranians a distinct nation in the Middle East as the Persian language and literature have a great impact on the constitution of the Iranian national identity. Persian language creates a sense of belonging among all Iranians and contains a set of values, expressions, proverbs, and even cognitive structures that reflect the ancient Iranian culture. Persian is a literary language and is considered the essence of Iranian character.[53] It is rich in proverbs, maxims, and metaphors that garnish communication and make the meaning sophisticated, pleasant, and nuanced. Furthermore, the Persian literature acts as a source of intellectual and artistic inspiration for all Iranians even for other linguistic groups. Iranians regularly read their classic literature and know by heart many poems of their literary masters such as Saadi, Ferdowsi, Rumi, Hafiz, and Omar Khayam. Torn between Arabic as the language of Islam on the one hand and English and French as the languages of modernity on the other hand, the Persian language has shown a good degree of resilience; it has found a way to survive, evolve, and innovate. Not surprisingly, both Pahlavi and Islamic Republic regimes have emphasized the significance of the Persian language as a foundation for national unity.

Azeris constitute more than 24 percent of Iran's population and are considered the largest ethnolinguistic minority. They speak Azeri, are fervent nationalist Shia, and are found largely in northwestern Iran along the borders with the Republic of Azerbaijan, Armenia, and Turkey. Despite their linguistic differences, the Azeris are well integrated into Iranian society, business, and politics.[54] For instance, the current supreme leader Ayatollah Khamenei and many other high ranking officials and clerics are ethnic Azeris. As zealous nationalists, Azeris had major contributions to the formation of modern Iranian identity in the past 500 years. For instance, the founder of new Shia Iran dynasty, Shah Ismail Safavi, was an Azeri. Similarly, Azeris played a fundamental role in the Iranian Constitutional Revolution (1905–1907). After the Islamic Revolution, the Azeris have participated in the Iranian government very actively as much as any other groups.

The Kurd ethnics are supposed to constitute around 7 percent of Iran's population. They are generally Sunni Muslim and live in the northwest part of the country. Much of the Kurdish territory shared among Iran, Turkey, Iraq, and Syria had been historically administered by Iranian rulers between the 10th and the 16th centuries. In 1514, Iran lost most of this Kurdish territory to the Ottoman rule. The Kurdish language is closely related to Persian,[55] but the Kurds have resisted the central government's policies to incorporate them into the typical Iranian life. Occasionally, they have been involved in skirmishes with the central government before and after the Islamic Revolution. The Kurdish problem is not limited to Iran because the Kurds in Turkey and Iraq have much more radical claims. In 2003, after the invasion of Iraq by the American-led forces and the creation of a semiautonomous state in northern Iraq, the Turkish and Iranian governments have been concerned about the independent tendencies among their own Kurdish minorities. The ethnic Kurds are present in the private and public economic sectors as well as in Iran's military and civilian establishments and apparently are becoming more integrated into the Iranian society.

The Arab minority is estimated to be around one million people who reside mostly along the Iranian–Iraqi border in the southwest Iran.[56] The Arabs came to Iran during the seventh and eighth centuries and speak some dialects of Arabic. They are predominantly Shia Muslims and do not have serious civil or territorial claims. Most of the Iranian Arabs are mixed with the Persians and Turks and often intermarry. The Arab minority has been living in Iran for many centuries and has a cordial relationship with the rest of the country. During the Iran–Iraq War, the

Arabs of Khuzestan fought on the side of the Iranians against the Iraqi Arabs.[57] The Gilakis are other Iranian groups who speak a particular Persian dialect and are settled mainly in the Caspian Sea area.[58] The Turkmen ethnics are estimated at less than 2 percent of Iran's population, speak Turkic languages, are mainly Sunni Muslims, and reside in the northeast of the country. The Lurs are dwelling in the western mountains of Iran and consist of mainly seminomadic tribes. They constitute less than 1.5 percent of the Iran's population and are supposed to be the descendants of the aboriginal inhabitants of the country. The Lurs speak some dialects of Persian language. The Baluchis comprise less than 1.5 percent of Iran's population, are mostly Sunni Muslims, and reside in the Sistan-Baluchistan province along the Pakistan border.[59] The Sistan-Baluchistan is believed to be the least developed part of Iran and is lagging behind in all socioeconomic measures such as employment and education. Due to tribal affinities of the Iranian Baluchis with their Pakistani brothers, the control over the province has been a daunting task for the central government. Generally, the Baluchis are not persecuted unless they are involved in illegal activities.[60] In the past years (2008–2014), a rebel Baluchi group called Jundallah has attacked government officials and civilian targets. The Iranian government maintains that some foreign countries like Saudi Arabia entice such ethnic clashes.

The Conditions of Ethnic and Linguistic Minorities

In theory, the Iranian Constitution guarantees the rights of ethnic minorities,[61] but in practice, Persians are mostly at an advantage to benefit from economic and social development programs. While the government does not discriminate against the race and origin,[62] the ethnic minorities lag behind in employment, education, and economic opportunities. Since the 1970s the ethnic groups have increasingly entered into the mainstream Iranian society and have improved their standards of living. Both Pahlavi and Islamic Republic policies have been relatively successful in assimilating ethnic minorities into the Iranian society. The Pahlavi Shahs through modernization and coercion, and the Islamic Republic by revolutionary and Islamic programs, have tried to overcome the ethnolinguistic differences and build a strong national identity. It seems that these efforts have been quite effective. Overall, despite some sporadic events, Iranian minorities are not considered major threats to the political stability of the country. Azeri minority is so large that practically it is a core component of Iranian identity. Azeris are well represented in the government, the religious institutions, and Iran business community.[63] The relationship between the Kurds and the Iranian state has been more problematic, partly because of geopolitics. While the Kurds are divided among Iran, Turkey, Syria, and Iraq, they have a strong affinity with Iranian culture and Persian language. Other minorities do not have any viable alternative to claim secession from the mainland. The solidarity of all ethnicities in the defense of Iranian territory during the Iran–Iraq War (1980–1988) is an indication that Iran has mainly succeeded in building a solid national identity that surpasses ethnic and tribal cleavages.[64]

Religious Minority Groups

Under the secular and modern regime of Pahlavi dynasty, the religious groups were not essential in determining the minorities' identities; however, it seems that under the Islamic Republic, the religious groups and affinities have gained more importance.[65] Nearly 89 percent of Iranians including Persians, Azeris, and Gilakis are Shia Muslims and 11 percent are categorized as Sunnis, Christians, Zoroastrians, Jews, and Baha'is.[66] According to Iran's constitution, only three religious minorities are officially recognized, namely Christians, Jews, and Zoroastrians.[67] The followers of these three religions are permitted within the limits of the law to perform their religious rituals and ceremonies and to act according to their own canon in matters of personal affairs, marriage, and religious education. Sunni Muslims are the largest religious minority in Iran and include ethnic groups such as Kurds, Baluchis, and Turkmens.[68] Also, it is estimated that a minority of Arabs and small communities of Persians in southern Iran are Sunnis.[69] While Iranian Shias completely respect their Sunni brothers, they consider their religion less refined. Since the Islamic Republic hinges upon the Shia principles, the government does not welcome the public show of Sunni religion.[70]

Baha'ism constitutes the largest non-Muslim minority in Iran. It is estimated that there are more than 350,000 Baha'is in Iran.[71] Most of Baha'is are middle class urban Persians and are dispersed across the country. Baha'ism appeared as an offspring of Shia Islam, claiming social reforms in the 19th century Iran. The leaders of Baha'ism were persecuted by political and religious authorities during the rule of Qajar dynasty in the 19th century. Under the Pahlavi rule in the 20th century, the conditions of Baha'is were improved and they enjoyed freedom to practice their religion, open their temples, and hold government positions.[72] Under the Islamic Republic, Baha'is are not recognized as a valid religious minority, rather they are seen as apostates and for that reason, cannot practice their religion openly.

Iran's Christians are estimated to be around 280,000 Armenians and Assyrians who are concentrated in urban regions such as Tehran, Esfahan, Tabriz, Arak, and Orumiyeh. Iran's Christians have not been mistreated; rather they have been well accepted as religious minorities by the Iranian Constitution under the Pahlavi rule as well in the Islamic Republic. Currently, they are permitted to choose their own representatives to the Parliament and can have their own schools and exert their own religious laws. In general, they have enjoyed a good standard of living and have contributed to the development of the Iranian society particularly through commerce, art, and industry. It is important to mention that while the Islamic Republic recognizes the Iranian Christians as a legitimate religious group, it does not tolerate evangelical services in Persian language and prevents Muslims from converting to Christianity.

It is interesting to note that Iran is home to the largest number of Jews anywhere in the Middle East outside Israel. The Iranian Jews are estimated at a community of 50,000 people concentrated in the Capital Tehran, and a few large cities such as Esfahan, Shiraz, and Hamadan. They date back to some 2000 years ago when the Achaemenid rulers liberated Jews from captivity.[73] Over the course of centuries, the Iranian Jews have been merged with Iran's mainstream society. They speak Persian as their mother language and have adopted the Iranian culture. Similar to Iran's Christians, they have been accepted as a religious minority by the Islamic Republic Constitution and overall have enjoyed a good standard of living. Under the Islamic Republic, they are entitled to elect their representatives in the parliament, have their own cultural and educational centers, and exert their own laws regarding marriage and family issues. After the

Table 1.2 The composition of ethnic, linguistic, and religious groups in Iran

Ethnic groups	Religious groups	Linguistic groups
Persian (58%)	Shia Islam (89%)	Persian (58%)
Azeri (24%)	Sunni Islam (9%)	Turkic (26%)
Kurd (7%)	Baha'ism	Kurdish (9%)
Arab (3%)	Christianity	Luri (2%)
Lur (2%)	Judaism	Arabic (1%)
Baluch (2%)	Zoroastrianism	
Turkmen (2%)		

Islamic Revolution, many of Iranian Jews migrated to the United States or Israel. While the Jews enjoy the same degree of freedom as the Christians, they are regarded with some suspicion as they have family and business connections with Israel.

There are only about 32,000 Zoroastrians in Iran but Zoroastrianism occupies an important place in the Iranian society. Zoroastrianism is one of the oldest religions of the world and was practiced as the official state religion in Iran during the Sassanid Empire. After the conquest of Persia by Arab Muslims in the seventh century, the inhabitants of Iran converted from Zoroastrianism to Islam; nevertheless they preserved many Zoroastrian customs and traditions that are still present in Iran's culture. Zoroastrianism consists of a monotheistic worship of Ahura Mazda (the Lord of Wisdom) and an ethical dualism opposing good and evil spirits. Many of the concepts of Zoroastrianism such as paradise, hell, devil, angels, the afterlife, and the last judgment are believed to have shaped Abrahamic religions including Judaism, Christianity, and Islam.[74] While Zoroastrians have not been subjected to harassment, they have suffered lower economic and social status and have migrated mainly to India in the 19th century. Under the Islamic Republic, the Zoroastrianism is accepted as an official religious minority whose followers are permitted to practice their religion freely, have their own cultural and educational centers, and exert their own laws with regard to marriage and family-related matters.

CHAPTER 2

Salient Themes and Trends in the History of Iran

Iran has been described as a historical nation because Iranians are constantly haunted by the shadow of their long history. As such, an examination of the Iranian history is a prerequisite to comprehend its current social and economic conditions. Moreover, a historical perspective provides insights into Iran's twisted relationship with other nations particularly with the Western powers. Obviously, a detailed account of the history of Iran is beyond the scope of this chapter, but in the following pages, I will try to review some salient chronological trends that remarkably continue to shape modern Iran.

Ancient Times and Pre-Islamic Era: The Divine Right to Rule

Around 559–530 BC, Cyrus the Great united the Aryan tribes on the Iranian plateau and founded the Achaemenid Empire. He described his empire as *Iran-shahr* and himself as the *king of kings*.[1] Achaemenids established an efficient bureaucratic system across their vast empire and built many roads, ports, and underground irrigation systems. For over two centuries, the Persians became the world dominant power and ruled the world from Egypt to India. The Achaemenid Empire was conquered by Alexander of Macedonia around 331 BC and Iran went under the Greek rule. Subsequently, a group of Iranian people called Parthians rejected the Hellenic influence and claimed for themselves the divine right to rule the country. Around 224 AD, a Persian called Ardeshir I overthrew the Parthians and founded the Sassanid dynasty. The Sassanid kings revived the Persian culture and Zoroastrian religion and returned to the Achaemenid government model. Zoroastrianism was founded by the Iranian prophet and reformer, Zoroaster in the sixth century BC and had a considerable influence on the Iranian art, culture, and society. The Sassanid rulers relied hugely on Zoroastrianism to justify their rule as ordained by Ahura Mazda (Zoroastrian God) and established a caste system that served their social and political agenda.

The Arab-Islamic Conquest: The Resilience of Iranian Identity

Despite all its military and administrative strengths, in the mid-seventh century, the Persian Empire was rapidly defeated by the Arab tribesmen who were armed with a new faith. After the collapse of the Persian Empire, Iranians converted to Islam and became part of the Arab-Islamic Empire. Around 750 AD with the help of Persians, the Islamic capital was relocated from Damascus to Baghdad where Persians could closely supervise the Islamic world.[2] The conquering Muslim Arabs had less experience with the government and empire organization, therefore they relied on the Persian tradition in governance, politics, bureaucracy, and fiscal system. Likewise, in cultural and scientific fields, the Persian Muslims brought numerous scholars and thinkers who wrote mainly in Arabic and made significant contributions to the advancement of science and art in the Islamic civilization. After the ninth century, the Arab rule over Persia waned gradually, and as a result, many Iranian monarchs emerged across the country. Persian language was again employed by government officials and administrators. The Persians adopted Islamic faith, but preserved their own culture and emerged as a distinct society within the Islamic civilization. In the end, the Iranian identity proved to be strong and resilient.[3]

Mongol Invasion: A Terrible Shock and Resilience

In 1220, Genghis Khan of Mongolia attacked Persia. The attack was terrible, brutal, and extremely destructive. Major cities were sacked and their inhabitants were cruelly slaughtered. Buildings, schools, libraries, mosques, and hospitals were totally annihilated. Eventually, Mongol invaders converted to Islam and became reliant on native Iranians to rule over their vast Empire. Regardless of its destructive effects, the Mongol Empire facilitated the exchange of ideas and goods among major civilizations namely China, India, and Persia.[4] During this time, some of the greatest poets and thinkers of the Persian literature, such as Hafiz and Rumi, appeared. Once again, Persians conquered their conquerors and the Iranian identity survived the wave of violence and brutality.[5]

Safavid Dynasty: Making of the Iranian Shia Identity

In the 15th century, a young Shia called Shah Ismail Safavi conquered the city of Tabriz in Azerbaijan province and gradually took control over entire Iran. Shah Ismail established the Safavid Dynasty, made Shia the official religion of state, and reinforced the function of Shia clergy. Since then, Shia became the cornerstone of the modern Iranian national identity and the clerics gained much social influence. Safavids emphasized some elements of Shia religion such as martyrdom, commemorations, and passion plays. Interestingly, the claim of Shah Ismail as the Shia ruler was in accordance with the Persian culture, which historically embraced the divine right of kingship. One of the most influential Safavid monarchs, Shah Abbas the Great, developed a disciplined army and defeated the Ottomans. He chose Isfahan as his capital and contributed to the advancement of different disciplines of art, science, architecture, and craftsmanship. The Safavids are considered the founders of modern Iran, because they unified a large territory under Shia religion, distinguished Iran from Sunni Ottomans, and established a powerful and glorious empire extending from Tigris to India.

Humiliation by the West and the Constitutional Revolution

In the 18th century, the Qajars dynasty took control over the country. During this time, Iran like many other Eastern nations lagged behind Europe and was extremely weak and impoverished. Faced with the industrial revolution and increasing power of the European countries, Iran could not defend its national interests. The British and Russians intervened in Iran's internal affairs and gained considerable influence in the country's political and economic domains. In the 19th century, Iran was humiliated and defeated by the Russian armed forces and consequently lost huge areas in the Caucasus and Central Asia including Georgia, Armenia, and parts of Azerbaijan.[6] On the other hand, the British government forced Iran to give up all its claims on Afghanistan. In addition, the Iranian trade was dominated by the Europeans, and Qajar Shahs or Princes were often bribed or forced to cede many unfair and exclusive concessions to the British and Russian companies.[7]

The economic crisis and rampant government corruption led to demands for curbing royal authority and establishing constitutional rule in 1904.[8] In 1906, Iran established the first parliamentary system and deputies of people came to play a role in the political governance. However, due to many internal tensions and the British and Russian meddling, two decades of turbulence and chaos followed the parliamentary rule. In 1907, the Anglo-Russian Agreement forced Iran to split up into three zones: the north to Russia, the southwest to Great Britain, and the remaining areas as neutral zones. Apparently, this aggression was intended to allow for the two major powers to prepare against German influence.[9] Russian forces occupied the northern parts of Iran in 1911 and the Russian-supported troops shelled the parliament and suspended the constitutional rule.[10] By 1917, Britain gained a significant influence over Iran and kept a tight political and economic control over the country undermining Iran's national sovereignty.[11] The restraint of the Iranian Constitutionalist movement by Great Britain and Russia and their meddling and aggression were interpreted as the foreign and Western animosity toward the nation.[12] Iranians became increasingly suspicious of the harmful influence of foreigners and Westerners on their society and considered them as serious threats to national sovereignty, culture, tradition, and religion.[13] This sentiment paved the way for the latent radical and Islamist movements.

Pahlavi Dynasty and the Accelerated Modernization or Westernization

During the 18th and 19th centuries, Iranian politicians managed to protect the independence of the country, but they were hugely under the British and Russian influence. By the end of World War I, Iran was plunged into a state of political, social, and economic chaos.[14] The country was suffering from civil war, foreign occupation, and ethnic uprisings, which demanded a strong leader.[15] In 1921, the British encouraged Brigadier Reza Khan to stage a *coup d'état.* He replaced the last Qajar Shah in 1925 and established the Pahlavi Dynasty. Reza Shah Pahlavi chose a nationalistic and authoritarian agenda and launched some drastic socioeconomic reforms.[16] In 1935, Reza Shah requested all foreign governments to no longer refer to his country as Persia, but as Iran. He emphasized Iranian nationalism and revitalized the pre-Islamic Persian identity. Undeniably, the most important objective of Reza Shah was modernization of Iran at any cost. To this end, he imitated the Western model and introduced substantial social changes. He centralized the decision making, severely crushed ethnic and tribal rulers, and revolutionized judiciary, education, army, transport, health care, and economy. In accordance with his modernization agenda, Reza Shah forcibly abolished the wearing of the veil and brought women to the workplace. As a result of his reforms, the Western educated lawyers replaced mullahs and the French Civil Code took the place of Islamic laws. Likewise, Reza Shah restricted religious festivals, commemorations, passion plays, and other practices that affected public life.[17] Obviously, these reforms aimed at socioeconomic development, but they were in clear contradiction with the traditional Iranian and Islamic values and, for that reason, received criticism from religious leaders. Indeed, Reza Shah's socioeconomic reforms decreased the influence of clergy in judicial, economic, and educational spheres and created resentment among conservative Islamists.[18] In his final years, Reza Shah developed friendly relations with Germans partly to counter the influence of Great Britain. With the outbreak of World War II, Iran was occupied by Great Britain and the Soviet Union. Subsequently, Reza Shah was sent into exile and his son Mohammad Reza was appointed the Shah of Iran.[19] Once again, the development in Iran was interrupted by foreign invasion and big powers' meddling.[20] On the whole, the rule of Reza Shah was marked by an accelerated modernization and Westernization, socioeconomic development, and emergence of Iran as a centralized nation-state.

Mohammad Reza Shah and the American Organized *Coup d État*

After World War II ended, Iran struggled for national autonomy, especially against the Soviets and the British.[21] During this time, oil was becoming an important issue in international relations and the state was relying more and more on revenues from exports of oil. From 1951 to 1953, Prime Minister Mossadeq led the oil nationalization movement and ultimately the parliament passed a law to liberate Iran's oil from British control. The Americans and the British governments plotted against the democratically elected Prime Minister Mossadeq and overthrew him in a jointly organized coup in 1953.[22] This event sullied the image of America in the Iranian collective consciousness. The Islamists, nationalists, and particularly the leftists viewed the role of American and British intelligence services in organizing the coup as another example of Western meddling in Iran's internal affairs. The nationalists, Islamists, and communists, despite all their ideological and political differences, agreed upon the animosity of Western powers toward Iran. The coup had a traumatic effect on the Iranian public opinion, which has continued to the present day.[23] After the coup, fearing Soviet aggression and internal opposition, the Shah built close relations with Great Britain and the United States. Moreover, the United States needed the Shah as a barricade against the expansion of the Soviet influence in the Persian Gulf.[24] Thanks to the support of the United States, Iran moved to become a major economic and military power in the Middle East. Relying on his throne, the Shah became increasingly autocratic and embarked on some rapid socioeconomic reforms. In 1962, he introduced his White Revolution that consisted of major programs such as land reform and women's suffrage. His reforms were in clear contradiction with the traditional and Islamic values and resulted in resentment from the clergy, the conservative groups, and even the middle class citizens. The majority of clerics were critical of the land reform program, liberalization of laws concerning women, and the extension of government institutions. In 1963, Ayatollah Khomeini described the Shah's White Revolution as a direct assault on Islam and preached in Qom by harshly criticizing Shah's socioeconomic reforms. The government severely suppressed the ensuing riots and Khomeini was exiled first to Turkey and then to Iraq. As a result of his opposition to Shah's social reforms, Khomeini emerged as a well-known Islamist dissident.

After 1963, encouraged by the support of the United States and enriched by oil revenues, the Shah found the audacity to end the democratic statute. He established an authoritarian rule and crushed all opposing groups including secular nationalists, communist movements, and Islamist clerics. Relations with the United States and other Western nations were warm, and moreover, Iran embarked upon trade and cultural relations with a wide range of regions and countries including Eastern Europe, the Soviet Union, France, Germany, and Scandinavia. Altogether, the 1960s and 1970s were marked by significant economic growth, modernization, rapid urbanization, and social transformation.[25] The land reforms reduced the power of feudal lords and empowered small farmers who mainly migrated to large cities and became middle class urban citizens. Between 1970 and 1977, the gross national product increased to an average annual rate of 7.8 percent.[26] Consequently, the standard of living rose dramatically and Iran's infrastructure improved rapidly. The Shah relied on oil revenues to finance the massive development plans. After all, he intended to lead Iran toward the Great Civilization, which was an allusion to the glory of ancient Persian Empire.

Islamic Revolution: The End of Monarchy

Despite economic prosperity and higher standards of living in the 1970s, the discontent with the Shah's regime was constantly growing. On one hand, his reforms were not aligned with the traditional Iranian and Islamic values, and on the other hand, Shah's accelerated modernization had led to numerous social problems such as mass urbanization, widening social gap, bribery, corruption, and inflation. By the late 1970s, opposition to the Shah grew from a wide range of political affiliations including bazaar merchants, seculars, liberal Muslims, leftists, communists, and guerrilla groups. All dissident groups gradually united behind the charismatic leadership of Ayatollah Khomeini whom they called *Imam*, an allusion to Imam Mahdi who according to Shia Islam will return and liberate the world from tyranny and injustice. In 1978, a powerful opposition movement to the Shah's regime was built up. A few months later, Khomeini returned to Iran triumphant and shortly after, in February 1979, took over. The Shah who was overthrown by the Islamic Revolution died in Egypt a year later. After 2500 years of monarchy, the Islamic Republic of Iran was born.

The First Decade of Islamic Republic: War and Domestic Violence

The first years of the new republic were marked by conflict, turmoil, unrest, bloodshed, and eight years of war with Iraq. During the Iran–Iraq War (1980–1988), the country experienced negative rates of real economic growth, decline in oil production, high levels of inflation, and international isolation.[27] The Islamic Revolution was reversing many of the Shah's political, social, and economic reforms. The emphasis on Persian nationalism was suddenly replaced by a revolutionary emphasis on Islam. Fundamentalist measures were taken and revolutionary committees patrolled the streets, enforcing Islamic codes of behavior. Due to turmoil and anti-Western sentiments, most of the educated elites fled the country. A wide range of political groups were competing for political power, pushing their agendas, and creating conflict and disorder. During the first year, the revolutionary Prime Minister Mehdi Bazargan and the first Islamic Republic President Abolhassan Bani-Sadr were expelled by radical forces. Anti-American sentiment was strong and the revolutionary students took control of the United States embassy in Tehran. The following months were marked by both internal and external threats. In September 1980, Iraq invaded parts of the southwestern oil-producing Iranian province of Khuzestan. On the domestic front, the Islamic government took harsh measures to eliminate any political and social opposition and moved toward the consolidation of political and military power. Remorseless executions of anitrevolutionaries, royalists, Marxists, seculars, and other opposing groups' supporters panicked the population. The Mojahadein-Khalgh, a strong Islamist-Marxist terrorist group stepped up a campaign of bombing throughout the country killing many clerics and high ranking government officials. The war with Iraq turned out to be a long and bloody battle in which both countries' populations suffered severely. After nearly eight years, in 1988 both sides withdrew to their respective borders and accepted a ceasefire. Following the death of Ayatollah Khomeini on June 3, 1989, the Assembly of Experts met in an emergency session and elected Ali Khamenei as the new supreme leader.

The Second and Third Decades of Islamic Republic: Construction, Reform, and Counter Reform

A few months after Khomeini's death, presidential elections took place and Ali Akbar Hashemi Rafsanjani was elected as president. Rafsanjani began the process of rebuilding the war-torn economy. Considered a pragmatist, he favored a policy of economic liberalization, privatization of industry, and a rapprochement with the West that would encourage foreign investment. After Rafsanjani's presidency, the unexpected victory of reformist Mohammad Khatami in 1997 brought high hopes among the population.[28] Khatami promised political and social reforms, civil liberties, and economic prosperity; therefore, he received overwhelming support from young middle class Iranians and women. He was reelected in 2001, but his reforms were hindered by the powerful Guardian Council. For the first few years of Khatami's presidency, it seemed the voices of reform were heard, but the hopes gradually waned and finally the reform movement was crushed. In 2005 Mahmoud Ahmadinejad was elected president of Iran and decided on hard line policies at home and abroad. In June of 2009, Ahamdinejad was reelected, but the election's results created a controversy, and supporters of the opponent, Mir Hossein Moussavi, took to the streets to protest the election was fraud. Ahamdinejad who enjoyed full support of the Supreme Leader and conservative clerics, undertook some drastic measures to reverse the sociopolitical reforms of his predecessors, adopted chaotic policies, and ultimately led the country to economic recession and further isolation.

Salient Themes and Trends in the History of Iran

A reflection on the history of Iran reveals some salient themes and trends that continue to impact its society. In the following pages, I briefly review some of these themes such as the Persian pride and ambition, sentiment of the lost glory, spirit of resilience, Iranian loneliness, belief in conspiracy theories, distrust of foreigners, centrality of religion and its impacts on politics, charismatic leadership, and recurrence of social movements and revolutions.

A chief theme in Iran's history is the Persian pride. As a nation, Iranians are conscious of the ancient Persian greatness and regret their lost status in the world affairs. They consider themselves and their culture as refined, glorious, and subtle and they develop lofty aspirations. As we have seen in the previous sections, by referring to the past Persian glory, Mohammad Reza Shah ambitiously intended to make Iran one of the most powerful nations of the world. After the Islamic Revolution, this trend continued under another label. Indeed, the Muslim clerics overwhelmingly relied on a combination of the Persian and Shia pride to push their revolutionary agenda and yearned for the leadership of Muslim world. As such, it is possible to claim that the Pahalavi and revolutionary regimes pursued some similar lofty goals with dissimilar approaches.[29] While Iranians consider themselves devoted Muslims, they underline their historical contribution to the Islamic civilization; they boast of their scholars and scientists such as Avicenna, Al-Khwarizmi, and Razi who significantly enriched the Islamic civilization.

Very closely associated with the Persian pride is the spirit of resilience and durability. Among Iranians, it is widely accepted that Iran has a resilient culture that has endured all the past aggressions and adversities and will overcome future threats. Iranians maintain that in the past they have conquered their conquerors by culture, art, and soft power and have persianized their invaders such as the Mongols.[30] At the same time, they have a sentiment of their lost glory as the size and influence of the Persian Empire has been declining steadily. Since the 17th century, Iran has lost control of Bahrain, Baghdad, the Caucasus, western Afghanistan, Baluchistan, and Turkmenistan. While Iran has not been formally colonialized, in practice it has gone under the control of the Britain and Russia during the 19th century. These losses have resulted in depressing impressions in the Iranian collective psyche.

An important characteristic of Iran as a nation is its ethnic and religious loneliness. As a Persian speaking nation, Iranians are linguistically or ethnically different from their neighboring countries. In addition, Shia represents a minority among all other Islamic branches. As we discussed previously, for the past five centuries, after the Safavid Dynasty, the Iranian identity has been deeply interwoven with the Shia creed. For all these differences, Iran has few natural friends in the Middle East and suffers from a severe cultural, linguistic, and historical loneliness. After the Islamic Revolution, Khomeini relied on a pan-Islamic rhetoric to export revolution, but despite all his material and moral efforts, he remained isolated and witnessed little success in other Islamic countries.

A central theme in the Iranian history is related to the foreign and especially Western meddling in Iran's internal affairs.[31] As mentioned previously, the history of Iran is marked by many foreign brutal attacks by the Greek, Muslim Arabs, Ottomans, Mongols, and Russians. In modern times, the Iranians have severely suffered from the British and American meddling. For that reason, they have a strong tendency to attribute many social, economic, and political problems to *outsiders*. They believe in conspiracy theories and always see some hidden hands behind every phenomenon. Average Iranians put blame on foreigners for any ill in their history and society and particularly see the Westerners' hands in every turmoil. After the Islamic revolution, the conspiracy theories targeted the American influence and Khomeini pointed to the United States as the *Great Satan* and the source of Iran's pains. After all, the Western meddling has left a deep scar on the Iranian social psyche that continues to shape Iran's destiny.[32]

Another prevalent theme in the Iranian history is religion, its pervasiveness, its close relation with politics, and its implications for the social life. Obviously, the Islamic Revolution was an astonishing phenomenon that incorporated religion into all aspects of sociopolitical life. In Michel Foucault's language, it was an expression of a spiritual and godly movement rejecting secular and material politics. While the Islamic Revolution was an astonishing religious movement, we should underline the close relationship between religion and politics throughout Iran's long history. As discussed earlier, the Sassanid rulers relied hugely on Zoroastrianism and Ahura Mazda (God) to legitimize their royal rule. Similarly, in the 15th century, Shah Ismail Safavi unified Iran under the flag of Shia Islam and knotted the Iranian national identity with this faith. Even Mohammad Reza Shah, who considered himself a modern and secular leader, relied on godly inspirations to justify his rule.[33] Cyrus was the first to establish a tradition of absolute kingship, which subsequently attained a godlike clout. The Ferdowsi's epic poems, *Shahnameh* (Book of Kings), portray the evolution of the divine right through which Iranian kings ruled.[34]

Despite a rigid hierarchical social system, the Iranian history is marked by the prevalence of revolutionary and social movements.[35] A review of Iran's history reveals a constant quest for social justice and revolutionarism. In Persian language, numerous words are used to describe different categories of revolutionary and social movements. For instance, enghelab (revolution), harj-o-marj (anarchy), ashub (disturbance, turmoil), naa-arami (unrest), shouresh (rebellion), eghteshash (rioting), ghiyam (rebellion), khizesh (jump), degargooni (change), harekat (movement), nehzat (movement), and jombesh (movement), and fetneh (crisis) are some terms that are referred to social and political unrest.[36] This revolutionary spirit is seen in many patriotic militants or groups such as Abu-Muslim (eighth century), Babak and Mazyar (ninth century), the Assassins (11–12th century), the Constitutional Revolution movement (1905), the oil nationalization (1951–1953), anti-Pahlavi movements (1960s–1970s), and the Islamic Revolution (1979). This propensity for revolution might be attributed to the activism of both Zoroastrianism and Shia Islam and their eternal quest for justice across the world.

CHAPTER 3

Current Issues

Steady Socioeconomic Development

A remarkable achievement of Iran has been its steady social and human development in the last 40 years, particularly after the Islamic Revolution.[1] According to the United Nations' reports, significant improvements have taken place in Iran in areas such as health, literacy, poverty reduction, gender equality, education attainment, female and child mortality, and life expectancy.[2] For instance, the adult literacy rate has increased from 14.5 percent in 1960 to 57 percent in 1988 and to 77.1 percent in 2001.[3] The gap between adult men and women has been constantly narrowing. As a result of these improvements, the living standards have continuously increased and the Human Development Index (HDI) has grown from less than 0.6 in 1980 to 0.719 in 2001. Iran's HDI value for 2012 was 0.742, positioning the country in the high human development category. In other words, after the Islamic Revolution between 1980 and 2012, Iran's HDI value increased by 67 percent.[4] Based on the same data, between 1980 and 2012, Iran's life expectancy at birth increased by 22.1 years, mean years of schooling increased by 5.7 years, and expected years of schooling increased by 5.7 years.[5] There have been major improvements in food security and as a result, the number of people suffering from hunger has been steadily declining. Indeed, Iran's Global Hunger Index measured by the Food International Policy Research Institute has fallen from 8.5 in the 1990s to less than five in 2012. Similarly, Iran's Gross National Income (GNI) per capita has increased by about 48 percent between 1980 and 2012.[6] As shown in Figures 3.1 and 3.2, the long-term growth of Iran's HDI has been well above a neighboring country such as Pakistan.

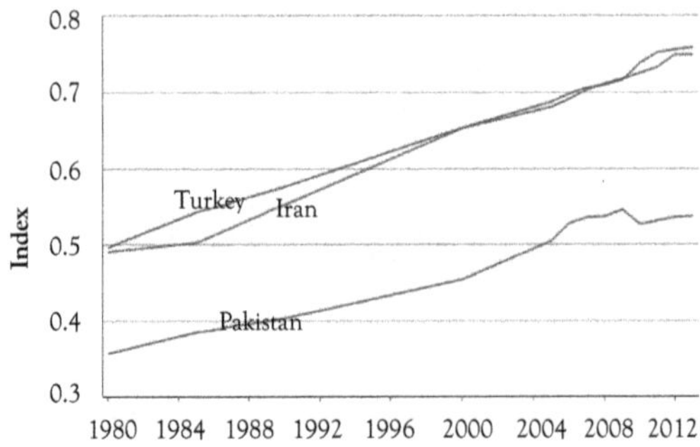

Figure 3.1 Trends in Iran's Human Development Index between 1980 and 2012

Source: Malik.[7]

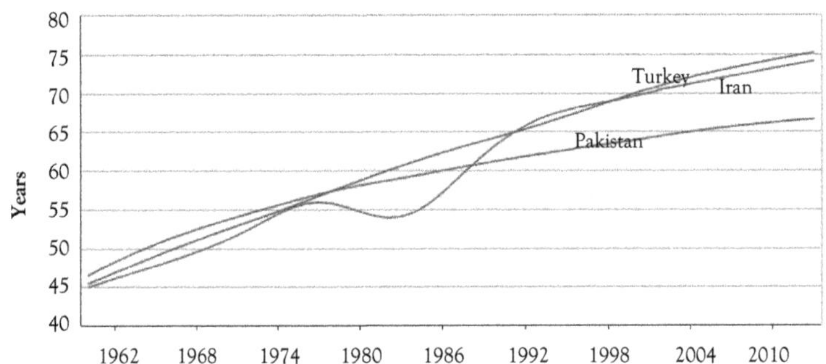

Figure 3.2 Trends in Iran's Life Expectancy in comparison with Turkey and Pakistan between 1962 and 2012

Source: Malik.[8]

A Modernizing Society

According to Inglehart's theory, the modernization process involves substantial changes including economic development, rising educational levels, higher occupational specialization, smaller families and higher rates of divorce, changing gender roles, and increasing emphasis on individual autonomy.[9] In that sense, it is appropriate to categorize Iran as a *modernizing society* or a traditional society that is in transition towards modernization. In the 20th century and particularly during the Pahlavi era, substantial changes happened in the Iranian education, economy, politics, jurisprudence, public administration, and even dress codes. During this period, the government was determined to take harsh measures to push the country toward an accelerated and even forced modernization. These changes led to the pervasiveness of Western values in Iran that were, for the epoch, in conflict with the traditional values.[10] At the time, many prominent Iranian intellectuals and religious leaders underlined the incompatibility between Iranian and Islamic culture and the Western modernity. For instance, in his book *Gharbzadegi* (Translated as Weststruckness), Ale-Ahmad (1962) a well-known writer and thinker insisted passionately on the corrupting influence of the West on the Iranian society.[11] Some scholars like Samuel Huntington suggested that the Islamic Revolution of 1979 was essentially a backlash to the accelerated modernization and Westernization of Pahlavi era.[12] According to this view, the Islamic Revolution emerged, largely, as a coalition of traditional forces to protect the traditional values confronted by modernization and Westernization process. After the Islamic revolution, the Iranian society has been affected by the interaction of both traditional and modernization forces. On the one hand, the religious and revolutionary agenda has pushed the society officially toward traditional values of Islam such as family, collectivism, deference to hierarchy, gender segregation, and religiosity. On the other hand, the same religious rule has led to the rise of modern values through public education, economic development, urbanization, and higher participation of women in labor market. For example, the Islamic government has extended the educational facilities to many rural zones and telephone, electricity, and health care services have become available in remote parts of the country.[13] In 2003, Iran's literacy rate was around 80 percent, and the country had more than 230 universities enrolling a total of nearly 1.6 million students.[14] Similarly, the quality of public health care has been improving considerably after the Islamic Revolution.[15] The weight of educated urban youth population has increased significantly, the number of women in schools and workplace has skyrocketed, and more importantly religiousness has become less attractive than before.[16] With all these changes, the current Iranian society is very different from what the Islamic clerics had expected.[17] Simply put, the effects of Islamic Revolution have been paradoxical. It seems that after three decades, the austere Islamic restrictions have backfired and the pace of modernization in Iran has been accelerated.[18] Currently, there is a widening gap between the population and the formal political structure. While the society, as a whole, has moved toward modern and secular values in the past 30 years, the political structure has remained extremely traditionalist and Islamist.[19] The reformists' movement in the 1990s and the Green Movement in 2009 could be seen as examples of two unsuccessful movements that sought a more modern, pluralistic, and open society. One may speculate that the increasing gap between the formal structure and population's culture may bring up major social movements in future.

The Paradox of Women's Conditions

The improvement of women's conditions began under the rule of Reza Shah Pahlavi in the 1930s and continued with his son Mohammad Reza Shah Pahlavi in the 1960s and the 1970s. During the Pahlavi era (1925–1979), the Iranian women were highly encouraged to participate in the public sphere and were granted the right to vote as well as the right to an equal voice in court. A family protection law was created in 1963 providing women with considerable rights in divorce matters and setting the marriage age for young girls at 18 years. Additionally, the women were offered the opportunity to attend all the educational and professional institutions.[20] In short, before the Islamic Revolution, the government policies aimed at improving the women's conditions by removing the traditional and religious barriers to their education, employment, and public participation.[21] Brusquely after the Islamic Revolution (1979), much of the rights women had enjoyed were lost. The revolutionaries abolished many of the Pahlavi's reforms and adopted such policies as the return of child custody to the father, the legalization of child marriage, the shift from an obligatory to the voluntary and contractual limitation on polygamy, and the authorization of men's unilateral right to divorce.[22] Also the Western-style dress was declared corrupt and the veil became obligatory. The Islamic government enforced gender segregation in most public places, women were required to ride in a reserved section on public buses, and on some occasions, adulterous women were given the death sentence. Despite all these conservative policies, in the postrevolutionary Iran, the women adequately managed to gain access to education, job market, and active public participation.[23] Currently, after three decades of Islamic rule, the number of women graduating from Iran's universities is overtaking the number of their men counterparts. The female literacy and school enrollment rates have increased tremendously and women make up 65 percent of all university students.[24] Iranian women occupy positions in almost all fields and are involved actively in workforce. While Iranian law and politics openly favor men, Iranian women have a highly noticeable role in public life, much more noticeable than in many other Islamic or Middle Eastern countries. Despite all the apparent restrictions, the postrevolutionary Iran has produced a large number of prominent female artists, filmmakers, journalists, publishers, authors, scholars, mathematicians, engineers, researchers, physicians, scientists, lawyers, human rights activists, managers, and university professors.[25] Therefore the condition of women in the postrevolutionary Iran seem very paradoxical. On the one hand, we witness the imposition of some harsh Islamic and traditional restrictions shortly after the Islamic Revolution; on the other hand, we find out that the Iranian women have had great achievements in different areas including education, business, and public participation.[26] Simply put, the Islamic restrictions have led to women's empowerment! There are two main reasons that can explain this paradox:

1. Modernization: Women's empowerment and the subsequent gender equality are closely associated with the modernization process and its implications, such as the shift from agriculture to manufacturing or service-based economy, urbanization, increasing life expectancy rates, declining infant mortality and fertility rates, and the improved population health.[27] For instance, declining infant mortality and fertility rates liberate women from the yoke of childbearing and create opportunities for women to actively participate in the social life.[28] Likewise, a manufacturing or service-based economy demands more educated female workforce[29] and urbanization in general leads to higher levels of gender equality. Therefore, we may suggest that despite all the postrevolutionary restrictions, the socioeconomic

development taking place in the postrevolutionary Iran has acted as the driving force behind women's empowerment.

2. The undesired effects of Islamization: We may propose that some of the postrevolutionary policies or restrictions such as sex segregation and women dress code (hijab) were in accordance with the Iranian traditional culture and for that reason turned out to be beneficial for a large number of women. After the Revolution, Iran's Islamic government persuaded even conservative rural families that it is culturally and religiously appropriate to send their daughters away from home to study and work.[30] Interestingly, for a traditional society such as Iran, the Islamic policies became liberators as they opened the school and workplace doors to the daughters of very conservative families who started to view women's education and work as being religiously acceptable.[31]

In summary, while the Iranian women still face many restrictions, they enjoy more empowerment than their counterparts in other Middle Eastern or Islamic countries, and they seem relatively satisfied with their way of life. It is important to emphasize that the Iranian legal and political structures are considerably lagging behind the everyday realities and the Iranian women are lawfully facing multiple obstacles. The future will prove whether the Iranian women can improve the formal political and legal structures and enjoy the rights they deserve.

Iranian Intellectuals: Torn Between Islam and the West

Over the course of the past two centuries, Iranian intellectuals have been inspired and motivated by two major sources: Shia Islam and Western ideas. This is quite understandable, because since the 19th century, many young students were sent to the European countries such as France, England, Belgium, and Germany to get education in new sciences and technologies. Upon their return to Iran, these graduates who generally belonged to Shia Muslim families became critical of their homeland and its backwardness. In searching for a solution, some viewed the West as the perfect model to be applied in Iran. Others argued that the Western model is not applicable to the Iranian context and opted for adaptation of the Western technologies to their indigenous values. In addition, inspired by the Russian revolution, many intellectuals embraced Marxism and tried to contest the influence of Islamist clerics.[32] The Iranian Communist Party particularly played a major role in shaping intellectual life by attracting a large number of writers, poets, translators, journalists, academics, artists, and high ranking scholars. After the coup in 1953, a new generation of religious intellectuals emerged. Disappointed by Western ideas, this group of intellectuals emphasized the importance of Shia Islam in the Iranian history and argued that the Iranian modernization should be based on original values of Islam. In some cases, there was an attempt to reconcile Islamic values with Marxist concepts of social justice and egalitarianism.[33] While these intellectuals were influenced largely by Western ideas, they were basically close to clerics' perspectives. Among this strand of intellectuals, Jalal Ale-Ahmad, Mehdi Bazargan, and Ali Shariati are recognized as intellectual pioneers of the Islamic Revolution.[34] Under the influence of religious scholars such as Morteza Motahhari and Mahmud Taleghani, the Islamic dimension of intellectual life grew substantially and cast a shadow on the communist ideas. After the Islamic Revolution of 1979, the Islamists took control of the government institutions and harshly eliminated the influence of leftists, Marxists, and Western-inspired intellectuals. The outbreak of war with Iraq was another reason for the revolutionary government to attack non-religious thinkers and eliminate them physically or ideologically. During the 1980s, the secular thinkers were sidelined and the Islamist strand took a radical position by criticizing the West for all ills and corruption in Iran and across the world.[35] In the postwar 1990s, there were signs of moderation among some Islamist thinkers such as Mahammad Khatami who was elected president in 1997. For a while it seemed that the radical Islamist agenda could not provide cure for an ailing Iranian society. The poor performance of revolutionary government, a long and terrible war with Iraq, and increasing social and economic problems made reformism the dominant trend in Iran's intellectual life during the 1990s.[36] The controversial presidency of Ahmadinejad between 2005 and 2013, and exclusion of reformers from the centers of power and universities may be viewed as a *counter attack* on the reformism that apparently lost momentum with the election of President Rohani in 2013. Currently, reformism is still the dominant intellectual strand. The proponents of the reformist trend emphasize the importance of indigenous and Islamic values, but they openly question the applicability of Islamic guardianship and advocate some liberal values pertaining to civic society, individual freedom, women emancipation, and freedom of speech.

Family

For most Iranians, the primary building block of society is family, and marriage is a common and blessed convention to create a family. Family is associated with honor, social status, wealth, and success. For that reason, loyalty to one's family is extremely important. Like other Middle Eastern countries, Iranian families are patriarchal, meaning that the head of the household is generally the husband or father who expects respect and obedience from the members of his family and is responsible to support them.[37] Children are central to the family and receive a good deal of attention especially in the middle classes. Yet, they are supposed to respect elders, act in conformity with their expectations, and take care of them in their old age. Compared with Western families, children may remain dependent on their parents' emotional or financial support even until their thirties. The relationship between husband and spouse is by and large much less egalitarian than Western societies. After the Islamic revolution, the government tried to revitalize some old fashioned practices in the Iranian families through changes in civil code and marriage regulation. For instance, according to the Islamic law women are denied the right to divorce their husbands. Despite all their efforts, the Islamic government did not succeed in restoring traditional family rules.

Marriage is considered an important path toward building a successful family and raising kids. In accordance with the traditional and Islamic values, premarital sexual relationship and cohabitation are not ethically acceptable and having children out of marriage is seen as improper. Most of the girls and boys stay with their families until marriage. The average ages at first marriage for women and men are 23 and 26 years respectively, however, there are some differences across the country and between small and large cities. For instance, the Baluch and Lur ethnic groups are marked by the lowest ages at first marriage and are more likely to have consanguineous and arranged marriages.[38] In urban regions, wedding ceremonies are held lavishly as they are intended to show off financial and social status. Flower decoration, food, cake, the wedding dress, photography, and other services are becoming increasingly trendy and expensive in large cities. Conventionally, the bride's family provides her with a dowry though the groom and his family are responsible for paying the wedding expenses and providing a home. Divorce is culturally undesirable, but in the recent years divorce rates have been increasing particularly in urban regions. There are other important cultural and structural differences between rural areas and large cities with regard to family issues. Families in large cities tend to be smaller and are characterized by higher levels of income, urban culture, higher level of literacy and education, and more modern values. In contrast, families in rural areas and small towns tend to be larger and are scored lower in education and income. Families issued from these areas are marked by more traditional and religious values. In rural areas, women have children shortly after marriage, but urban couples often delay their pregnancies to have more leisure time and money. Tests for genetic and contagious diseases are carried out before marriage and couples can use professional services including fertility and genetic counseling across the country.

Sexual Conduct

Khomeini had mentioned that the Revolution of 1979 was a return to puritan Muslim values. Accordingly, the Islamic government took some drastic measures to desexualize the society and fight what they called impurity, misconduct, and corrupt Western behavior. These measures were various and touched on social, political, cultural, artistic, and even private spheres of citizens' lives. In the early 1980s, the morals police could arrest people in their own homes for accusations such as corrupt or immoral sexual behavior. Both the arrest and punishment remained very arbitrary and depended largely on the circumstances. The punishment could range from small fines to incarceration, lashing, and even execution. The campaign of Islamic government against immoral misconduct culminated during the war against Iraq. After the war and during Rafsanjani's presidency (1989–1997), as a result of the liberalization of society as a whole, the government decreased the level of pressure on citizens. Moreover, the new generations who were entering their adulthood became increasingly moderate, and gradually distanced themselves from the orthodox revolutionary behavior. Faced with a young society and their sexual desires, the Islamic government desperately sought solutions. Subsequently, a range of quick fixes and superficial measures were promoted including temporary marriage and financial subsidies to young couples. Neither of these measures proved to be effective. Financial incentives were not considerable enough and they targeted the wrong groups. The idea of temporary marriage, which was suggested in Friday prayer ceremony by the ex-president Rafsanjani, was out of favor by the majority of people especially women, young, and middle class families. Even many clerics opposed to it as a provisional solution that could engender bigger social and cultural problems such as sexual violations, unwanted pregnancies, illegal abortions, and sexually transmitted diseases.

Overall, the conjugal and sexual behavior in the postrevolutionary Iran is marked by a combination of traditional, religious, modern, Western, and common sense practices. It is possible to identify three main types of sexual behavior within the Iranian society. Type 1 is the orthodox Islamic Republic recommendation. Accordingly, no heterosexual contact out of marriage is permitted, and both men and women should adhere to the strict puritan conducts and dress codes as outlined by the government. While this type of behavior has its roots in the Iranian tradition and Islamic teachings, it is not very popular among Iranians especially in the urban areas. Type 2 sexual conduct is marked by more laissez-faire and Western values and is increasingly popular among the postrevolutionary young generation. Finally, Type 3 is a middle ground between Types 1 and 2 and is based on common sense and pragmatism. As a general rule, while promiscuity is not widely accepted in the Iranian society, the common sense heterosexual socialization is widespread in the urban areas. Dating in the Western sense does not take place in Iran, but boys and girls could mingle and flirt in schools, universities, and parks. The concept of temporary marriage and polygamy are uncommon and disliked, and young girls' virginity is still an important and sensitive issue.[39] For many people, virginity is an indication of women's purity and their future loyalty. However, the younger generations are becoming less sensitive to virginity and may negotiate it before marriage.

Dress Code: A Constant Battle

One of the most contentious issues about the postrevolution Iran is the imposition of an arbitrary dress code on all Iranians particularly on women. Shortly after the Islamic revolution, hardliners argued that an Islamic country should be 100 percent Islamic and waged a full-fledged war against all symbols of corruption. They took some strict and even irrational measures to impose a uniform dress code on women consisting of a loose coat and headscarf or chador in black or grey. Similarly, they put in place mainly implicit standards for a dress code for men. For instance, Western style, colorful, and short-sleeved dresses were banned. Faced with considerable resistance from the population, the Islamic government relied on paramilitary forces (*Basij*) and morals police to impose the so-called Islamic dress code and crack down on what was labeled as *improperly-clad* citizens. The streets of Tehran and large cities became the battlefield between improperly-clad men or women and the police forces. Many were arrested or cautioned by police over their dress, some were obliged to sign formal statements that they would do better in the future, and some faced court cases.[40] It seems that even after 35 years of Islamic rule, the government and religious bodies have not been successful in implementing their intended dress code. The Iranian women have found new ways of expressing their individual freedom and in the past years the Islamic *hijab* has become less appreciated among ordinary Iranians. For example, women have begun to wear more fashionable colored dresses rather than dark chadors.[41] Currently, despite some sporadic crackdowns, the Islamic hijab is much more lenient in comparison with that prevalent in the 1980s. Over the course of the past 10 years (2005–2014), women have gradually altered the standard form of their outfit and made it shorter, tighter, and more colorful. To express their discontent with the imposed dress code, young women have transformed the recommended dark headscarf into a fashionable shawl in different colors and designs that makes them even more attractive. The more Westernized women may expose body parts or choose sexy dresses but the traditional and religious women prefer modest and conservative dress codes with darker colors and little make up.[42]

Most of the Iranian men do not have beards, but since the Islamic Revolution (1979), beard has become a sign of association with religiosity or theocratic government. Growing moustaches has been conventionally very popular among men and has been connected with manhood and chivalry. While moustaches are still admired, it seems that in the past 20 years, they are becoming less popular. Ties for men in public places are forbidden and most men wear casual clothing like trousers and long- or short-sleeve shirts. Young men prefer jeans and t-shirts, but the religious men distinguish themselves by wearing loose shirts that are buttoned up. On the whole, Iranians dress well and are quite careful about what they wear. Their dress codes diligently communicate their tastes, their values, and whether they belong to modern, traditional, educated, *bazaari*, or conservative religious groups.

Education System: Learn to Leave

For many centuries, the primary and secondary educational schools in Iran were administered by clergymen. In the 19th century, with the advent of modern times, these schools found themselves under growing pressure as they could not adopt new sciences in their curricula. Unavoidably, the modern social and technical changes led to reform in the Iranian education systems and gradually some secular schools were established. Under the Pahlavi rule (1925–1979), Iran's education system was rapidly modernized; all the religious primary schools disappeared, and the religious secondary schools were dedicated solely to training the clergy and Islamic scholars.[43] Worried about the preservation of traditional and Islamic teachings, the clerics and conservative religious people expressed their criticism of the Western style education system. After the establishment of the Islamic Republic (1979), the transformation of schooling system in general and universities in particular has been a major preoccupation of the revolutionary authorities. The postrevolutionary transformation aimed at both politicizing and Islamizing education system in order to generate a new generation whose values and beliefs come in accordance with the ideology of the ruling power. Accordingly, the authorities took drastic measures to fire those teachers who were opposed to the Islamic Revolution, put certain restrictions on girls, changed the textbooks, and introduced a series of religious practices in schools. Despite all these measures, the postrevolutionary educational model kept almost the same Western structure that existed under the Pahlavi rule, chiefly in order to respond to technical and economic needs. Furthermore, the Islamic Republic apparently continued Pahlavi's commitment to offer free, public, and mandatory elementary education to both boys and girls.

Currently, the schooling system consists of three cycles: primary, middle (guidance), and secondary education, which cover grades 1 to 5, 6 to 8, and 9 to 12, respectively. The middle cycle or guidance provides students with general education that will be used in choosing their concentration in the secondary cycle. The secondary education is divided into two main branches: academic and technical and vocational branches, which respectively lead to university education and job market. Iranian families spend extensively on educating their children considering it as an investment for their future. In the past 15 years, higher education has become very pervasive and 80 percent of high schools graduates enter universities. Due to a large number of applicants, admission to universities is through a nationwide entrance examination called *koncour* (from French *concours*). The *koncour* examination is very competitive and only the most talented students can enter state funded universities. In 2009, almost 1.2 million applicants took the *konkour* entrance exam. The last three years in high school are all about preparation for *konkour*. If the applicants are not among those accepted into prestigious state universities, then they may attend one of the private colleges or Azad Islamic Universities that exist across the country. There are more than 200 state universities and 250 institutes of higher education in the private sector, which is a large number going by the standards of developing countries. state-run universities are free and may pay some financial aid to their students, but private universities (Azad Universities) necessitate substantial tuition fees. In general, parents pay the costs of study and only a very small number of students work. The number of research institutions has grown dramatically since the Islamic Revolution. For instance, by 1982 there were 86 research institutions in the country, and 10 years later, in 2001, the number climbed to 191.[44] Since the 1990s, Iran's government has undertaken specific policies to reorient research towards industry and application.[45] Nevertheless, education, success, and income do not always go together, and due to high unemployment rates many of the university graduates end up being unemployed or underemployed. Every year, large numbers of educated young Iranians leave the country to work or study in other countries mainly in Canada, the United States, and Australia. According to the International Monetary Fund (IMF), Iran tops the list of countries in losing their academic elite, with a net loss of 150,000 to 180,000 specialists per year, which is equivalent to an annual capital loss of $50 billion.[46] Another report by the World Economic Forum ranks Iran 107 out of 142 countries in retaining and attracting talented people.[47]

Youth

The youth had a major role in the revolution and establishment of the Islamic Republic. Many high ranking revolutionary officials were very young, sometimes under 30 years of age. Ironically, the Islamic Republic has had a tense relationship with young Iranians, especially those born after the revolution. Politically, the Islamic regime oppressed young dissidents from opposition groups, particularly from the leftist parties. At the social level, the youth have been restricted from civil liberties and have been subject to stern dress codes and guidelines. At the economic level, the youth have suffered from hyperinflation, unemployment, increasing cost of living, and lack of professional and educational opportunities. Most of the young Iranians compare themselves with their peers in developed countries and blame the government for all their social, economic, cultural, educational, and professional shortcomings. This attitude has been leading to an implicit opposition to the government policies and resorting to an underground youth culture. It is important to mention that there are major differences between urban youth and those in smaller towns and villages, as the former group is more Westernized.[48] The urban youth persistently look for ways to reject harsh boundaries. While they remain mainly religious, the government extremism has pushed them towards a much more liberal orientation, which is in stark contrast with hard line clerics' worldview. It seems that the younger generations are more hedonistic and do things that were not permissible for the previous generations.[49] House parties, aggressive alcohol drinking, wild drug use, and sexual promiscuity are quite common behind closed doors in urban centers. These parties are considered not only as entertainment but also as political and ideological dissidence. On the whole, the typical urban Iranian youth are very different from their revolutionary parents who lived 30 to 40 years ago. Today, the Iranian youth are enlightened, disillusioned, and depoliticized. While they have a positive attitude toward the West in general and the United States in particular, they are extremely nationalistic. Despite all their economic or social hassles, they take great pride in being Iranian. They are receptive to Western modernity, but they think that there should be national solutions to all the problems of the country.

CHAPTER 4

The Various Causes and Features of the Islamic Revolution

The Islamic Revolution and Its Charismatic Leader

Despite economic growth and social development, there was an increasingly popular opposition to the Shah and his policies during the 1970s. The opposition came from a wide range of political and ideological orientations, but it was led by Ayatollah Khomeini who lived in exile in Iraq. In 1977 the declarations of Ayatollah Khomeini were circulated in Iranian cities and his name was synonymous with opposition to Pahlavi's regime. On January 9, 1978, a group of religious students in the city of Qom protested the visit of the American President, Jimmy Carter and demanded the return of Ayatollah Khomeini to the country. Shortly after, an insulting article in a daily paper against Ayatollah Khomeini caused a demonstration in Qom. The police opened fire on the protesters and killed many of them.[1] Forty days after the massacre in Qom, people took to the streets to commemorate the martyrs according to Shia traditions and showed their anger at the government actions. Once more, the police opened fire on the protesters and many people were killed in Tabriz, in the Azerbaijan province. The commemoration of Tabriz martyrs sparked protests in other cities such as Yazd and Isfahan and the ensuing chain of nationwide revolutionary demonstrations defied Shah's authority. The demonstrations were inspired mainly by traditional Shia culture, labeling the Shah as the tyrannical *Yazid* and encouraging resistance through sacrifice. The mass demonstrations were often led by men wearing white shrouds to indicate their willingness for martyrdom. By August 1979, demonstrations had become an undeniable reality in all Iranian cities.

The Shah tried to calm the situation by appointing new prime ministers but all these attempts turned out to be too little, too late, and surely ineffective. The revolution was already in progress and the Shah had lost control over the country.[2] In all these demonstrations, the name and picture of one person was always heard and seen: Ayatollah Khomeini. Khomeini aimed at Islamizing all aspects of society such as politics, state, culture, education, law, and economy.[3] During his exile in Najaf (Iraq), he had developed his ideology of absolutist theocracy, but in 1978 he was deliberately silent about this doctrine and pretended to be a spiritual man who envisioned progressive and democratic rule. On many occasions, Khomeni had mentioned that he would not be a leader of the government.[4] From his exile in France in 1978, Khomeini was effectively leading the uprising. He declared that "the struggle will continue until the establishment of an Islamic Republic that guarantees the freedom of the people, the independence of the country, and the attainment of social justice."[5] By 1978, he has gained unquestionable popularity and all dissidents, including Marxists, leftists, and seculars, respected his leadership.

On February 1, 1979, Khomeini returned to Iran after 14 years of exile. As the leader of the revolution, he received a warm welcome from millions of enthusiastic Iranians at the airport. Only 10 days later, after some skirmishes in the capital Tehran, the revolutionary forces took control over the country. On February 11, 1979, the Iranian radio feverishly announced the victory of the revolution and claimed the end of monarchy. By referring to their Shia beliefs, many Iranians were seeing the Hidden Imam in Khomeini and were dreaming of creating a utopian society. In an irrational ecstasy, millions of people rushed into the streets and celebrated the beginning of a supposedly heavenly era. On April 1, 1979, after a national referendum, Ayatollah Khomeini officially declared Iran to be an Islamic Republic and became the supreme leader of Iran. The Islamic Revolution happened swiftly; it seemed multidimensional, complex, and most of all, irrational.

The Aftermath of the Revolution

The euphoria of the celebration did not last for a long time. Shortly afterward, the revolutionary courts were established and hundreds of the previous regime's officials were ruthlessly executed. The country became the scene of disorder and power struggle among different political and ideological factions including fundamentalist Muslims, liberals, Marxists, leftists, and nationalists. While there was an interim government in place, the central authority had broken down. In fact, the semi-independent revolutionary committees were performing a variety of functions across the country and did not accept the authority of the central government. Thanks to his charismatic influence, Ayatollah Khomeini intervened in all spheres of government responsibilities, made major decisions, and established new institutions without consulting his revolutionary prime minister. In addition, the country was overwhelmed by ethnic conflicts as minorities such as Kurds, Arabs, and Turkmens claimed ethnic autonomy. Faced with internal turmoil, Khomeini created the Revolutionary Guards as a special military force loyal to the clerical leaders in order to protect the Islamic Revolution. Furthermore, the revolutionary regime took some drastic measures not only to stifle dissidents, but also to ban opposing newspapers and restrict civil liberties. Those who had complained of lack of freedom under the Pahlavi rule were disappointed by the new dictatorship that seemed much harsher.

Externally, the nascent Islamic Republic was involved in multiple disputes with neighboring and Western countries. The relations with the United States were especially litigious, as the Islamic regime was demanding extradition of the Shah. On November 4, 1979, Iranian students stormed the United States embassy in Tehran and took American diplomats as hostages. The incident led to a political crisis, and as a result, Prime Minister Mehdi Bazargan resigned. Subsequently, the diplomatic relations between the revolutionary regime and the United States were cut off and Iran was engulfed in an increasing foreign and domestic turmoil. In the belief that Iran was too weak to resist, Saddam Hussein took advantage of the revolutionary chaos to wage a massive war against Iran. Enjoying the full support of the United States, on September 22, Iraqi military forces crossed the Iranian border and rapidly invaded parts of the Iranian territories. While Iran was a revolutionary and isolated country, Iraq had cozy relations with all Western countries especially with the United States. Indeed, Iraq received direct military support from all Western countries, the Soviet Union, and all Arab countries except Syria. During the early stages of war, the situation for Iran was extremely difficult, as the Iranian army was disorganized, the military equipments were not sufficient, and the regime was fighting insurgencies and internal opposition groups. Yet, the Islamic regime adroitly managed to take advantage of both religious and nationalistic spirits to mobilize a huge army of enthusiastic young volunteers who were ready to defend their nation. These young volunteers (Basiji) were not well trained, but fought heroically and were fully committed to the Islamic Revolution. In the beginning, the Iraqi forces were dominant; however an apparently diluted Iranian army attained unexpected defensive success. It seems that Saddam Hussein had not taken the Iranian human factor into consideration. Despite all their domestic and foreign problems, the revolutionary regime overcame the adversary. By summer of 1982, the Iraqi military forces were driven out of Iran. Contrary to Saddam's predictions, the war became long and bloody and cost more than a million lives on both sides. After eight years of horrific conflict, the two countries finally accepted a ceasefire in 1988.

The war with Iraq resulted in radicalization of the Islamic regime. The moderate figures of the revolution were gradually sidelined or eliminated. Subsequently, the regime took some extreme measures to reinforce the Islamic values by modifying the legal system, segregating sexes, curbing media, and purging government institutions and universities from seculars or liberals. Despite the substantial external threat, the war with Iraq strengthened the Islamic regime by uniting Iranian society and by providing the regime with a strong pretext to stifle the domestic opposition.[6] In the 1980s, the Islamic regime was fighting on both external and internal fronts. The external front was the war against Iraqi invaders, but in fact, it had a wider scope and included an ideological conflict with all the Western and Arab countries that supported Saddam Hussein's regime. The internal front was even more threatening and consisted of a full-fledged conflict with the domestic opposition groups ranging from Muslim liberals to seculars, monarchists, Marxists, and ethnic separatists. For the young Islamic Republic, both threats were existential. Therefore, the Islamic regime did not differentiate between the internal and external oppositions and fought on both fronts with the same tactics. The war volunteers (Basiji and Islamic Revolutionary

Guards) who have been fighting against Iraq were skillfully utilized to stifle any kinds of social, civil, or political discontent inside Iran. At some points nearly all opposing groups were labeled traitors and were subject to execution by revolutionary courts. The exact number of executions is not known, but it could hover around 20,000 to 50,000 between 1980 and 1995. As a result of mass executions, opposition groups were practically eradicated or fled abroad. Perhaps the reigns of terror and violence are inherent in all revolutions, particularly in an Islamic one.

Once the war with Iraq was over, the Islamic regime had to veer to a more moderate and pragmatic path to respond to the population's increasing expectations such as economic growth, employment, education, and health care. Following the death of Ayatollah Khomeini on June 3, 1989, the Assembly of Experts elected Ali Khamenei as the supreme leader. Subsequently, Ali Akbar Hashemi Rafsanjani was elected president. The new government led by Rafsanjani took some substantial measures to revive the Iranian economy that had been devastated by the war and poor planning. During the 1990s, the Islamic Republic concentrated on social and economic reconstruction, health care and family planning, and education and literacy programs. The reconstruction programs continued after the election of Mohammad Khatami as president in 1997. During his tenure, in addition to economic planning, Khatami initiated significant political reforms to create a more open society. Khatami's policies met tough opposition from the supreme leader and his conservative supporters. He was exceptionally successful in normalizing relations with the West and neighboring countries. The era of Khatamai ended in 2005 when hardliner Mahmoud Ahmadinejad was elected president and claimed a return to the revolutionary principles of the 1980s. To some extent he tried to follow a hard line in both domestic and foreign policies. He was not successful in reviving the 1980s principles, but adopted chaotic, populist, and confrontational policies. In June 2009, Ahmadinejad was re-elected president for a second term. Supporters of the opponents, Mir Hossein Moussavi in particular, took to the streets to protest the fraud. In the end, the Islamic regime managed to use police and paramilitary Basij forces to suffocate the unrest and restore the calm.

The Complex Nature of the Islamic Revolution

The collapse of monarchy came as a surprise not only to foreign observers, but also to Iranian people and Shah's close associates.[7] The revolutionary movement swept through the country in less than a year and quickly overthrew the most stable regime in the Middle East.[8] In that sense, the Islamic Revolution of 1979 can be qualified as astonishing, extraordinary, and influential. It was not just a simple rebellion or protest; it was quite similar to other great popular upheavals, for example the French and Russian Revolutions.[9] The Islamic Revolution may be labeled as a social revolution since it was certainly one of the most popular uprisings in the world.[10] It was the result of a mass-based social movement that aimed to overthrow the Shah's political, cultural, and economic order.[11] It brought substantial changes to the state of the country, class structures, and governing doctrines.[12] It reversed the course of Westernization process of Iran that had been started under the Reza Shah Pahlavi rule and instead revived the Islamic ideology as a source of inspiration for other Islamic movements in the Middle East and across the world. The uniqueness of the Iranian revolution resides in its Islamic ideology that fueled the uprising and offered an alternative model for the Muslim world that was opposed to the political and cultural hegemony of the United States and the West. The complexity of Islamic Revolution resides in its multifaceted nature, in its popular support, in its far-reaching ramifications, in its breadth and depth, and especially in its contradicting features. While the Revolution was essentially Islamic, it was supported by a wide range of secular intellectuals, nationalists, and also the leftists and communists. The Revolution was basically a democratic movement, but it created one of the most authoritarian regimes in the Iranian history. It promised freedom and equality, but ironically it brought hate, intolerance, and bloodshed. Surprisingly, many of the early revolutionaries became the first prisoners in the new regime. How can we explain such contradictions? Perhaps, these contradictions have originated from the Iranian national identity. The Iranian identity is, by itself, highly complex and paradoxical; it oscillates between modernity and tradition. It is Islamic, but at the same time it is pre-Islamic and Persian. It embraces the future, but it is haunted by the shadow of the past.[13] Likewise, the Iranian Revolution was a combination of progressive and modern forces mixing up democracy, freedom, equality, justice, and leftist ideology with theocracy, bigotry, intolerance, and backwardness. In other words, the Islamic Revolution was a blend of tradition and modernity, intellectuals and clerics, nationalism and God, communism and Islam, reactionary and progressive forces, and tolerance and violence. The Pahlavi regime was brought down by an alliance of heterogeneous groups including traditionalist bazaar merchants, radicalized clerics, young students, leftist-communist forces, intellectuals, nationalists, and middle class urban citizens.[14] All these dissimilar forces rallied behind Ayatollah Khomeini against the Shah, but in fact they had different agendas and pursued conflicting objectives. As Kissinger pointed out, revolutions take place when a variety of forces unite to assault an unsuspecting regime. The broader the revolutionary coalition, the greater its destruction, and the more sweeping the change, the more violence is needed to reestablish order and authority.[15]

The Various Causes and Features of the Islamic Revolution

Revolution as a Backlash Against the Accelerated Modernization or Westernization

Historically, the roots of the revolution can be sought in social reforms that took place in the 1930s when Reza Shah Pahlavi launched some ambitious modernization initiatives.[16] Both the Pahlavi monarchs were impatient to transform an undeveloped, agrarian, and traditional Iran to a modern, strong, and developed society.[17] Reza Shah focused much energy on state-building by developing military, bureaucracy, and education system.[18] He ordered military conscription in which all Iranians from different ethnicities were required to speak Persian and to carry identity cards with family names. He created a strong centralized government and swiftly moved to secularize Iranian society by building modern education institutions, universities, courts, banks, and government organizations. He replaced the Muslim lunar calendar with a solar one, banned tribal and traditional clothing, and advocated women's rights.[19] For that reason, Reza Shah is often recognized as the great modernizer. Likewise, his son Mohammad Reza Shah was obsessed with socioeconomic development and had lofty ambitions to move Iran to the rank of the five most industrialized nations.[20] During the 1960s and the 1970s, the Shah launched his famous White Revolution and land reforms, which resulted in depriving landowners and clergy of their considerable traditional and religious privileges.[21] Under his rule, women's rights were greatly improved and the educational system had a significant overhaul.[22] Agricultural, educational, and legal reforms created modern and Westernized institutions replacing the religious institutions. At the same time, Shah's cultural modernization program aimed to reduce the importance of Islam by revitalizing the ancient Persian culture. In 1971, he organized the celebrations of the 2500th anniversary of the establishment of the Iranian dynasty with great fanfare and introduced new national holidays derived from the ancient history of Iran. Most of these reforms caused discontent with the Pahlavi regime among the population.[23] The clerics and traditional bazaar merchants were particularly disturbed by the modernization and socioeconomic reforms as they were losing much of their influence and interests. Because of the close association between modernization and Westernization, the clerics targeted Shah's policies and labeled him as a traitor to the Iranian nation and an agent of anti-Islamic imperialist forces. In the 1960s and 1970s, much of the Khomeini's rhetoric was directed at Shah's modernization or Westernization policies that according to him were menacing Islam. Khomeini threatened that if the regime continued their reforms, he would ask the people to expel the Shah.[24] In response to Shah's reforms, he repeatedly preached that Islam was under threat. In his view, the threat to Islam stemmed from an accelerated and ruthless social modernization undertaken by the Shah. The Shah who was raised with Western education had a totally different perspective and sought to modernize Iran at any cost. In his opinion, the clerics represented the *dark reactionary forces* blocking the path of Iran's progress. While the Shah insisted on his accelerated modernization and dreamt of building the Great Persian Civilization, the traditional forces were developing their networks of resistance. Khomeini's message was gaining popularity not only among clerics, but also among the newly urbanized population who were not comfortable with the modernization programs. The Shah's reforms pushed the population to the arms of the Shia clergy who mobilized them with traditional and religious values.[25] As the Shah pushed his Westernization or Modernization agenda, population's discontent grew and many Iranians saw him as an evil that was committed to the destruction of the Iranian religious and traditional identities. After all, they felt that to get rid of the Western influence, they needed to overthrow the Pahlavi regime.[26] As some scholars have pointed out, the Islamic Revolution can be described as a clash between the accelerated Westernization or modernization process and the traditional or religious forces.[27] In that sense, the Islamic Revolution was the victory of traditionalism over modernization. The history showed that the Shah had underestimated the power of the traditional forces.

Rebellion Against Dictatorship

Although Iran was a constitutional monarchy, the Shah ruled the country as an absolutist monarch.[28] The political power was concentrated in the ruling class that consisted of high ranking bureaucrats, capitalists, and influential families.[29] The Shah had built a system centered on his person and was directly involved in every important decision making. He personally made all major resolutions, appointed officials, initiated reform programs, and was even openly involved in domestic and foreign investments.[30] All decisions required his approval,[31] and especially during the last decade of his rule, he had become enormously arrogant and stubborn. Despite all the astonishing economic reforms, the political transformation and exercise of the democratic process had not taken place in the country. In 1975, the Shah created a single-party political system to dictate his own policies. Naturally, the centralization of power resulted in his political vulnerability.[32] While his political rule did not enjoy the popular support,[33] the Shah wrongly relied on his strong army and ruthless secret police forces. Due to his secret police cruelty, opposition groups went underground and became increasingly radicalized.[34] In addition to the regime's cruel oppression, the rampant corruption, inefficiency, and social injustice, contributed to the population's dissatisfaction with the Shah's authoritarian rule.[35] In the end, the criticism was directed to his Excellency and he finally became the common enemy of the diverse groups such as nationalists, seculars, Marxists, Islamist, leftist, intellectuals, and clerics. The Shah's political dictatorship and repression can be described as the main causes of the Islamic Revolution. It is not surprising that during 1977 to 78, all the social resentment was directed to the Shah's absolutist rule and the main slogan of the revolutionaries was *Death to the Shah*. Since all decisions were concentrated in the hands' of the Shah, high ranking officials and military officers were literally incapable of saving the monarchy in 1978.[36]

Economic Causes

The state of Iran's economy was not so terrible that it warranted revolt by itself, but the Shah's massive reforms led to economic discomfort among large portions of the Iranian population and ultimately created an opportunity for an uprising.[37] For instance, the Shah used the state power to promote industrial capitalism and badly embarrassed the powerful traditional bazaar merchants (bazaaris).[38] Similarly, the Shah's agricultural policies led to massive migration to large cities and resulted in high urban employment. The Shah paid much attention to Iran's oil industry, but neglected other sectors of economy, particularly agriculture.[39] The farmers were suffering and often had to migrate to Tehran and other large cities because farming was not a reliable job for them in the countryside after the land reforms. Meanwhile, the urban unemployed population grew rapidly in Tehran and other large cities.[40] The reforms and inappropriate economic policies resulted in the formation of spawning slums around the cities and the creation of a huge class of urban poor.[41] On the other side, the rising oil revenues brought about inflation, concentration of wealth, increasing social gap between the rich and the poor, and rampant corruption in the centers of power.[42] Furthermore, much of the economic reforms seemed like superficial programs that did not rely on sound planning and did not pave the road to Iran's industrialization or development.[43] From an economic perspective, the Islamic Revolution might be seen as a revolt by the urban middle class workers, the unprivileged groups, and the traditional merchants (Bazaaris) who were losers of the Shah's economic reforms. The Revolution provided some opportunities for abolishing privileges of the dominant groups, confiscating their possessions, and tearing down the institutions that supported them.[44]

Nationalism and the Third-Worldist Perspective

Along with the previous explanations, it is possible to view the Islamic Revolution as a genuine popular assertion of Muslim and Iranian identity against the Western political, technical, economic, and cultural domination.[45] Remember that the Shah was installed into power by an American-British organized *coup d'état* in 1953 that toppled Iran's democratically elected Prime Minister Mossadegh.[46] Furthermore, the Western intervention in the Iranian domestic affairs during the 19th and 20th centuries had created a bitter memory in the Iranian collective psyche. The Shah was widely seen as an American agent who was promoting the Western interests. As such, the Islamic revolution can be seen as a third-worldist movement, attempting to liberate the country from the Western imperialism. After all, the main characteristics of the Islamic Revolution were hostility to the West and an emphasis placed on the indigenous economy and culture.[47] The new revolutionary ideology had an Islamic-nationalist dimension that was a reaction to the Western colonial influence.[48] Not surprisingly, the Islamic Revolution was a source of inspiration for many Middle Eastern and third-world countries in their opposition to the Western hegemony.

Revolution and the Need for Spirituality

For some observers, the mass protests of middle class urban citizens, merchants, and well-dressed university students against the Shah took place in absence of any clear social or economical basis. According to this perspective, the Iranian Revolution was derived from a need for something novel, spiritual, and divine. The late leader of the Iranian Revolution, Ayatollah Khomeini, once said: "Our revolution was the explosion of light," emphasizing that the revolution was not simply seeking material and economic improvement, rather it aimed at religious and spiritual betterment. In addition to the socioeconomic and cultural explanations, it is possible to view the Islamic Revolution as a *spiritual movement* aiming at liberating politics and society from the materialism. This is in line with what the French philosopher Michel Foucault introduced as *political spirituality* in the 1970s.[49] In other words, the Islamic Revolution was an attempt to overthrow the materialistic power of the Shah by relying on spiritual forces.[50] The Islamic Revolution promised to the Iranian people something moral that would drastically change their *subjectivity*.[51] Indeed, many supporters of the Islamic Revolution eagerly sacrificed their well-being to establish a spiritual and religious society, free from the corrupt and materialistic vices of Western liberal democracies. It is well known that the Iranians who support the Islamic Revolution often call it a *Revolution of Values*.[52] As Ayatollah Khomeini has famously said:, "People did not rise up to get cheaper melons."

Revolution and Conspiracy Theories

Iran is located in a very critical part of the world, more precisely in the Middle East between the Persian Gulf and the former Soviet Union. In addition to this strategic location, the country sits on abundant oil and gas resources and plays a crucial role in energy markets. This geopolitical and energetic importance naturally makes the country prone to foreign meddling. As a result, some suggest that the great powers in general and the Soviets, Americans, British, and even the French might have been involved in influencing or organizing some factions of the Islamic Revolution. This perspective is very rampant among the Iranian royalists who believe that the Islamic Revolution was a conspiracy against the Iranian nation to create political and social turmoil and ultimately impede the rise of Iran as a great regional power. Princess Ashraf Pahlavi once commented that there were foreign countries that saw Iran under the Pahlavi rule as a rising power and they did not want the emergence of another Japan in the Middle East.[53] The supporters of the conspiracy theory are suspicious of President Carter's human rights policies and his lack of support to the Shah.[54] They are suspicious of the unhelpful role of France in giving residency to Ayatollah Khomeini in 1977 at the height of turmoil. They are distrustful of the destructive and anti-Pahlavi programs of the BBC Persian Radio in 1977. More importantly, they are suspicious of the speed at which the revolution gained momentum and overthrew such a well-established monarchy. They see the chain of events before and after the Islamic Revolution with great suspicion and ask why Shah's strong and loyal armed forces did not intervene to defend the royal regime or at least, to protect their own families. They cannot believe that the strongest army in the Middle East was defeated by an urban guerilla movement in less than two days.

CHAPTER 5

The Distinctive Features of Iranian Shia

Shia and Sunni Muslims

Historically, religion has a special place in the Iranian society. Ancient Iran was the birthplace of Zoroastrianism, which is believed to have influenced Judaism, Christianity, and by extension, Islam. Currently, around 90 percent of the Iranians are Shia Muslims, but there are many other religious groups in the country including Christians, Jews, Zoroastrians, and Baha'is. The Constitution of Iran recognizes Shia Islam as the official religion of the country. Sunni Muslims represent only about 6 to 8 percent of the Iranian population.[1] A majority of Kurds, Baluchis, and Turkmens, and a minority of Arab ethnicities are Sunnis. In addition to Iran, Shia Muslims live in other countries such as Azerbaijan, Iraq, Lebanon, Yemen, Bahrain, Saudi Arabia, and parts of the central and southern Asia. Saudi Arabia has a substantial Shia minority estimated at 10 percent of its population. Altogether, it is estimated that Shia Islam is practiced among approximately 10 to 15 percent of the world's Muslim population.[2] While the majority of Muslims in the world are Sunnis, the Iranian Muslims are largely Shia. In fact, Shia confession is an important component of the Iranian national identity. After the conquest of Muslim Arabs in the seventh century, most of the Iranians gave up Zoroastrianism and converted to Islam. Despite their natural affinity with Shia, for many centuries the inhabitants of Iran, like other Muslim countries, officially professed the Sunni form of the Islamic faith and Sunni Muslims constituted majority of the Iranian population.[3] Between 1501 and 1735 AD, Iran came under the reign of Safavid dynasty that passionately united Iran under Twelver Shia faith. Henceforth, the national identity of Iran has been interwoven with Shia Islam and Iran has been distinguished from the neighboring Muslim countries.[4] Under the Safavid kings, the Shia shrines in Iran and Iraq were reconstructed and many Iranian Shia clerics settled in Iraq's holy cities such as Najaf and Karbala. Similarly the relations between Iran and other Shia countries such as Lebanon grew stronger as many Lebanese Shia scholars moved to Iran and developed the basis of Iran's Shia clerical establishment.[5]

Regardless of their historical and political differences, all Muslims—both Sunni and Shia—share similar principles as they believe that the Prophet Mohammad was the messenger of God (Allah) and the Koran contains the words of God revealed to the prophet some 1,400 years ago. All Muslims abide by the rules of Islam as stated in the Koran. Islam as a religion hinges upon five pillars: (1) Shahadat—the belief that "There is no God but Allah, and Mohammad is His Prophet;" (2) five obligatory prayers in a day; (3) giving alms to the poor; (4) fasting during the month of Ramadan; and (5) making a pilgrimage to Mecca once during a lifetime, if one can afford it.[6] In theory, Islamic faith has the mission to bring salvation, liberation, and justice to the world. In that sense, Islam is a religion from God and oriented toward humanity.[7] It involves both worldly and godly teachings. For Muslims, Islam is not a manmade institution; the Koran contains the words of God, and its commands are literally correct and practical even in modern times. More importantly, Islam is considered an all-encompassing creed governing every aspect of life: public, private, political, and economic. These features make Islam rather an intolerant and inflexible religion that imposes its traditional commandments on the contemporary social life and resists reform and modernization. The Islamic jurisprudence is based mainly on the Koran and Prophet Mohammad's teachings and conducts.

Depending on their reactions to the modern world, Muslims can be divided into two main camps: the reformists and the fundamentalists.[8] The reformists emphasize the importance of religious teachings, but try to reinterpret the Islamic teachings by adapting them to socioeconomic and technological circumstances.[9] They underline that Muslims could improve their lives by reconciling Islam and rationality. For instance, the Iranian reformists such as Assad-Abadi and Ali Shariati did not dislike the Western ideas; rather they tried to incorporate them into the Islamic thought to build a beneficial and practical formula for Muslim societies.

In contrast, the Islamic fundamentalists are known by their enthusiastic opposition to secularization and social modernization.[10] They underline that Islam has unalterable teachings for all aspects of personal and social life that should be applied in political, cultural, and economic matters. Most importantly, the fundamentalists stick to a literal understanding of the Koran and believe that Islamic teachings and traditions should be precisely executed regardless of the modern time and circumstances.

The Shia-Sunni Divide

Shias and Sunnis share similar theological and legal tenets. The major differences between the two sects reside in their disagreements over the succession to the Prophet Mohammad and the leadership in the Muslim community.[11] When the Prophet Mohammad died in 622 AD, there was disagreement among his followers on selection of his successor. Sunni Muslims recognize Mohammad's father-in-law, Abu Bakr as the leader of the Islamic community. By contrast, the Shias believe that the Prophet had appointed his cousin and son-in-law Imam Ali as his successor because of his superior qualities and devotion. In particular, the Twelver Shia Muslims believe that the real leadership of the Muslim community passed from the Prophet Mohammad to Imam Ali and then to 11 of his direct descendants. Shia Muslims denounce the persecution and martyrdom of the rightful Imams by the reigning Caliphs who, in their view, deprived them of their rights to assume the prescribed religious leadership. In contrast, Sunnis reject this idea and believe in another course of leadership for the Muslim community. Sunni Muslims recognize the first four Caliphs including Imam Ali as faithful followers of the Prophet Mohammad, but do not accept the Shia Imams as the right leaders of the Muslim community. In short, while the Sunnis regard the previous caliphs as legitimate leaders of the Muslim community, the Shias view them as illegitimate rulers and believe in a line of Imams descended from the Prophet.[12] In addition to these historical differences, Shia Muslims attach importance to Ali, not only as the First Imam (Caliph), but also as a devoted Muslim who was a close associate of the Prophet Mohammad. The Shias maintain that Imam Ali had outstanding qualities as he was the first one who converted to Islam and subsequently became Prophet's closest companion. For that reason, they glorify Imam Ali and consider him as *the friend of God*. In their view, he and his descendants inherited some of the Prophet's supreme qualities and can be seen as the best interpreters of Islamic teachings and tradition. Furthermore, the Twelver Shias believe that the Twelfth Imam who is in occultation will return and will eventually establish justice across the world. Shia Islam has a few sects. After the Twelver Shia, the Ismailis are the second largest Shia sect whose followers recognize only seven Imams. Ismailis are found mainly in parts of India, Pakistan, and Afghanistan.[13] Similarly, the Zaydis represent another Shia sect whose adherents are found mainly in Yemen. Other Shia sects such as the Alawites and Druzes are found in parts of Syria, Lebanon, and Turkey.[14] Similarly, the Sunni Islam has many branches and subdivisions; among them the four schools of Hanafi, Shafii, Maliki, and Hanbali are notably important. In the past decades, the Hanbali School has been transforming to radical movements such as Wahhabism and Salafism in Saudi Arabia.[15] Figure 5.1 depicts the major branches of Islam and their relative sizes.

Due to their minority status, the Shia communities in other countries such as Afghanistan, Bahrain, Pakistan, and Lebanon have historically sought spiritual and material support from Iran.[16] Despite their historical and political differences, there were no considerable conflicts between Sunni and Shia Muslims in the last three centuries. Indeed, the relations between Shia Iran and its Sunni rival, the Ottoman Empire and other Arab countries and communities were quite peaceful during the 18th, 19th, and 20th centuries.[17] Sunni and Shia Muslims have lived peacefully together for centuries and commerce, socialization, religious congregation, and intermarriage between the adherents of two sects have been quite common. In the recent decades, with the rise of Wahhabi Islam in Saudi Arabia, Shias have been subjected to harassment, persecution, and massacres in many countries including Bahrain, Pakistan, Afghanistan, and Saudi Arabia. For example, the Taliban massacred 8000 Shia Hazaras in 1998, and more recently, Sunni extremist groups have systematically targeted and slaughtered Shias in Iraq, Pakistan, and Bahrain. The violence against Shias has contributed to the empowerment of Sunni terrorist groups like Taliban, al-Qaeda, and the Islamic State of Iraq and Syria (ISIS). Facing the anti-Shia doctrine of Wahhabism

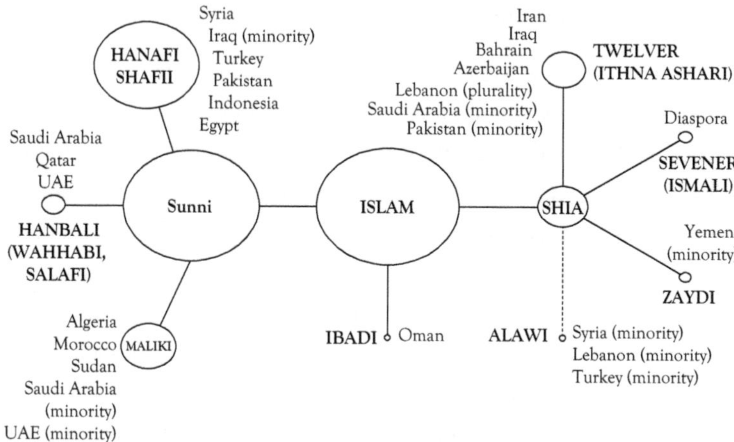

Figure 5.1 The main branches of islam and their relative weights

Source: "The Sunni-Shia Divide."[18]

in some Arab countries, Iran has remained conciliatory and instead has underlined 71 Sunni–Shia relations.[19] One may suggest that in addition to socioeconomic and demographic changes in the Middle East, the Iranian Islamic Revolution, and the Wahhabis' interpretation of Islam in Saudi Arabia have contributed to increasing tensions between Shia and Sunni Muslims over the course of the past decades.[20] After the Iranian Islamic revolution, Saudi Arabia has accelerated the promulgation of Wahhabism as a puritanical and antagonist version of Sunni Islam. In the absence of effective measures to curb radical Islam (both Shia and Sunni faiths), the sectarian conflicts between Shia and Sunni communities may lead to large scale and destructive political and military conflicts in the greater Middle East.

The Shia Salient Features

Regardless of their disagreement over the succession to Prophet Mohammad and the leadership in the Muslim community, there is very little theological and legal difference between the two sects.[21] Nevertheless, certain matters and principles receive more attention in Shia Islam and have different meanings and implications. For instance, guidance and emulation, the Hidden Imam, mourning rituals, and the JURIST GUARDIANSHIP are peculiar to Shia and are not seen in Sunni Islam.

Guidance and Emulation

Shias believe that the Muslims always need guidance in religious matters. This guidance is offered first by the 12 Imams or dependents of the prophet Mohammad, and afterwards by the qualified clerics (Faghih) who assume the responsibility of religious guidance. Those high ranking and qualified Shia clerics who have the authority of religious guidance are called marja (literally the reference for religious matters). There is no formal procedure for being accepted as a marja, but the prominent Shia clerics from religious schools in holy cities such as Najaf, Karbala, Mashhad, and Qom may reach this rank. The essential qualifications of a marja include an extensive knowledge of jurisprudence proven by many years of teaching and scholarship along with exceptional piousness and spirituality.[22] The qualified Shia clerics may be promoted to the rank of marja upon the recommendation of their fellow clerics and acceptance of their devoted followers.[23] The faithful Shia may choose their preferred religious guides (marja) and follow their instructions throughout their lives. Furthermore, the devoted followers pay their religious taxes to their chosen marjas who supposedly take care of financing Islamic schools and charity organizations. Therefore, the high ranking and qualified Shia clerics (marja) exert a significant degree of influence over their followers.

Clerical Organization and Interpretation of Religious Teachings

In Shia Islam, the body of the clerical institution is very hierarchical and well-structured moving from modest preachers to high ranking ayatollahs and grand ayatollahs with significant influence over their followers. In other words, Shia religious hierarchy seems similar in structure and religious power to that of the Catholic Church. Conversely, in Sunni Islam, the clerical organization is less centralized, and the clergy exert less power and influence over their followers. Furthermore, while the sources of religious interpretation are similar among Shia and Sunni believers, the Shia legal interpretation is more dynamic as it permits some degree of individual reasoning by high ranking clerics.[24] Thus, a characteristic of Shia Islam is the constant discussion and reinterpretation of its doctrine by high ranking clerics.

Martyrdom

While the idea of martyrdom is found in all Islamic factions, it is in Shia Islam that it receives a good deal of attention. The Shias believe that all their 11 Imams have been martyred to defend their faith. Every year, they commemorate Imam Hossein, the Ali's younger son who was martyred near Karbala in Iraq in 680 AD. His death symbolizes martyrdom for the sake of God, righteousness, and Islam. The martyrs believe that fighting and dying for the holy cause of virtue is part of their religious obligations.[25] For many centuries martyrdom was a dormant idea reserved for prophets, Imams, and saints, but the Islamic Revolution and the war with Iraq revived it and brought the martyrdom idea to Iranians' daily lives.[26] During the war with Iraq (1980–1988), millions of young volunteers who called themselves Basiji poured to the war zones to defend their homeland, their Islamic Revolution, and their faith. Thanks to the unimaginable heroism of these young volunteers, the Islamic Republic neutralized the internal and external threats and emerged as a strong regional power.

Jihad

The concept of Jihad occupies an important place in both Shia and Sunni Islam. The word Jihad literally means to strive.[27] According to Islamic-Shia teachings, Jihad may have two forms; the first form is fighting one's own evil inclinations and the second one consists of fighting unfaithful aggressors.[28] Therefore, a faithful Muslim should make efforts to defend the faith and Muslim community against internal and external attacks. For the obvious reasons, the second form of Jihad is what is well known in the West. The Shia idea of Jihad is associated with historical suffering and grievances of the Shia Imams, especially the martyrdom of Imam Hossain.[29] It is important to emphasize that in Shia Islam the Jihad requires the return of the *Last Imam* who is in occultation. Therefore, Shia Muslims should not resort to Jihad; rather they should be patient and wait for the return of their promised Imam.

Commemoration and Mourning Rituals

Shia Muslims are marked by the commemoration of their Imams and mourning rituals. Every year for 10 days (Ashura), they mourn the Battle of Karbala and martyrdom of Imam Hussein with many flamboyant rituals including chanting, passion plays, whipping, and chest beating. During these festivals, Shia men and women dressed in black march through the streets, slap their chests, and chant in the memory of martyrs and their sufferings. Faithful men may remember the suffering of Imam Hussein by flagellating themselves with chains, and some mourners may cut their foreheads until blood streams from their skin.[30] In Iran, many passion plays and theatrical performances (*tazieh*) take place on the streets during Ashura to highlight the spirit of sacrifice, heroism, and resistance of Imam Hussein. Similar commemoration and passion plays take place in Iraq, Bahrain, and India.

Ceremonial and Practical Differences

There are minor practical and ceremonial differences between Shia and Sunni Muslims. Shias, like Sunnis, emphasize: "There is no god but Allah, Mohammad is the messenger of God," but in their call for prayers, they add that "Ali is the friend of Allah." Likewise, Shias perform prayer a little bit different from Sunnis and place the forehead onto a piece of hardened clay and not directly onto the prayer mat when prostrating. In addition, they tend to combine prayers and generally pray three times each day instead of five. Glorification of the Prophet Mohammad and pilgrimage to his shrines is another distinctive feature of Shia Islam.[31] There are other minor differences in tradition and historical narratives between the two sects. For example, Shia Islam permits fixed-term or temporary marriage, which was permitted at the time of the Prophet but is currently forbidden by the Sunnis

The Hidden Imam and Apocalyptic View

As mentioned earlier, the Twelver Shias believe that the Twelfth Imam or Mahdi is in occultation and will eventually return to establish the rule of justice. They consider that Prophet Mohammad was the last messenger of God, but Imam Mahdi will come to correct the religion's deviations. In other words, Shias consider the rule of Imam as an extension of Mohammad's prophecy and believe that the Muslim community should be provided God's guidance via an Imam. They expect the return of Imam Mahdi as a world reformer who will revive the authentic Islamic teachings.[32] In accordance with this principle, the Shia traditional world-view is very pacifist and maintains that any effort in founding a legitimate religious government before the return of the Hidden Imam is heretical. In other words, due to the occultation of the Twelfth Imam, Shia tradition suggests that no expansionist Jihad can be fought.[33] Apparently, this Shia's view was altered by Ayatollah Khomeini and his idea of the Jurist Guardianship.

Velayat Faghih or the Jurist Guardianship

The idea of *Velayat Faghih* or the Jurist Guardianship did not exist in the Shia tradition and was developed by Ayatollah Khomeini during the 1970s. Velayat Faghih can be considered as an extension of the leadership of the Muslim community. Accordingly, Ayatollah Khomeini suggested that in the absence of the Hidden Imam, the Shia's jurists (Faghih) should assume the responsibility of establishing an Islamic government by providing the social and political leadership that the Prophet and the Imams had offered.[34] The Jurist Guardianship entails that the Shia clergymen, by virtue of their religious knowledge, are the best qualified to rule the society of believers.[35] It is important to note that not all Shia Muslims or clerics accept this idea. Some Shia Muslims believe that clerics should provide guidance for the faithful to interpret Islamic law but should remain outside the realm of politics.[36] For example, Ayatollah Shariatmadari (1904–1985), a prominent Shia cleric, regarded the Jurist Guardianship to be a deviation from the true Shia Islam. The idea of Velayat Faghih was introduced in the postrevolutionary constitution and provided a conceptual framework for the revolutionaries to build the Islamic Republic of Iran under the rule of Ayatollah Khomeini as the first Supreme Leader. The Iranian Constitution emphasizes the clerics' rights to assume the political authority and to enforce the Islamic law in the country.[37]

The Shia Religious Organization: Clerics, Mosques, Religious Schools, and Shrines

The Iranian Shia religious organization consists of a large number of clerics who are involved in a complex network of mosques, religious schools, meeting-halls, and shrines across the country.[38]

The Iranian Shia clerics include nearly 300,000 members ranging from low-ranking preachers and religious students to high-ranking clerics and grand ayatollahs.[39] As mentioned earlier, the Shia Muslims believe that after their holy Imams, religious jurists have the exclusive right to understand and interpret religious knowledge to the Muslim community.[40] Therefore, they have a much more elaborate and powerful religious hierarchy than the Sunnis. Laymen and junior clerics are supposed to choose and follow a high-ranking cleric (*marja* or *mojtahed*) who masters the religious jurisprudence and theology. Generally, to become a *mojtahed*, a clergyman should spend many years to complete religious studies and receive an authorization from other experienced authorities. The prominent clerics who become grand ayatollahs may attract millions of followers and enjoy an unquestionable financial and moral support. Ayatollah Khomeini was a prime example of a grand ayatollah who skillfully capitalized on his followers' support to ignite the political and social unrest in the 1970s. Due to the length of such studies, most religious students cannot complete the full curriculum to attain *marja* or *mojtahed* distinction. In such cases, the students who have not completed the advanced levels make a more humble religious career by serving as low ranking preachers, prayer leaders, teachers, and mosque administrators. Historically, the Shia clerics have been independent from the state and for that reason they have preserved their financial and organizational freedom. However, this independence has been waning after the Islamic revolution, as most of the clerics were employed by government institutions as administrators, counselors, advisors, auditors, judges, university professors, radio and television speakers, representatives, members of parliaments, and political officials.[41] In addition to employment, many of the high ranking clerics have access to public or private funding in the form of endowments, religious taxes, and donations. In contrast to the Western-style educated intellectuals, the clerics are available to the ordinary population, speak their language, and understand their preoccupations. They are skillful public speakers and master effective communication tactics to touch on the interests of the audience. In small towns, the clerics are considered as trustworthy and respectable and are financially and logistically supported by the traditional bazar merchants. In particular, the clerics with black turbans who are allegedly descended from the prophet Mohammad, receive a good deal of respect and financial support.

Mosque is a place for congregational prayers. It is estimated that there are about 6,000 mosques in Iranian towns.[42] The mosques are equipped with a special chair used by religious preachers or mullahs. Husainiyeh is another Shia congregation place serving as a site for religious ceremonies, especially during the anniversary of Imam Hussain's martyrdom. The mosques' preachers talk mainly about religious topics, but thanks to their close ties with the community, they touch on many social, economic, and political issues. In addition to mosques and meeting halls, Shia Islam has shrines as the holiest sites. Shrines are generally mausoleums of the venerated Imams or their relatives. The most important Shia shrines are located in Iraq; however, there are more than 1,000 small and large shrines across Iran.[43] The most important shrines in Iran are those of Imam Reza in Mashhad and Hazrat Masoomeh in Qom. These shrines consist of many peripheral institutions such as mosques, religious seminaries, museums, hospitals, and libraries. Many shrines are open 24 hours each day and receive a large number of pilgrims from all over the country. In almost all Iranian towns, there are many smaller shrines called *imamzadeh* that honor Imams' offsprings and those quasi-saints who are known for their faithfulness and pious lives. The movement of pilgrims creates a coherent religious network across the country and serves as a medium of cultural and social exchange among different ethnic groups. It should be noted that the pilgrimage to Imams' shrines is a Shia custom and is not seen in Sunni Islam.

CHAPTER 6

A Hybrid and Complex Political System

A Hybrid Political System

In the aftermath of the Islamic Revolution (1979), Ayatollah Khomeini and his supporters proposed that in the absence of the 12th Shia Imam, the clerics are the most qualified to rule the country.[1] Based on this idea, the clerics proclaimed an Islamic Republic and assumed control of the state and its institutions. Nevertheless, since the Islamic Revolution was a popular movement, they had to recognize the democratic right of the population in electing representatives for government functions and institutions.[2] This resulted in a hybrid political system that hinges upon religion on the one hand and population's elected institutions on the other. Likewise, the Iranian Constitution is a blend of the theocratic principles inherited from Shia Islam and the republican ideas borrowed from the Western political systems. The Constitution emphasizes the importance of Islam as an all-encompassing ideology that should serve as the foundation of governance, but at the same time recognizes some democratically elected representatives. Another complexity of the Islamic Republic is incorporating Islam and Iranian identity and envisioning the governance over both Muslim community of believers and the Iranian nation.[3] This combination seems quite difficult to maintain because the Muslim community is essentially transnational and includes multiple countries, ethnicities, and nations with diverging or even opposing interests.

The Components of the Islamic Republic

The Islamic Republic of Iran is an exclusive state with a high concentration of political, administrative, economic, and military power. As a hybrid political system, it includes both elected and unelected institutions and components.

The Supreme Leader

The Supreme Leader or *Vali-Faghih* is appointed for life by the Assembly of Experts, sits at the top of the power pyramid, and embodies the spirit of theocratic rule in Iran. In theory, the Supreme Leader assumes the Muslim's community leadership in the absence of the 12th Imam and as a result, his authority is based on his mastery of religious knowledge. The current Supreme Leader, Ayatollah Khamenei, was selected by the Assembly of Experts upon Ayatollah Khomeini's death in June 1989. Despite his junior position within the Shia clerical hierarchy, he was suddenly promoted to the rank of ayatollah. Since then he has proved to be quite effective in accomplishing the tasks. According to the Iranian Constitution, the Supreme Leader is responsible for the creation and supervision of "the general policies of the Islamic Republic of Iran."[4] In addition to his spiritual leadership, he holds major executive functions including declaring war or peace, planning the foreign policy, appointing the head of judiciary and the guardian council members, monitoring the national broadcasting organizations, and even reinstating the president. As the commander in chief, the Supreme Leader appoints the high ranking army officers and the Islamic Revolutionary Guards Corps' commanders who remain fully accountable and loyal to him. He closely supervises the intelligence and security services.[5] He also appoints Friday-prayer speakers and numerous representatives in the government, provinces and towns, universities, and in all religious and cultural institutions across the country.[6] The Supreme Leader's representatives are responsible for scrutinizing their respective institutions and ensuring that the Leader's decrees are fully observed and properly implemented.

In fact, the Supreme Leader enjoys more power and influence than the former king, Mohammad Reza Shah Pahlavi. While the function of the Shah was mainly political, the supreme leader benefits from political, religious, spiritual, and even emotional influence altogether. Interestingly, the word *Vali* in Farsi is used in the sense of *tutor of a minor*. Therefore, it seems that the supreme leader is an elderly father who is supposed to lead, control, and reprove the Muslim community under his rule. These features seem in accordance with the typical Iranian leader who is a two-faced father: compassionate and stern.[7] During the past decade, the power of the Supreme Leader Ali Khamenei has been contended by many other political players such as the reformist president Mohammed Khatami (1997 to 2005), the reformist fractions of the parliament, and an increasing number of religious and nonreligious thinkers. More recently, the religious and spiritual authority of the supreme leader has been relying on various footings such as financial and economic power, the Islamic Republic Broadcasting Agency, and military and paramilitary forces.[8] For instance, the supreme leader directly appoints the directors of the large Islamic foundations (*bonyads*) that function as powerful economic entities.[9]

The President

As the head of the executive branch, the president is the second most powerful figure in the Iranian political system.[10] While the president is elected directly by popular vote, all the presidential candidates should be approved by the powerful, unelected, and conservative Guardian Council.[11] For example, in the 2005 presidential elections, more than 2,000 individuals applied for candidacy, but only eight were qualified. The president holds office for a period of four years and is responsible for executive and economic matters by choosing the ministers and forming the cabinet that must be approved by the parliament. His tasks include the administration of the country's budget, implementation of the laws passed by the parliament, and supervision of the foreign policy and international affairs. It should be noted that the president's legitimacy is subject to the Supreme Leader's and parliament's endorsements. Therefore, the status of the president is similar to that of the prime minister under the Shah. He should fulfill the Supreme Leader's and parliamentarians' demands. While the Supreme Leader remains the most important figure in the country, the president still represents a key political actor especially with respect to foreign policy and economic planning.[12] The boundaries between the president's and the Supreme Leader's power spheres are not always clearly demarcated, and on many occasions, they might clash with each other. For example, during Khatami's presidency (1997 to 2005) there were many tensions between the patriarchic and religious rule of the Supreme Leader and the reformist policies of the president office. Mahmoud Ahmadinejad was elected the sixth president of the Islamic Republic in June 2005 and was controversially re-elected in June 2009.[13] Ahmadinejad enjoyed the Supreme Leader's support especially during his controversial re-election in 2009. The current president, Hassan Rouhani, was elected in June 2013 and tried to take moderate and judicious policies that are sometimes at odds with the Leader's approbation.

The Council of Guardians

The Council of Guardians is a very powerful body in the Islamic Republic. It consists of six clergymen and six jurists. The six clergymen or half of the Council of Guardians are directly appointed by the Supreme Leader for six-year terms. However, the six jurists are appointed by the Parliament at the recommendation of the head of the judiciary who is in turn appointed by the Supreme Leader.[14] The Council of Guardians has two major functions: on the one hand, it exerts a complete control over the elected representatives and their legislations; on the other hand, it preselects all the presidential and parliamentarian candidates. The Council of Guardians is responsible for screening all proposed legislations by Parliament in order to verify their compatibility with Islamic law and the Iranian Constitution. The council has the authority to block any legislation under the pretext of contradiction with Islam or violation of the Constitution. In the case of any stalemate between the Council of Guardians and Parliament, an *Expediency Council* appointed by the Supreme Leader, intervenes. The Council of Guardians has the power to design the elections in such a way that the voters must choose from a short list of preselected and preapproved candidates. Naturally, the Council of Guardians uses this authority to approve only those candidates who are fully loyal to the Supreme Leader. In the past 30 years, a vast majority of parliamentary and presidential candidates have been disqualified. In fact, by appointing the Council's clergymen, the Supreme Leader and his advisors exert direct control over all elections and legislations in the country. Therefore, the

Council of Guardians is often seen as a major obstacle to the democratic process in Iran.

The Parliament

The Iranian Parliament or Majles Shoora Eslami is a unicameral legislative institution that consists of 290 members who are publicly elected every four years. Similar to the presidential elections, all parliament candidates should be approved by the Council of Guardians. In addition to political competency, the parliament candidates should acknowledge their unquestionable loyalty to the Islamic Republic and the Supreme Leader. On many occasions, the Council of Guardians has used its right to preselect the parliamentarians. For example, during the 2004 elections, a large number of parliament's candidates, especially reformists, were disqualified from participation.[15] Despite all these filters, the Iranian parliament remains one of the most democratic institutions in the Middle East where some heated debates take place. Parliament members are representatives of different Iranian provinces or towns and are elected by a popular majority. In addition, the Iranian Constitution has made provisions for the representation of the minority communities of Zoroastrians, Jews, and Christians. The parliament is responsible for drafting legislation, ratifying international agreements, and scrutinizing the effectiveness of the president and his cabinet ministers. The parliament's legislative function is subject to the approval of the Council of Guardians, which can reject any proposed legislation that is judged in conflict with Islamic law or Iran's constitution.[16] Indeed, while the parliament represents the core of Iranian democracy, its real authority is curbed by the powerful Council of Guardians whose cleric members are directly appointed by the Supreme Leader.

The Assembly of Experts

The Assembly of Experts is a council consisting of 86 religious clerics approved by the Council of Guardians and elected by the popular vote to eight-year terms. The Assembly of Experts is responsible to select the Supreme Leader and has the potential power to oust him.

Since the Supreme Leader is an Islamic jurist (Faghih), all members of the Assembly of Experts should be senior clerics. For that reason, the Assembly of Experts represents an extremely conservative body whose values and outlooks are very different from the mainstream Iranian society. An important feature of the assembly is its secretive meetings taking place behind closed doors and not published anywhere. There are little insights into the activity and decision making of the Assembly of Experts.

The Expediency Council

The Expediency Council is a body that serves as a mediator between the Council of Guardians and the Parliament in the case of friction, divergence, and stalemate.[17] In addition, the Expediency Council may advise the Supreme Leader on his constitutional responsibilities and domestic policies.[18] The Expediency Council consists of around 40 permanent members appointed directly by the Supreme Leader. While the major function of the council is to mediate between the Council of Guardians and the Parliament, upon the request of the Supreme Leader, it can get involved in resolution of other important disputes.

The Judiciary

Under Iran's constitution, the judiciary is considered as an independent branch of the Islamic Republic along with the executive and legislative branches.[19] The judiciary is supposed to execute and enforce the Islamic law. For that reason, the head of judiciary, who is generally a clergy, is appointed directly by the Supreme Leader for a five-year term. As mentioned previously, the six nonclerical jurists of the Guardian Council are appointed by the head of judiciary. Therefore, a close relationship between the Supreme Leader and the judiciary is important in shaping the configuration of the Council of Guardians. Most of the members of the judiciary are ultra conservative clerics. There are three different courts in Iran: the Public Courts, the Revolutionary Courts, and the Special Clerical Courts. All civil and criminal cases except revolutionary or security-related issues are addressed by the Public Courts. Those cases involving crimes against national security, narcotics, and smuggling are sent to the Revolutionary Courts. In addition to regular and revolutionary courts, the Special Clerical Court serves as a powerful instrument for imposing regime's will on the senior Shia clerics.

Structure, Power Relations, and Decision Making

As shown in Figure 6.1, the formal political structure of the Islamic Republic is very complex and relies on equilibrium between the democratic and the undemocratic forces deriving from the elected and unelected institutions.[20] In addition to the official power structure, the Iranian politics is shaped by a complex web of personalities, religious organizations, influential families, and shadowy clubs. This informal structure has a considerable influence on political decision making. To ascend the political ladder, individuals should build strong relationships (*ravabet*) with influential clubs and get acceptance from power centers. Many ministers, parliamentarians, provincial governors, mayors, and even the Supreme Leader himself are part of these networks and are involved in complex mutual dealings. The political relationships (*ravabet*) are often reinforced by marriage and family-related links. In this respect, Iran is not different from many other Eastern countries characterized by nepotism and informal power circles. Former president, Rafsanjani, once expressed that Iranian

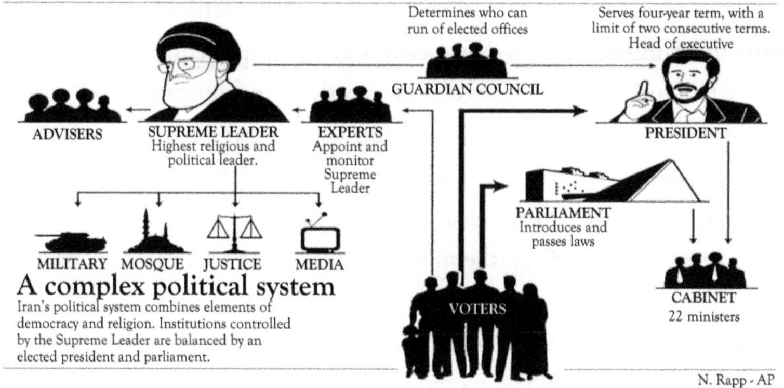

Figure 6.1 The structure and components of Iran's political system

Source: National Democratic Institute.

politicians prefer to form informal relationships instead of political parties, because in this way they can escape accountability.[21] The Supreme Leader controls many shadowy but influential organizations that have not been mentioned in Iran's constitution including the Office of Supreme Leader's representatives, the Association of Friday Prayer Leaders, and the Special Court for the Clergy.[22] The representatives of the supreme leader are seen in all state, civilian, and military institutions.[23] Other examples include the *bonyads* (foundations) or powerful revolutionary and religious foundations that control large parts of the nation's economy and are responsible to protect the Islamic and revolutionary principles. In theory, the *bonyads* aim at offering charity and social services,[24] but in practice, they are engaged in various lucrative business activities including import and export of products, and construction projects.

The political parties are not well established, but there is an ongoing power struggle among different revolutionary factions. It is possible to think about two important factions within the regime: conservative principlists and moderate reformists. Both factions fall within the framework of Islamic Republic but have different approaches. In other words, while united under the Islamic Republic, the two factions are ideologically different.[25] The conservative principlists literally believe God has delegated his political sovereignty to the Supreme Leader. Thus, they emphasize cultural conservatism, adhere to a highly orthodox interpretation of Shia Islam, and do not regard democratic rule as essential.[26] In foreign policy, the conservative principlists distrust the West and prefer isolation or restricted international relations. This faction is more aligned with the Supreme Leader Khamenei and his Representatives.[27] In contrast, the moderate reformists consist mostly of technocrats who insist on the importance of popular vote and consider Iran as a nation-state whose interests should be primarily protected. The moderate reformists have a pragmatic approach to political problems and intend to modernize the country. In foreign policy, the moderate reformists seek national interests and search deal-making occasions with the Western powers and neighboring countries.[28] The reformists were dominant in the political scene between 1997 and 2005 when they were controlling both the presidential office and parliament.

The complexity and chaotic nature of the Iranian political system are the results of a large number of formal and informal organizations, family ties, personal relationships, overlapping institutions, and most of all, the mixture of religion and politics. Even so, this complexity is often mitigated by a cultural emphasis on harmony and collectivism. While the political debates are often violent, the decision making is largely based on collective agreement and consensus among the leaders.[29] This kind of decision making explains why despite their apparent differences and disputes, the Islamic Republic leaders seldom confront each other.[30] Due to the apparent chaos and complexity, the outsiders may have the wrong impression that the political leaders are either powerless or confrontational. It should be noted that the Islamic Republic leaders are religious people and are naturally inspired by the Islamic teachings, still their decision making is often pragmatic and realistic. As mentioned previously, the Shia clerics have a good degree of freedom to interpret the Islamic teachings and make concessions on the basis of rationality or self-interest.

The Iranian Regime and the Iranian Identity

In many respects, the Islamic Republic may be viewed as the natural outcome of all forces that shaped the Iranian history. Two fundamental elements of the Iranian history, namely *religion* and *kingship*, are extraordinarily incorporated into the fabric of the Islamic Republic. For instance, the idea of a Supreme Leader (Vali-Faghih) is a Shia tenet that is analogous to the concept of Persian Shah and therefore nicely touches on the Iranian psyche. The Supreme Leader, first and foremost, is a spiritual man who is a moral teacher, who guides his kids like a father, who decides for them, and occasionally punishes them. The word *Vali* in Farsi means tutor and is used mainly for those minor children who are not able to discern their own interests. That is why, Ayatollah Khomeini was seen as a godly Persian father.[31]

The Islamic Republic cannot be considered as a full-fledged democracy but it relies on the popular support. Indeed, Iran is the only example of an Islamic state established by a popular revolution.[32] The fact that despite all international pressures the regime has shown a remarkable resilience that can be interpreted as an indication of its popular support. According to a study conducted for the World Values Survey in 2000, the Iranians rate their political system quite positively, averaging 5.84 on a scale of 1 to 10.[33] Over the past decade, especially after the controversial presidential elections of 2009, the regime has taken a harder stance and has distanced itself from the population's desires, but as a whole, the Islamic Republic has adequately responded to the realities of the Iranian society. Although there is an important element of authoritarianism in internal politics, the Islamic Republic, unlike many of its neighbors, has developed important institutions of participatory democracy. Apart from the 2009 presidential vote, Iran's elections have been generally fair and free. As a recent Oxford University study suggests, with the exception of Turkey, overall there is more progress toward democracy in Iran than in any other country in the Middle East.[34] One may suggest that by the Middle Eastern standards and in comparison with other Muslim countries, the Islamic Republic is a quasidemocratic political system.

Opposition, Resilience, and Survival

Several dissident groups have been seeking to overthrow the Iranian regime. Among them, the People's Mojahedin is a left-leaning Islamist-Marxist group, which was originally formed in the 1960s, aiming at overthrowing the Shah.[35] The Islamic Republic ruthlessly arrested and executed large numbers of People's Mojahedin members for their role in massive assassinations and terror-related operations in the 1980s. The People's Mojahedin Organization has lost legitimacy and approval, as people and especially the younger generations are embracing liberal values and are gradually distancing from both Islamic and Marxist ideologies. In addition to this organization, many Iranian elites in the United States and other Western countries like a change of political regime in Iran. These opposition groups are dispersed across the world and include dissimilar and even conflicting viewpoints ranging from royalists, pan-Iranists, and communists to seculars and intellectuals. The Green Movement opposition group was formed spontaneously after the presidential elections of 2009 and led to major demonstrations across the country and ultimately shook the very existence of the Islamic Republic. In the late 2009, it was believed that the Green Movement could pose a serious threat to the Islamic Republic, but the authorities relied on a combination of strategies like counter-demonstrations, show of force, and intimidation to stifle the opposition movement, and ultimately they regained control over the political arena.[36]

So far the Islamic Republic has successfully battered the opposition groups. We may attribute this success to multiple factors. First of all, it is important to note that the opposition groups have dissimilar political and ideological orientations and cannot cooperate with each other to overthrow the Islamic regime. Second, the Islamic Republic enjoys a high degree of resilience due to its dual legitimacy stemming from both Islamic and republic values. The political system consists of some elected and some appointed functions that supply stability and flexibility at the same time. On the one hand, the Islamic Republic is an authoritarian theocracy characterized by limited pluralism, dominant ideology, and strong and unelected leadership. On the other hand, it is a republic relying on regular parliamentary and presidential elections in which voters have a true but limited choice. The elections in the Islamic Republic aim to legitimize the semiauthoritarian political system while preventing unwanted people from penetrating into the power structure. The elections are instrumental in reducing internal tensions and manipulating the population.[37] Ironically, the elected positions enhance the Islamic Republic's legitimacy and pave the way for an authoritarian rule. Depending on the circumstances, the political leaders have used an effective combination of hard and soft powers to handle critical situations. Another major cause of the regime's resilience can be attributed to the mounting foreign pressure and the hostility of Western countries especially the United States. For example, the Bush Administration allocated $400 million in 2007 for conducting covert operations against the Islamic Republic.[38] These operations included supporting separatist groups, directing terrorist attacks inside Iran, and helping political dissidents.[39] Ironically, the increasing animosity of the Unites States has served the Islamic Republic to gain legitimacy, to boost the nationalist agenda, and ultimately to stifle any voice of domestic opposition. The Iraq aggression against the Iranian territory in the 1980s, the international economic and political sanctions, the American campaign for regime change, and the military threat by the United States and Israel have indirectly helped the Islamic Republic represent itself as a legitimate, nationalist, and powerful regime. A very successful tactic of the Iranian regime in suppressing the voice of domestic opposition is to connect them to foreign powers. In that sense, the so-called campaign of regime change advocated and financed by the United States has been a very precious gift to the Islamic Republic. After all, it seems what has not killed the Islamic Republic has made it constantly stronger.

The Islamic Republic sustainability despite the internal opposition and foreign threats confirms that regardless of their Islamic rhetoric, the ruling clerics behave quite rationally. Over the course of the past 35 years, the Islamic Republic has managed to accomplish its key functions in providing order and security in one of the most tumultuous regions of the world.[40] While the Islamic Revolution has not fulfilled its lofty aspirations, to some extent, it has offered social development and economic welfare to the underprivileged and rural population. Thanks to these economic reasons and more importantly because of its religious and cultural affinities with the population, the Islamic Republic has continued to rule the country for more than three decades. The current political system may continue to function in the future, unless it cannot meet the socioeconomic expectations of the population especially those of the younger generations. In the past decade, economic problems like inflation, unemployment, and brain drain have posed major threats to the very existence of Islamic Republic. One may suggest that the Green Movement of 2009 and the ensuing popular uprisings were rooted in the socioeconomic factors. Some authors speculate about the possibility of a Chinese model for Iran, consisting of a combination of economic reforms and cultural liberalization alongside political authoritarianism.[41] It is hard to predict the future trajectory of Iranian politics, but considering the centrality of a Supreme Leader, it is plausible to suggest that the personality of the next Supreme Leader will be of paramount importance.[42]

CHAPTER 7

Iran and the World

The Postrevolutionary Iran

Before the Islamic revolution, Iran was a member of the Western alliance against the Soviet Union and communist ideology. It maintained cozy relations with the Western countries, enjoyed their military and technological support, and defended their interests in the Persian Gulf region.[1] Shortly after the revolution, Iran's Islamic regime rejected the regional and international status quo and called for an Islamic uprising. The postrevolutionary Iran actively sought to export its ideology to other Muslim and Middle Eastern countries and as a result, clashed with the so-called corrupt and pro-Western regimes in the region.[2] Iran's revolutionary ambitions did not involve territorial claims, rather they were purely ideological. Iran supported revolutionary groups in Iraq, Lebanon, Bahrain, Saudi Arabia, and Kuwait, and denounced the pro-Western regimes as corrupt.[3] As a consequence, Iran increasingly distanced itself from the international community, took a defiant approach to the world and neighboring countries, and fell into isolation. In its early days, the Islamic Republic used to have a strong tendency toward an ideologically-planned foreign policy, but in the recent years, it has become gradually pragmatic and rational. The new generations of Iranian policy makers are more pragmatic and less committed to the revolutionary ideology.[4] For instance, Iran cooperated with the United States in Afghanistan and Iraq as it viewed the stability of the neighboring countries in its own national interest.[5] Furthermore as a major energy producer, Iran should interact carefully with the Organization of Petroleum Exporting Countries' members and oil customers, which are the industrialized or emerging countries. This importance of oil implies that even though it is a revolutionary country, Iran should operate within the existing international political and economic frameworks.[6]

In general, it is possible to distinguish two important orientations in Iran's behavior toward the international community: Revolutionary Islam on the one hand and national interests on the other. The advocates of the first orientation aim at exporting the revolutionary doctrine to other Islamic and even non-Islamic countries and underline the importance of revolutionary rhetoric in international relations.[7] Accordingly, they suggest that the Islamic Republic should refrain from rapprochement with Israel, the United States, and other imperialist or Western countries.[8] By contrast, the proponents of the second orientation argue that Iran as a nation-state should maximize its own national, strategic, and economic interests. They emphasize rational decision making instead of confrontation and inflammatory approach and they seek international trade and cooperation.[9] In practice, Iran's foreign policy is a mixture of both ideologically planned and nationally-motivated concerns.

Iran's diplomatic decision-making apparatus is very complex and includes a large number of institutional and noninstitutional actors and influential personalities.[10] To implement its foreign policy, the country utilizes a wide range of mechanisms and tools including oil, pipelines, Shia and Islamic ideologies, anti-imperialist rhetoric, financial aid, trade, populism, and public diplomacy.[11] In the past three decades (1990–2010), Iran has had tense relations with most of the Western countries, the United States, Israel, and its Arab neighbors. Iran's increasing ties with the principal competitors of the United States including China, India, Russia, and Europe has undermined the American hegemonic power.[12] At the same time, Iran has reinforced its links with Syria and has increased its position in Afghanistan, Iraq, and Lebanon.[13] Additionally, Iran has taken advantage of the neo-Bolivarian tendencies to develop relations with some Latin American countries such as Venezuela, Ecuador, Nicaragua, and Bolivia.[14]

The Middle East and Neighboring Countries

Israel

Israel has a special place in the Islamic Republic foreign policy. Under the Pahlavi regime, relations between Iran and Israel were very friendly and the two countries were involved in close commercial, technological, and military cooperation. However, the postrevolutionary Iran has viewed Israel as its number one enemy and has shown a staunch opposition to peace negotiations between Israel and the Palestinians.[15] For the past

35 years, Iran and Israel have had no diplomatic and commercial relations. The Islamic Republic labels the Israeli regime as "occupier" and argues that because of occupation of the Palestinian territories, Israel has no political legitimacy on the world stage. The Iranian leaders have often taken a harsh stance toward Israel, have promoted anti-Israeli discourse, and have offered moral and material support to the opponents of the Israeli regime such as Hamas, Palestinian Islamic Jihad, and Hizbollah.[16] Among these groups, Hizbollah is politically and ideologically close to Iranian leaders. Hizbollah maintains both political and military branches and holds many seats in the Lebanese parliament and government. The use of anti-Israeli discourse has been a deliberate strategy of Iran's post-revolutionary foreign policy. By choosing an antagonistic position toward Israel, the clergy hoped to bridge the Arab-Persian divides and take the leadership of the Muslim community across the world.[17] However, this confrontational approach has proved to be inefficient in building trust with Arab nations and instead has led to Iran's international isolation.

The Gulf Cooperation Council States

The ideology of postrevolutionary Iran was considered as a threat to autocratic and pro-Western regimes in the neighboring states such as Iraq, Bahrain, Kuwait, Saudi Arabia, and the United Arab Emirates (UAE).[18] In fact, the Islamic Revolution created a high level of insecurity among Iran's neighbors as they were afraid of the expansion of the revolution to their countries.[19] In 1981, the United States backed the creation of the Gulf Cooperation Council (GCC), consisting of Saudi Arabia, Kuwait, Bahrain, Qatar, Oman, and the UAE. The GCC aimed primarily at creating a balance of power against the influence of Iran[20] and to this end, it supported Iraq during the eight-year war against Iran. The relations between the GCC's members and Iran have been mostly bitter and unfriendly, but in 1997, when the moderate Khatami took office, Iran tried to normalize its relations with neighboring countries.[21] During the past decade, the GCC's countries have maintained normal diplomatic and commercial relations with Iran. While they have been concerned about the increasing political and economic influence of Iran, they have not openly supported the United States' conflict with Iran.[22] Iran's relations with Saudi Arabia are especially complex since the two countries are seen as ideological, religious, economic, and political rivals.[23] Saudis are anxious about the growing influence of pro-Iran forces in Iraq and in Lebanon and are fearful of Iran's nuclear program. In addition, Saudi Arabia is very concerned about the influence of Iran among Saudi Shia minorities.[24] The UAE has some territorial disputes with Iran over three strategically located islands in the Persian Gulf. Nevertheless, the UAE has significant trade and cultural relations with Iran and is hosting a large community of Iranian businessmen.[25] For instance, around 450,000 Iranians reside in the UAE; there are more than 200 flights per week between the UAE and Iran, and the two countries trade more than $10 billion worth of merchandise per year.[26] Dubai's proximity to Iran, its flexible regulatory regime, and large numbers of Iranian residents make it similar to what Hong Kong once was to China; a safe haven for both business and pleasure.[27] Among the GCC's members, Oman has maintained very warm relations with Iran. Kuwait's relations with Iran can be described as satisfactory, but there have been sporadic tensions over the operations of Iran's spies inside Kuwait's territory.[28] Qatar shares a huge natural gas field with Iran in the Persian Gulf and generally is not seeking any confrontation. Bahrain is the only Arab state that is home to about 60 percent Shias of Persian origin and the Bahrain government is especially fearful of the Iranian influence in its internal affairs. In 2009, a high ranking Iranian official created some tensions when he mentioned that Bahrain used to be an Iranian province.[29]

Overall, the GCC countries have an ambivalent attitude toward Iran as they are very concerned about their long-term security in the Persian Gulf. Indeed, formation of the GCC and Washington's alliance with the Gulf States were due to Iran's provoking behavior after the Islamic Revolution. While the GCC states view a revolutionary Iran as a threat, they fear that with a more moderate regime in Iran, their alliance with the United States could be shaken if not broken.

Iraq

The relationship between Iran and Iraq is very complex. The people of these two countries are connected by many social, cultural, economic, ethnic, religious, and family-related ties. Historically, the current Iraq or Mesopotamia has been the cradle of civilization, and for many centuries, it has been part of the Persian Empire. Majority of the Iraqi people are Shia and consequently share the mainstream Iranian religious customs and beliefs. Also, both Iran and Iraq are home to a large number of Kurds who interact with each other across the border. With all these ties, the two countries have fought against each other in a long and bloody conflict for eight years. Less than two decades after the war, it seems that the two nations have already forgotten the unpleasant memories. The United States' invasion of Iraq has pushed the two nations closer to each other. Thanks to the U.S. military intervention, Iran has gained popularity and influence in Iraq. The Iranian surrogates have built a considerable presence among the Iraqi politicians and religious leaders.[30] After the U.S.-led invasion of Iraq in 2003, Iranians initially aided some insurgency, but soon they changed their policies and supported the new Iraqi government.[31] The removal of Saddam Hussein offered Iran a great opportunity to push its own agenda. Currently, Iran is Iraq's largest trade partner. Iranian exports to Iraq include fresh and processed food, consumer goods, cars, and electricity. In return, Iraqis export crude and refined oil products to Iran. The volume of trade between Iraq and Iran has been constantly increasing in the past seven years and has reached about $12 billion in 2013.[32] The countries are poised to double their bilateral trade in the next few years.

Afghanistan

Very similar to Iraq, the Invasion of Afghanistan by the U.S.-led forces has resulted in an increasing influence of Iran in this country. Prior to the invasion, Afghanistan was ruled by Taliban who were ideologically and politically hostile to Tehran, therefore, the invasion of Afghanistan clearly served the Iranian national interests. The western and northern parts of Afghanistan have close sociocultural ties with Iran by virtue of common language (Persian), commerce, and ethnicity. Iran is mainly interested in expanding its cultural and economic ties in Persian-speaking eastern, central, and northern Afghanistan. The Iranian companies have been involved in a variety of construction and commercial projects in

Afghanistan. Despite all their political and ideological differences, both Iran and the United States are interested in a more stable Afghanistan.[33] While Iran supports a stable Afghanistan, its policy in this country is greatly affected by rivalry with the United States. As such, it is possible to describe Iran's policy in Afghanistan as multidimensional, pursuing different and sometimes contradictory objectives. For instance, while Iran is keen to help the Afghan government, it could support anti-U.S. militant groups within the country. Obviously, Afghan officials try to defuse the rivalry between the United States and neighboring Iran. In 2012, Wikileaks documents revealed that the Afghan president has been frequently receiving cash from Iran.

Pakistan

Thanks to their historical and cultural affinities, the bilateral relations between Iran and Pakistan have been mainly friendly. The influence of Iran led to the existence and prevalence of Persianized form of Islam in South Asia and particularly in Pakistan between the 13th to 19th centuries. Likewise, Pakistan's official language, Urdu, is heavily influenced by Persian. As the Pakistani author, Mujtaba Razvi, pointed out, after Islam, the Iranian cultural tradition exercised perhaps the most decisive and penetrating influence in fashioning the Muslim sociocultural ethos in Pakistan.[34] Pakistani politicians such as Zulfikar Ali Bhutto appreciated the help of Iran on many occasions and emphasized the importance of maintaining fraternal relations with Pakistan's eastern neighbor.[35] While both Iran and Pakistan are Muslim majority states, they have different religious perspectives as Pakistan has a Sunni majority while Iran has a Shiite majority. The bilateral relations between the two countries were strained in the 1990s when Pakistan supported anti-Iran Taliban in Afghanistan. In the recent years, Pakistan has moved closer to Saudi Arabia and has moved away from Iran and its shared cultural tradition. While Iran is still suspicious of the links between Pakistan and Sunni groups such as Taliban, it seems that the bilateral relations, especially after the U.S.-led invasion of Afghanistan, have been improving. As a whole, the bilateral relations seem peaceful because the two countries maintain diplomatic connections and cooperate economically and politically. The two countries have been cooperating to build a pipeline that would allow Iran to export 21.5 million cubic meters of natural gas per day to Pakistan.[36] In addition, Iran and Pakistan have signed several agreements such as Bilateral Trade Agreement; Bilateral Agreement on Cooperation in Plan Protection and Quarantine; Joint Economic Commission and Defense Cooperation, Preferential Trade Agreement; and most recently, the Joint Ministerial Commission on Security. Despite their intended political and economic cooperation, the bilateral relations have been strained by the pressure of the United States, Saudi Arabia, and the rise of radical Islamist groups.

Central Asia and the Caspian Region

Since the collapse of the Soviet Union, Iran has made some attempts to strengthen its influence in the new independent republics by means of substantial cultural, religious, and linguistic similarities with them. In this part of the world, Iran has to compete with Russia, Turkey, and the United States to gain influence. Iran was slow to take advantage of the opportunities in the ex-Soviet republics as it was preoccupied by its revolutionary rhetoric in the Middle East. Furthermore, Iran was not willing to support the radical Islamist groups in central Asia for sake of its own security and on the basis of confessional and ideological differences with these militant groups.[37]

Iran has always maintained important trade relations with the central Asian countries and has often helped the poorer states by offering them road, rail, and pipeline.[38] Furthermore, Iran is an observer member at the Central Asian security grouping consisting of Russia, China, Kazakhstan, Kyrgyzstan, Uzbekistan, and Tajikistan. The relations between Iran and neighboring Republic of Azerbaijan are particularly important due to their ethnic, religious, and historical commonalities.[39] The two countries have large number of Azeri ethnics and share Shia confession. Nevertheless, Iran has held good relations with Armenia, which is a Christian country, and has territorial disputes with the Republic of Azerbaijan. Among the Central Asian countries, Iran had significant achievements in gaining economic influence in Turkmenistan.[40] For instance, Iran and Turkmenistan have agreed to construct a gas pipeline between the two countries and to connect their railroads so that goods could be shipped from the Central Asian state through Iran to the Persian Gulf.[41] There is rivalry to Iran's activities by Russia, Turkey, and the United States.[42]

Syria, Lebanon, and Palestinian Militant Groups

As part of its grand policy toward Israel, Iran has been offering ideological and material support to some Palestinian militant groups. The United States has accused Iran of providing subsidy, weapons, and training to militant groups such as Hamas, and Palestinian Islamic Jihad. Iran's regional influence was enhanced by Hamas' victory and its takeover of the Gaza Strip. Similarly, Iran has developed a close relationship with Hezbollah group whose Shia members are greatly inspired by the Islamic Revolution. In the years especially after 2006, Hezbollah has emerged as a powerful military and political player in Lebanon. It is widely believed that Iran supplied Hezbollah with sophisticated weapons via Syria. Both Syria and Iran consider Hezbollah as an effective instrument to put pressure on Israel and achieve their regional objectives. After 1979, Iranian-Syrian relations have been extremely friendly. Iran, a Persian Islamic theocracy, and Syria, an Arab nationalist secular republic, represent quite different ideological orientations; but thanks to their regional interests, they have maintained a strong strategic alliance for more than 30 years.[43] Indeed, Syria was the only Arab nation that supported Iran against the Saddam Hussein regime between 1980 and1988, and thus prevented Iraq from portraying the war as an Arab–Persian conflict. In return, Iran provided Syria with cheap energy and invested heavily in the Syrian economy.[44] After the eruption of civil war in Syria in 2010, Iran in conjunction with Russia has been providing financial and logistic support to the regime of Bashar Al-Assad.

Turkey

Turkey and Iran are regional powers, competitors, and above all trade partners. The relations between the two countries have been peaceful and stable for more than three centuries. Turkey is a major exporter of goods to Iran and receives a large number of Iranian tourists each year. In return, Turkey receives its energy needs from Iran. The bilateral trade between

Iran and Turkey was estimated to be over $10 billion in 2008 and is expected to grow in coming years. It is estimated that over 2.7 million Iranian tourists visited Turkey in 2010.[45] In the recent years, Iranian businesses have seen Turkey as an ideal destination for their investments.[46] According to the Turkish government data, around 1,500 Iranian companies were active in Turkey by the end of 2010.[47] In addition to trade and investment, Turkey provides a convenient road to the European and international markets for importing machinery and products that Iran cannot import through legal channels. After the Islamic Revolution, as a result of Iran's diplomatic and economic isolation, the Iranian economy has increasingly relied on trade and business with Turkey.[48] Iran has seen Turkey as a strong economic and diplomatic partner that can defuse the international economic sanctions. By ignoring the U.S. warnings, Turkey has pursued its national interests in the Middle East and has been instrumental in helping Iran overcome the international sanctions after 2010.[49] Despite warm commercial and diplomatic relations, Iran and Turkey have major political and ideological differences. Turkey is a member of NATO and, obviously, is supported by the Western alliance; however Iran has close ties with Russia and opposes the Western influence. With regard to the Syrian conflict, the two countries have significant differences as Turkey openly supports anti-Assad insurgency, while Iran officially backs Bashar Al-Assad's regime. In addition, Iran and Turkey compete with each other over gaining influence in the Central Asia, the Caucasus, and more recently in the Middle East. While Turkey does not consider Iran a substantial threat to its security, it is still cautious about the Iranian nuclear program and its outcomes.[50]

The West: The United States and the European Union

The United States

As former secretary of state, Henry Kissinger, said "Here are few nations in the world with which the United States has less reason to quarrel or more compatible interests."[51] Iran was a close ally of the United States under the Shah who returned to his throne in 1953 through a coup d'état engineered by the Central Intelligence Agency (CIA). The Shah adopted a pro-Western policy, welcomed the American and Western investments, purchased advanced weapons from the United States, and most importantly, secured the flow of oil from the Persian Gulf to the Western economies. At home, the Shah modernized economy very rapidly and aimed at building a strong and stable nation. From the Western perspective, the Shah was a great leader who brought much needed security to the Persian Gulf region and opposed the expansion of the Soviet Union. With the advent of the Islamic Revolution in 1978 to 1979, the American–Iranian relations changed drastically. The Iranian revolutionaries held a grudge against the United States for many reasons, especially because of the extensive support of Americans for the Shah dictatorship and their direct involvement in the 1953 coup d'état. Furthermore, many revolutionaries believed that the United States was seeking to overthrow the Islamic regime like it did in the 1953 coup.[52] In November 1979, a group of Iranian students seized 63 hostages in the U.S. embassy in Tehran leading to a diplomatic stand-off and growing tension between the two countries.[53] Since then, the American-Iranian relations have been marked by hostility and resentment. On the one hand, the United States accuses Iran of harboring terrorists, discouraging the peace process in the Middle East, and harming American interests around the world. Americans label Iran as a rogue and outlaw country that does not abide by the international rules.[54] In addition, the U.S. reprimands Iran for its nuclear program, its military and defense projects, its human rights record, and its system of governance.[55] In the recent years, the U.S. government has used the Iranian nuclear program as a *casus belli* to make military threats and to increase pressure on Iran.[56] Some groups of American politicians led by the former Vice President, Cheney, believe that the U.S. policy should focus on using military confrontation with Iran or on changing Iran's regime.[57] On the other hand, Iran accuses the United States of undermining its revolutionary government, supporting dissident groups, helping Iran's enemies, and setting up harsh trade sanctions against its economic interests.

There are many grounds for the political standoff and bitterness between the United States and Iran: geopolitical, historical, regional, and cultural. From a geopolitical perspective, the U.S. policy toward Iran hinges upon a strategic framework aiming at containing Iran in the Middle East and particularly in the Persian Gulf.[58] As president Carter emphasized: "An attempt by any outside force to gain control of the

Persian Gulf region will be regarded as an assault on the vital interests of the United States of America, and such an assault will be repelled by any means necessary, including military force."[59] The Islamic Revolution ousted the Shah as one of the closest U.S. allies and brought to power a nationalist-Islamic popular government in 1979. For obvious reasons, instead of satisfying the U.S. economic and political expectations, the revolutionary regime in Iran took an independent trajectory and sought to maximize its own national and regional interests. That is exactly why the United States took a hostile stance toward the Iranian independent and nationalistic regime by labeling it as a rogue state, a threat to U.S. regional interests, a threat to regional stability, and even a threat to international security.[60]

The postrevolutionary Iran has chosen the opposition to Israel as its ideological trademark. The clerical regime is perhaps the most vocal opponent of Israel; they label Israel as the occupier of Palestine, they publicly condemn any peace attempts or agreements, and by extension they denounce the United States for supporting Israel. In addition to the revolutionary rhetoric, Iran has sponsored several Islamic groups and activities such as Hezbollah movement in Lebanon and Hamas in Gaza. Obviously, this attitude toward a very powerful and influential country such as Israel has created major barriers to friendly relations with the United States and many other Western countries.[61]

Some of the causes of resentment in the Iranian–American relations reside in the historical events. The United States is a young and optimistic nation; but Iran is an ancient nation and consequently is affected hugely by its long, glorious, and tragic history. Iranians remember their humiliations by the Western powers especially by the British and Americans. In 1953, the British and American secret agencies allegedly facilitated overthrowing of the popular and democratically elected Prime Minister Mosadegh. After the Islamic Revolution, the United States did not respect the new revolutionary regime in Tehran and took multiple actions to undermine its stability. In 1980, the U.S. government incited Saddam Hussein to attack the revolutionary Iran and offered him extensive support by attempting to block conventional arms sales to Iran, providing battlefield intelligence to Iraq, and even by fighting the Iranian naval forces.[62] In 1988, the United States shot down an Iranian civilian airliner with 290 passengers over the Persian Gulf and surprisingly prized the captain of the U.S., *Vincennes*, for these actions.[63]

While the regional and geopolitical factors are behind much of the antagonistic relations between the two nations, the effects of cultural and ideological causes should not be overlooked. Iran remains a traditional society,[64] and part of its hostility with the West in general and with the United States in particular can be attributed to the incompatibility between the modern and traditional values.[65] The Iranian leadership and the Iranian society as a whole see the West as a disturbing and corrupting power that demoralizes their pure religious values.[66] Iranian intellectuals and leaders frequently have used the terms such as *West-toxification*, *West-struckness*, or *cultural invasion* to point out the irksome influence of the American and Western culture.

While the diplomatic relation between the United States and Iran was disrupted by the Islamic Revolution, the informal exchange between the two countries has continued to grow in the postrevolutionary era. Due to extensive American–Iranian relations under the Shah, the United States was home to a large number of Iranian expatriates who kept in touch with the motherland. In the past three decades, a growing number of Iranian students or skilled workers have migrated to the United States and have made this country their home. According to Iranian Studies Group at Massachusetts Institute of Technology, in 2004, more than 700,000 Iranians or persons of Iranian descent were residing in the United States.[67] In 2007, a survey by the *World Public Opinion* revealed that while large majorities of Iranians have negative views of the U.S. government, they have favorable attitudes toward the American people and culture.[68] It seems that Iranians are particularly concerned about the U.S. foreign policy, which they consider a threat to the stability of the Middle East.[69] A large majority of Iranians and Americans support steps toward improving the U.S.-Iranian relations. A recent poll by the state-run National Institute for Research and Opinion Polls showed that 75 percent of Iranians favored a dialogue with the United States. Particularly, they support bilateral relations on issues of mutual concern, cultural, educational, and sporting exchanges, better access for journalists from the two countries, increased trade, and more tourism.[70]

The European Union

The European countries at first had an ambivalent attitude toward the Islamic Revolution, but rapidly took an antagonistic policy toward the revolutionary regime and offered their support to Saddam Hussein in his war on Iran.[71] After the war with Iraq, both Iran and the European Union (EU) tried to normalize their relations. The rapprochement between Iran and Europe was mutually beneficial. From the Europeans' standpoint, Iran was an attractive large market and a source of energy.[72] From the Iranians' standpoint, EU was a source of much needed investment and technology. In addition, the Europeans believed that engagement with Iran could strengthen the moderate elements of revolutionary regime and ultimately reduce the Islamic radicalism.[73] Hence, the bilateral economic and diplomatic relations were expanded and the Europeans sought to resolve their ideological and political differences with Iran by a critical dialogue. While the United States had no diplomatic relations with Iran, the European countries took the lead in negotiations with Iran over its controversial nuclear program. In 2003, the Foreign Ministers of Germany, France, and the United Kingdom travelled to Tehran in order to persuade the Iranian authorities to work more closely with the International Atomic Energy Agency inspectors. However, the bilateral relations were stressed after 2010 as the EU joined the United States and imposed some harsh sanctions against Iran over its nuclear program.[74]

European nations have different views towards Iran, but in general they are more unwilling to get involved in a military confrontation and see Iran's abundant energy resources and consumer market as opportunities for cooperation and trade. Occasionally, they have sought closer ties with Iran in order to take advantage of economic cooperation and at various points they have tried to promote and exploit reforms in Iran's political system. The French Peugeot, Renault, Alcatel, and Total, the Swiss Nestlé, the Swedish Svedala Industri, the Norwegian Statoil, the Italian ENI SpA, the German Siemens, and many other European corporations have been doing business in Iran. Overall, the relations between Iran and the EU have been driven by short-term, mutual interests. It seems that while the two parties are interested in expanding their cooperation, the ideological, cultural, and geopolitical differences keep them apart.

Asia, Latin America, and Africa

China

China a communist country and Iran a theocratic regime represent dissimilar and even opposing ideologies but they have maintained very friendly bilateral relations. In addition to cultural and civilizational affinities, the postrevolutionary Iran turned to Asia and particularly to China to offset the standoff with the Western powers. As early as the 1980s, Iran was receiving technological and military help from China. Subsequently, Iran developed strong economic and trade relations with China to neutralize the U.S. sanctions and maintain its geopolitical independence. In the absence of Western rivals, the Chinese companies have successfully penetrated into the Iranian market and gained considerable market share in different sectors such as oil, gas, urban infrastructure, and construction. China has viewed Iran as a stable country in the Middle East that could ensure its huge energy needs.[75] As a permanent member of the Security Council, China has regularly used its political weight and veto right to defend Iran's nuclear program. There is considerable military cooperation between the two countries and, reportedly, China has provided Iran with dual-use technology that could be used for the development of weapons. In short, China and Iran relations are based on solid geopolitical and economic mutual interests.

India

Iran and India have been traditionally bordering civilizations, trade partners, and regional allies. The two countries have significant cultural and political commonalities and have been pursuing mutual interests with regard to regional security, terrorism, and Islamic radicalization. Before the Islamic Revolution and during the Cold War period, Iran and India had good relations, but they belonged to two different geopolitical poles: India developed strong military and economic links with the Soviet Union whereas Iran had close cooperation with the United States.[76] After the Revolution, the relations between Iran and India have been strengthened as the two countries have identified their mutual interests and moved to expand cooperation in several key areas including energy, geopolitical and strategic interests, counterterrorism, regional stability, and defense. India is one of the main buyers of Iran's oil and the two countries have considered some methods to transfer Iran's energy reserves to India. For instance, the two countries have considered the construction of an ambitious pipeline that would transfer Iran's gas to India via Pakistan.[77] Additionally, the two countries are working on the North-South Transportation Corridor to link Mumbai via Bandar Abbas (Iran) with Europe.

Africa

There are many reasons that Iran is becoming interested in expanding relationships with Africa. In addition to enormous economic and political opportunities, the Islamic Revolution discourse is primarily anti-Western and anticcolonial pretending to defend the interests of oppressed masses across the globe including Africa. Iran is mostly interested in relations with the East African countries as, thanks to their location, they can serve Iran's regional plans.[78] By relying on the Islamic and revolutionary ideology, Iran has been seeking to attract local Muslim populations and gradually has established a permanent presence in the East African countries. Iran can threaten the Western sea lanes at the entrance to the Red Sea. Also, Iran may use the East African countries such as Sudan to transfer military equipment through Egypt to the Hamas-controlled Gaza Strip.[79] In pursuing its grand African policy, Iran has been involved in a variety of projects in agriculture, energy, construction, and infrastructure. In 2009 and 2010, Iran's president visited many African countries such as the Comoro Islands, Djibouti, Kenya, Uganda, and Zimbabwe. Iran has expressed its willingness to help African countries liberate from the Western oppression.[80]

Latin America

As part of its anti-American strategy, Iran has been developing cozy relationships with Latin American countries, especially those who challenge the U.S. hegemony. Cuba, Venezuela, Nicaragua, Bolivia, and even Brazil are among those countries that Iran's presidents have visited in the past six years. Iran and Venezuela have been involved in many joint projects in banking, oil production, construction, and technology transfer. Hugo Chavez, the late president of Venezuela, visited Iran on many occasions and became one of Iran's closest allies. To increase its political influence in Latin America, Iran has been opening offices in several countries. Allegedly, Iran has offered Bolivia $1 billion in financial aid and investment and has been looking for new ways to strengthen its ties with Brazil. The Unites States is concerned about the marriage of Iran's Islamist ideology with Latin American anti-U.S. policy and the ensuing effects on security.

Russia

Due to its proximity and immensity, in the past three centuries, Russia has played an important role in Iran. Russia and Iran fought multiple wars in the 18th and 19th centuries. In the 19th century, Russia annexed the northeastern provinces of Dagestan, Azerbaijan, and Armenia. For more than two centuries Iran was involved in the great game between Great Britain and Russia. In World War II, the Russian forces invaded the northern parts of Iran, and in the 1940s, Stalin made serious attempts to separate the northwestern part of Iran. During the COLD WAR, Iran was a member of the Western Alliance and naturally was protected by the United States against Russian aggression. The attitude of Iranians towards the Soviet Union and Russia has been ambivalent. While the northern neighbor has been a source of threat and invasion, most of the Iranian leftists and intellectuals viewed its geopolitical role as positive. After the Islamic Revolution, the Soviet Union and later the Russian Federation gradually established close relations with Iran and, in the absence of the United States, provided Iran with technological and military provisions. The collapse of the Soviet Union bridged the apparent ideological gap between the communist regime and the Islamic Republic. Iran's rapprochement with the post-Soviet Russia evolved very quickly as it turned to a close security and trade partner of Iran.[81] Russia's proximity and its influence in the international community made it a valuable partner of Iran. In the past two decades, thanks to hostility between the United States and Iran, Russia has continued to develop lucrative diplomatic and trade relations with the Islamic Republic.[82] Russia has provided Iran with arms and has been actively involved in the design and construction of Iranian nuclear facilities.[83] In return, Russia has opposed a military solution to the issue of Iran's nuclear program and as a member of the United Nations Security Council, has used its diplomatic weight to neutralize the effects of international resolutions against Iran. Despite the increasing bilateral economic and security cooperation, the two countries have significant conflicting interests. Russia has shown a hesitant support for Iran and supposedly does not like a strong Iran south of its border. Similarly, Iran has been historically concerned about the expansionist intentions of its northern neighbor. The two countries have unsettled and serious differences about naval borders on the Caspian Sea. What is more, the two countries hold the world largest gas reserves and Russia sees Iran as a serious rival in exporting natural gas, especially to Europe.

PART 2

Making Sense of Iranian Business

CHAPTER 8

Structure and Components of Iran's Economy

A Historical View

Between the1960s and the 1970s, Iran's economy enjoyed growth rates of 10 percent per year along with growth in per capita income and low inflation.[1] In the late 1970s, Iran was flourishing and had accumulated enormous amounts of surplus to invest. The 1979 Islamic Revolution suddenly disrupted the business activities, strained the existing social relations, and led to political and economic anarchy. Shortly after the revolution, the Islamic government nationalized large manufacturing and financial enterprises and the Revolutionary Islamic courts confiscated property of the so-called antirevolutionaries and capitalists.[2] Banks and major industries like mining, transport, telecommunication, and utilities were forcefully nationalized. Very rapidly, the Islamic Revolution transformed the country into an Islamic state with a public sector dominating all economic sectors. With the Iran–Iraq War from 1980 to 1988, Iran faced sharp declines in oil production, high levels of inflation, and negative economic growth for more than eight years.[3] After the war, the country embraced some timid economic reforms and tried to attract international investment. From March 1989 to March 1994, Iran followed the first five-year plan and undertook more liberal economic reforms that reduced state control.[4] In the 1990s, the President Rafsanjani's political and social reforms provided a more welcoming environment for business activities. As a result, the Islamic regime emphasized the security of capital and private property rights and gradually moved away from its revolutionary economic discourse.[5] The second and third five-year plans continued until 2004 and advocated more ambitious economic programs and more privatization efforts.[6] Between 1997 and 2005, President Khatami followed essentially the economic liberalization policies of his predecessor. Under Khatami the government launched extensive reforms such as tax policy changes, unification of the exchange rate, liberalization of imports and exports, and adoption of the regulations to attract investment. The election of Ahmadinejad in June 2005 and his reliance on a superficial populist discourse led to adoption of increasingly chaotic economic policies. Ahmadinejad had no clear economic agenda and represented one of the most reactionary factions of the Islamic Republic. Hence, his political and social policies resulted in rising internal stagnation and growing international pressure on Iran. Many of Ahmadinejad's economic policies have been messy. For instance, his government continued Khatami's reforms such as tariff reductions and privatization of state-owned enterprises, but increased the state control over the economy.[7]

An Overview of Iran's Economy

Iran was the 19th largest economy in the world in 1980, but with the Islamic Revolution and during war with Iraq, it suddenly fell to the 39th rank in 1994. According to the Central Intelligence Agency Factbook, the Iranian economy has risen again to the 19th largest in 2013.[8] Despite small contractions in 1993 and 1994, the Iranian economy has been growing constantly since 1989 (after war with Iraq), with an average annual growth rate of 5.4 percent (See Figure 8.1 and Table 8.1). Especially in the past decades (1990–2010), Iran's economy has been growing very rapidly with an average annual rate of 6.4 percent.[9] A significant portion of this growth is attributed to energy sector and increases in oil revenues. For instance, between 1999 and 2006, the Iranian oil revenues tripled. In addition to energy, other sectors such as services, agriculture, and manufacturing have significantly contributed to the national economic growth. For the period from 2012 to 2017, Iran aims at keeping the annual economic growth around 6 percent, the inflation under 12 percent, and the employment under 7 percent. Furthermore, the country aims at reducing economic dependence on oil and gas, privatizing state-owned companies, and increasing the nation's research budget to 3 percent of GDP.

In 2012, Iran's GDP (calculated at purchasing power parity [PPP]) was estimated at $1.002 trillion. Due to harsh Western sanctions, in 2013

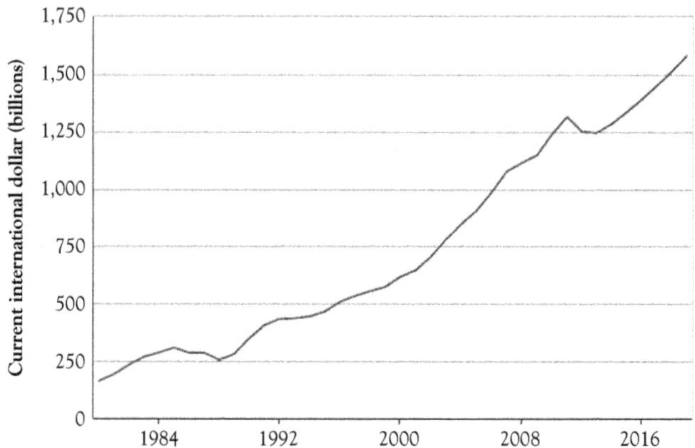

Figure 8.1 Iran—gross domestic product based on PPP

Source: IMF World Economic Outlook, October 2014.

Table 8.1 Annual GDP growth based on PPP

Year	Value ($)	Change (%)
2014	1,283.63	3.16
2013	1,244.33	-0.45
2012	1,250.01	-4.89
2011	1,314.24	6.09
2010	1,238.77	7.93
2009	1,147.73	3.06
2008	1,113.69	3.51
2007	1,075.93	9.20
2006	985.33	8.93
2005	904.54	6.61
2004	848.49	8.60

Source: IMF World Economic Outlook, October 2014.

Iran's GDP contracted between 1.5 to 1.9 percent and fell to $987.1 billion.[10] The World Bank forecasted in its Global Economic Prospects report that Iran's GDP will grow by 1.5 percent in 2014. According to the same report, growth rates of 2 percent and a 2.3 percent have been predicated for 2015 and 2016, respectively. Similarly, the International Monetary Fund (IMF) has estimated growth rates of 1.3 percent and 1.98 percent in 2014 and 2015.[11]

With its estimated $12,800 GDP per capita in 2013, Iran is classified as an upper middle income country (See Figure 8.2 and Table 8.2). In 2005, Iran was included in the *Next Eleven* emerging countries by Goldman Sachs Financial Group. According to this report, in addition to BRIC (Brazil, Russia, India, and China), Iran is supposed to grow as one of the largest world economies by mid-century.[12] Likewise, the IMF is optimistic about Iran's long-term growth prospects. During the war with Iraq in the 1980s, Iran's current account balance was in deficit,

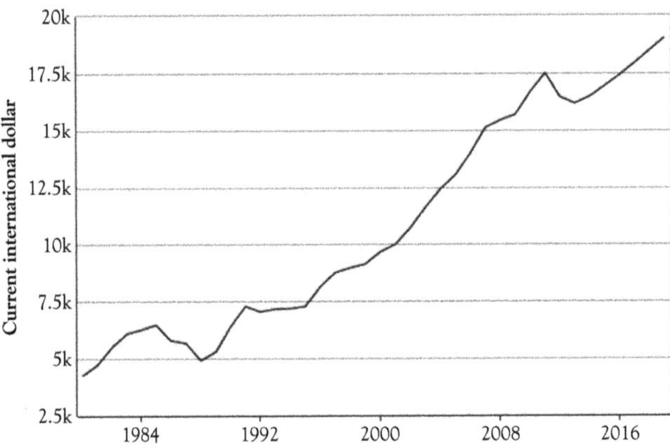

Figure 8.2 GDP per capita based on PPP

Table 8.2 GDP per capita based on PPP

Year	Value ($)	Change (%)
2014	16,463	1.85
2013	16,165	-1.72
2012	16,447	-5.95
2011	17,488	4.95
2010	16,664	6.28
2009	15,679	1.62
2008	15,429	2.22
2007	15,095	8.00
2006	13,977	7.22
2005	13,036	5.00
2004	12,415	6.96

but since the mid-1990s, Iran has constantly run a current account surplus. Iran's international reserves have been growing from $60.5 billion in 2006 to $81.7 billion in 2007 and $100 billion in 2008.[13] Because of high reliance on oil revenues, Iran's economy is highly exposed to periodical fluctuations in oil prices. To overcome these vulnerabilities, in 2001, the Iranian government created a special reserve fund to accumulate surplus oil revenues to smooth possible economic instabilities. The Reserve Fund has served the government to assert its political and military power, implement its expansionary monetary policies, finance construction projects, provide public subsidies, and even distribute cash among the poor. In a move to retaliate U.S. economic and political sanctions, the Iranian government has shifted its foreign reserves from American dollar to gold and other hard currencies such as euro and Japanese yen.[14] Apart from a political move, the Iranian government believes that replacing dollar with Euro and other currencies is financially justified. After December 2007, Iran stopped accepting payments in the U.S. dollar and asked for other currencies for oil export purchases by foreign countries.

Inflation and Labor Market

As shown in Figure 8.3, the postrevolutionary Iran has experienced persistent high consumer price inflation for more than 30 years. Since 2000, the average annual inflation rate has been hovering around 15 percent. This high rate of inflation may be attributed mainly to the ineffectiveness of the government in pushing the Central Bank to constantly increase the money supply. Furthermore, the government has shown a tendency to provide cheap and easy credits to politically powerful borrowers such as the Revolutionary Foundations (*bonyads*), state-owned enterprises, and influential politicians.[15] The interest rates for these borrowers are significantly below the market and in some cases are negative in real terms. To compensate for the difference between the real values of these loans and other expenditures, the government makes the Central Bank print more money and practically creates inflation. Other causes of inflation in Iran may be identified as the lack of government accountability, the government fiscal irresponsibility, corruption, lack of budget planning, and the expansionary fiscal policies. In all these cases, the government, via the

Central Bank, fills the deficit with freshly supplied money. In the recent years (2009–2014), the Western sanctions have crippled Iran's economy and have created additional inflationary pressures. For instance in 2013 and 2014, the annual inflation rate was hovering over 30 percent (See Figure 8.3, Table 8.3). The high inflation has led to lack of confidence in the national currency (rial) and pushed many Iranians to invest their savings in gold, real estate, and foreign hard currencies. More recently (2012–2014), spiraling prices have hit the population so badly that even the middle class families have been struggling with the mounting cost of food, housing, education, transport, and health care.

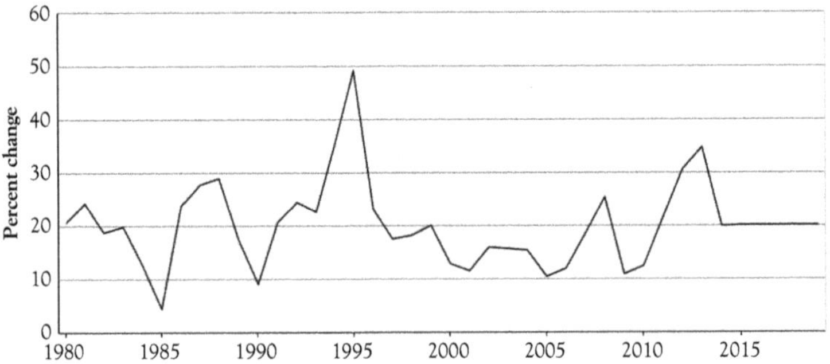

Figure 8.3 Consumer price inflation, annual percentage change

Source: IMF World Economic Outlook, October 2014.

Table 8.3 Consumer price inflation between 2004 and 2014

Year	Value (%)	Change (%)
2014	19.8	−42.81
2013	34.7	13.77
2012	30.5	41.91
2011	21.5	73.81
2010	12.4	14.62
2009	10.8	−57.39
2008	25.3	37.26
2007	18.4	55.15
2006	11.9	14.90
2005	10.3	−32.30
2004	15.3	−2.07

In addition to hyperinflation, high unemployment rate is recognized as another obstacle to Iran's economic prosperity. Indeed, some believe that unemployment remains the single largest hurdle to Iran's economic growth.[16] As shown in Figure 8.4 and Table 8.4, the economic growth has not kept pace with the population growth and as a result a large number of skilled or semiskilled workers have remained out of employment. It is estimated that each year, about 750,000 young Iranians enter the job

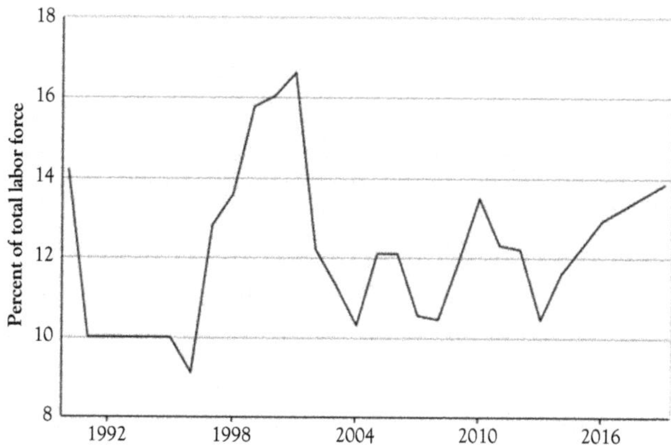

Figure 8.4 Unemployment rate

Source: IMF World Economic Outlook, October 2014.

Table 8.4 Unemployment rate between 2004–2014

Date	Value (%)	Change (%)
2014	11.6	10.89
2013	10.4	−14.43
2012	12.2	−0.81
2011	12.3	−8.75
2010	13.5	13.15
2009	11.9	14.00
2008	10.4	−0.94
2007	10.5	−12.76
2006	12.1	−0.07
2005	12.1	17.48
2004	10.3	−8.85

Source: IMF World Economic Outlook, October 2014.

market for the first time placing pressure on the government to create new jobs.[17] The Statistical Center of Iran has announced that the average unemployment rate for the Iranian calendar year that ended on March 20, 2014 hit 10.4 percent,[18] but some analysts believe that the real unemployment rate is much higher. The unofficial unemployment rates have been hovering over 15 percent in the past decade. Unemployment is considerably higher among the youth and excessively affects those under 30 years of age. In addition to unemployment, underemployment or working with high education or skill levels in low wage or skill jobs has become another major problem in the recent years. Due to rising educational and technical levels, a large number of Iranian youth cannot find the jobs that match their abilities and are forced to work in low skill and temporary employments. Under the increasing pressure of inflation and low wages, many workers may take up multiple jobs to make ends meet. The biggest employers are in the public sector including government, social services, education, agriculture, mining, trade, and transport areas. While the manufacturing sector employs almost 30 percent of the workforce, it makes a relatively small contribution to the gross national product.[19] According to the Iranian Finance and Economic Affairs Minister, Iran must create 8.5 million new jobs in the next two years.[20] Under these circumstances, many young and educated Iranians are forced to leave their home country in search of better professional opportunities. As reported by the IMF, Iran has one of the highest brain drain rates in the world.[21]

Economic Sectors

Industry is the largest sector and represents almost 45 percent of Iran's GDP. It includes oil and gas, petrochemicals, steel, textile, and car manufacturing. The service sector and agriculture respectively account for 44 percent and 11 percent of Iran's economy[22]. Despite its small size, the agriculture sector created 20 percent of jobs in 1991.[23]

Oil and Gas

With 10.3 percent of the world's reserves of oil, Iran is placed in the third rank after Saudi Arabia and Canada.[24] Furthermore, Iran has the world's second largest gas reserves. Iran was the second largest producer of Organization of Petroleum Exporting Countries (OPEC) in 2012 by an estimated production of four million barrels of crude oil per day. The main export markets for Iranian oil are Japan, China, India, and South Korea. Natural gas extraction is used for domestic needs and despite its immense reserves, Iran has very limited gas exports to the neighboring countries. Between 2002 and 2011, the country has greatly benefited from high oil prices and accumulated a sizeable hard currency surplus. However, the reliance on oil export revenues makes Iran's economy highly vulnerable to the volatility of international oil prices. An unexpected decline of oil prices under $40 per barrel for an extended period of time may bring about serious financial implications.[25] While natural resources in general and oil in particular contribute to wealth creation in a country, they can be detrimental to sustainable socioeconomic development as well. Many analysts believe that oil revenues have been responsible for deterring Iran's industrial competitiveness. For instance, empirical studies show that countries rich in natural resources tend to have slower economic growth than countries with a smaller endowment of natural resources.[26] The negative relationship between resource endowment and economic growth is particularly strong in countries with weak or corrupt institutions such as Iran.[27] Oil contributes to about 60 percent of government revenues and 30 to 40 percent of GDP.[28] As such, Iran's government can be described as a *rentier state* that does not depend on domestic sources of production, but rather is the primary distributor of wealth in the society.[29] Since the wealth creation is very largely independent of domestic production, the *rentier state* tends to violate the basic principle of efficiency in the society.[30] This economic pattern may lead to empowerment of a small group of privileged politicians and their associates, prevalence of corruption, and lack of accountability to the population.[31]

Manufacturing Industries

Before and after the revolution, the government has tried to diversify economy by investing oil revenues in several industrial sectors. Iran's manufacturing sector is more developed than those of other Middle Eastern countries; however, its share of GDP is still small relative to those of developing countries such as Brazil, China, India, and Mexico. In the recent years, industry sector has suffered due to increased exchange rates making the sector less competitive. Moreover, the Western imposed sanctions and three decades of political isolation have deprived Iranian industries from access to technological and managerial resources. Currently, Iran manufactures various products such as automobiles, telecommunications equipment, machinery, paper, rubber, steel, food products, wood, textiles, and pharmaceuticals. For instance, Iran is a main producer of steel in the world and the largest in the Middle East. Also, it produces different metals and nonmetal minerals such as coal, copper ore, lead, zinc, and aluminum. With two automotive giants (Iran Khodro and Saipa), Iran is the largest car maker in the Middle East and the 15th largest motor vehicle producer in the world.[32] Car makers are hugely dependent on foreign technology. Some companies from France and Germany have a considerable presence in the Iranian automotive market. In the recent years, the Iranian car makers have initiated joint ventures with foreign companies including Peugeot and Citroen (France), Volkswagen (Germany), Nissan and Toyota (Japan), Kia Motors (South Korea), Proton (Malaysia), and Chery (China).[33]

Iran has hugely invested in petrochemicals. Currently, the country is the second largest producer of petrochemicals in the Middle East. It is estimated that the petrochemical industry needs an estimated $30 billion in fresh investment.[34] Due to a large consumption market, in the recent years a growing number of medium sized companies have been involved in food products such as canned food, soft drink, meat processed food, fruit juices, and confectionary. These food-related products are consumed mainly in the domestic market; however, they have been marketed to other neighboring countries such as Iraq, Afghanistan, Persian Gulf States, Tajikistan, Azerbaijan, and Turkmenistan. Some Western companies such as Nestlé and Coca Cola have signed contracts with local Iranian businesses.[35]

Service Sector

The service sector accounts for 44 percent of Iran's GDP and includes a wide range of diverse activities in banking, financial services, education, and health care. Iranian financial sector is dominated by government intervention at all levels. Iran's Central Bank or the Bank Markazi of Iran is under the direct control of the government and follows its fiscal and monetary policies. In 1979, shortly after the Islamic Revolution, the government nationalized all banks and took control over the financial sector. However, in the recent years there has been a growing trend toward privatization and liberalization of the economy.[36] Consequently, some semi-private banks have emerged in Iranian financial sector. These banks belong mainly to the Revolutionary Foundations (*bonyads*) and the state owned enterprises. In some cases, the shares of public banks have been sold on Tehran Stock Exchange. Nevertheless, a few state-owned banks control the financial sector. Some analysts have questioned the effectiveness of public banks in providing appropriate financial services.[37] Moreover, private banks are restricted by complex and unstable regulations. In addition to the formal financial system, many individuals and small businesses rely on a complex network of trusted people to borrow, lend, and transfer money.

Agriculture Sector

The Islamic Republic has often emphasized the importance of agriculture as a means of economic and political self-sufficiency. Yet, in the recent years the weight of agriculture in Iran's economy has decreased constantly. While agriculture represents only 11 percent of GDP,[38] it is still the largest employer representing around 20 percent of all jobs in 1991.[39] Agricultural output is relatively low, due to poor soil, lack of adequate water distribution, low quality seed, and undeveloped farming techniques. Iran is a net importer of grains, especially rice and wheat, and a net exporter of some well-known agricultural products such as caviar, pistachio, saffron, rice, wheat, barley, and a variety of fruits. The agriculture sector is threatened by droughts, climate change, environmental pollution, and lack of professional farmers. The country usually uses oil export revenues to pay for agricultural imports, but in the recent years a combination of factors including droughts, population increase, and rising international food prices have put strains on food security.[40] Despite the emphasis of policy makers on agricultural sector, limitations of arable land and water practically prevent Iran from achieving complete food self-sufficiency.

International Trade

Despite the international sanctions, Iran's international trade has been increasing over the course of the past decade. Thanks to higher oil revenues, from 2004 to 2007 the volume of Iran's international trade doubled and reached $147 billion with a trade surplus of $36 billion in 2007. Nearly 80 percent of total export revenues result from oil and gas sectors.[41] Petrochemicals, carpets, and dried fruits account for the rest of export revenues. Top export markets for Iranian oil are Japan, China, India, South Korea, and Italy. Top markets for nonoil exports are the United Arab Emirates (UAE), Iraq, China, Japan, and India.[42] Because of limited domestic refinery capacity, the country is a major importer of gasoline. Iran's gasoline imports were estimated around $5.7 billion in 2006 and $6.1 billion in 2007.[43] Gasoline is subsidized by the government and is sold at a very low price, which leads to higher levels of fuel consumption. Major gasoline suppliers to Iran include India, Turkmenistan, Azerbaijan, the Netherlands, France, Singapore, and UAE. In addition to refined petroleum products, Iran imports a wide range of products such as industrial machinery, food products, and consumer goods. According to the IMF, in 2007 Iran's top trading partners included China, Japan, Italy, South Korea, and Germany.[44] As shown in Table 8.5, Germany, China, UAE, and South Korea are considered major suppliers of Iranian imports.

Table 8.5 Major trading partners, FY2007 (millions of U.S. dollars)

Country	Total trade	Exports	Imports	Trade balance
China	20,135	12,188	8,017	4,101
Japan	13,064	11,599	1,465	10,134
South Korea	8,421	5,139	3,282	1,857
Italy	8,039	5,215	2,824	2,391
Turkey	7,539	6,013	1,526	4,487
Germany	6,066	621	5,445	−4,824
UAE	5,915	747	5,168	−4,421
France	5,334	3,069	2,265	804
Russia	3,272	282	2,990	−2,708

Source: IMF, Direction of Trade Statistics.

As a result of tough economic sanctions, the U.S. trade with Iran is very limited and American companies are prohibited to invest in the country. This has provided golden opportunities for Japanese, Chinese, Russian, and European businesses. Many analysts believe that the United States sanctions against Iran are detrimental to American businesses and may deprive the United States of access to Iranian market.[45] European countries and particularly Germany have been marinating strong economic and trade relations with Iran. However, it seems that more recently Iran has been shifting its trade from European countries to emerging economies such as China, Japan, Russia, Turkey, and Central Asian countries. Iran's growing trade relationship with emerging countries is part of a reaction to political pressure from the Western countries. Furthermore, Iran has been seeking to use trade relations with countries like China and Russia to attract their political support on the international stage.[46]

As international sanctions have increased the difficulty of trade with Iran, UAE has become Iran's most important connection to the global economy.[47] Through this trade relationship, Iran overcomes the imposed international sanctions whereas UAE makes billions of dollars annually. Nonoil trade between UAE and Iran was officially estimated to be around $12 billion in 2007, but unofficial and often illicit trade volumes could be much bigger.[48] The large part of this trade involves re-exportation or supplying Iran with *repackaged* foreign products from, Asia, Europe, and the Unites States. The U.S. trade with Iran is restricted, but many U.S. products are available in Iran via UAE.[49] The trade relationship between the two countries is highly beneficial for UAE. For instance, in 2010, UAE exported over $9 billion worth of goods to Iran and imported only $1.12 billion worth of goods from Iran.[50] One may suggest that after the Islamic revolution, Iran's economic loss has been translated into UAE's prosperity. On many occasions, the U.S. government has tried to put pressure on UAE to restrict its trade with Iran; however it seems that these attempts have not been effective in reducing the trade between the two neighboring countries.

Key Players in Iran's Economy

According to Iran's constitution, "The economy of the Islamic Republic of Iran consists of three sectors: state, cooperative, and private, and is to be based on systematic and sound planning" (Article 44, Iranian Constitution[51]). In practice, Iran's economy is a mixture of central planning, state ownership of large enterprises, village agriculture, and small private firms.[52] The state sector includes all large-scale and mother industries such as foreign trade, radio and television, telephone services and aviation. The private sector consists of small and medium-size companies concerned with products and services that supplement the economic activities of the state. The contribution of private sector is estimated at about 15 percent of GDP.[53] The cooperative sector is practically insignificant and includes enterprises offering limited number of products and services. In addition, informal and other illegal activities constitute a considerable part of the Iranian economy. The Heritage Foundation has classified Iran's economy as the 173rd freest in the 2014 report.[54] In terms of economic freedom, Iran is ranked the last out of 15 countries in the Middle East and North Africa region and is known to have one of the closest economies in the world. The lack of economic freedom implies heavy state interference in many aspects of economic activity, lack of economic dynamism, and restrictive business and investment policies. In practice, the government controls economy through ownership and management of large state-owned companies, banks, Revolutionary Foundations (*bonyads*), and Islamic Revolutionary Guards.

Public Sector: State-Owned Companies, Bonyads, and the Islamic Revolutionary Guard Corps

The public sector consists of state-owned companies, *bonyads*, Islamic Revolutionary Foundations, and the Islamic Revolutionary Guard Corps. Shortly after the Islamic Revolution (1979), the State acquired ownership of large corporations in a variety of sectors including banking, insurance, telecommunication, energy, and transport. As a result of this rapid nationalization, the role of State in the Iranian economy was dramatically enhanced and all economic activities were run virtually by the government. Despite some timid liberalization efforts during Rafsanjani's presidency in the 1990s, the state-owned companies remain the largest economic entities.[55] Thanks to their significant influence, many of these large companies have received financial subsidies and business privileges from the government and have been protected from foreign and domestic competitors.[56] This has resulted in low levels of productivity and efficiency in the state-owned companies particularly in industries such as automotive, steel, and transport.

Bonyads or Islamic Revolutionary Foundations were created in 1979 to manage the properties of the Royal family and their capitalist dependents. On the basis of Ayatollah Khomeini's direct decree, the *bonyads* confiscated massive assets and suddenly became powerful semigovernmental organizations.[57] The raison d'être of these foundations initially was to serve the poor and social justice, but later they relied on their revolutionary power and generous fiscal and economic privileges such as low interest rate loans, monopolies, government loopholes, and tax exemption advantages to conduct extremely lucrative business activities across the country. Currently, the *bonyads* are under direct control of the Supreme Leader and are not required to report their income and operations to the public. Furthermore, the *bonyads* are not subject to the Iranian legal or parliamentary supervision and are exempt from any taxes. It is often suggested that economic and political reform in Iran will not be effective unless *bonyads* come under the parliamentary supervision.[58] The major problem with *bonyads* is that they intervene in all aspects of economic activity, compete with the private and state-owned enterprises, and are not accountable for what they receive from the public. Furthermore, it is very difficult to frame the *bonyads*, because they are obscure and complex foundations involved in a wide range of financial, social, charitable, religious, political, and cultural activities. Indeed, the exact magnitude of *bonyads*' wealth and power is not known. The *bonyads* may have hundreds of companies in diverse industries. The largest *bonyads* include Bonyad Shahid va Isaar-Garaan (Foundation of the Martyrs and Veterans) with over 100 companies, Bonyad Mostazafan (Foundation of the Underprivileged), and Astan Quds Razavi (Imam Reza Shrine Foundation) with revenues of $12 billion in 2005.[59] These *bonyads* are involved in both domestic and foreign economies in areas such as agriculture, construction, industries, mining, transportation, commerce, and tourism across Europe, Russia, Asia, the Middle East, and Africa.[60]

The Islamic Revolutionary Guard Corps (IRGC) is a military organization that was founded in 1979 to defend the new Islamic government and stifle any voice of opposition. The IRGC has emerged as a dominant power not only in defense and security matters but also in political and economic affairs.[61] The IRGC consists of five branches: the Grounds Force, Air Force, Navy, Basij militia, and Qods Force special operations.[62] After the war with Iraq, the IRGC crept into the Iranian economy through postwar reconstruction projects. Since then, the IRGC has benefited from the support of the Supreme Leader and has been involved in a variety of business opportunities like construction, oil, and gas projects.[63] Very recently, the IRGC has started to acquire large state-owned enterprises and has become a major player in banking and telecommunication industries.[64] Due to its control over Iran's borders and airports, the IRGC, or at least some of its officials, are very likely to be involved in smuggling prohibited products into the country. Market participants are concerned about the presence of the IRGC in business activities and have complained about their exorbitant privileges and profits. Some analysts suggest that the harsh Western sanctions have provided a pretext for the IRGC to extend their grip over Iran's economy.

Private Sector: Bazaaris, Industrialists, and Small Businesses

After the Islamic Revolution, the private sector has shrunk dramatically as many businesses were seized by the new regime and their assets were transferred to the Revolutionary Foundations (*bonyads*). The existing private businesses consist of mainly Bazaaris and family-owned companies that operate in trade and distribution, agriculture, small manufacturing, and mining. Since Iran's private companies have to compete with some powerful organizations such as the *bonyads* and the IRGC, they have small scale operations and limited prospects. Generally, it is possible to identify three major groups in the Iranian private sector: bazaaris, industrialists, and small and medium-sized businesses.

Bazaaris or urban traditional merchants work in the *bazaar,* which is a collection of shops and stalls in covered and open alleyways. According to Iranica Encyclopedia, the urban bazaar was and still is a social institution, comprising religious, commercial, political, and social elements.[65] In addition to shopping area, the Iranian bazaar includes mosques, schools, restaurants, tea houses, gymnasiums, and bathhouses where merchants can meet and exchange information. The bazaaris represent mainly conservative and traditional groups of the society and institutionally have close ties with the clergy and religious leadership.[66] After the Shah's White Revolution in the 1960s and the subsequent modernization of Iranian society, the economic weight of bazaaris diminished substantially. The resentful bazaaris opposed the Shah overwhelmingly and played a critical role in the Islamic Revolution by promoting and financing strikes and public demonstrations.[67] The bazaaris are engaged in a wide range of business activities such as importing, exporting, wholesaling, retailing, and lending money. Since Iran is a society of trade merchants with limited manufacturing sectors, the bazaaris have an important economic function.[68] They maintain a strong hold on Iranian economy and politics, and in order to protect their own interests, resist economic and social openness, foreign direct investment, and international competition.[69] Over the course of the past 50 years, the rapid economic modernization has reduced the traditional importance of the bazaar, but has not led to its demise. More recently, the bazaar merchants are becoming specialized in certain products such as carpets, jewelries, gold, and food products and are supplementing modern shopping areas.

The industrialists represent more educated or modernized entrepreneurs than bazaaris and are marked by their liberal socioeconomic values. They are involved mainly in manufacturing and technological sectors, which are not under the control of bazaaris or the government. The small and medium-sized businesses are owned and run mostly by the middle class individuals. They have limited financial, technological, and managerial resources and struggle to make a living. As a result, they cannot usually grow at the national and international levels.

Future Outlook

The Western and American economic sanctions have resulted in multiple and sometimes conflicting outcomes. On the one hand, the sanctions have created substantial barriers to doing business with Iran, have complicated its business environment, and have led to low levels of foreign investment. As a result, Iran has experienced significant difficulties in developing its oil and gas sectors.[70] On the other hand, the sanctions have generated golden opportunities for American rivals predominantly China and Russia in expanding and deepening their trade, business, and political ties with Iran.[71] Likewise, the Western sanctions have diverted Iran's trade and business from the Western countries to the emerging and Eastern countries such as India, Brazil, China, South Africa, South Korea, and Malaysia. Meanwhile, Iran has been able to circumvent the sanctions by transshipment from neighboring countries like UAE and Turkey.

It seems that there is no political will and social capacity to transform the country's rentier economy at least in the near future.[72] Therefore, Iran's economic growth remains highly dependent on the energy sector in short and mid-terms. Despite the government's attempts to diversify economy, oil and gas revenues still account for almost 80 percent of the total export revenues. Iran's oil and gas sector has huge growth potential and one may suggest that energy prices and the ability of Iran in developing and exporting its oil and gas resources will be central to its economic prosperity in the short term. In the past decade between 2004 and 2014, Iran enjoyed a high economic growth, but the prospect of such growth remains uncertain. If the country can overcome geopolitical and international risks, the overall economic growth seems quite positive.[73] Any sharp decline in oil prices below $90 per barrel may create serious challenges to the country's economic growth. In addition to international sanctions and energy prices, Iran's economy is highly affected by internal factors including domestic policies, stability, economic planning, and management or mismanagement of country's resources. The last eight years from 2005 to 2013 have been marked by economic mismanagement, high unemployment, hyperinflation, brain drain, and rising corruption at all levels. It is crucial for the government to take some macroeconomic measures to reduce inflation, increase non-oil output, and minimize the government fiscal dependency on oil revenues.[74] Some have a positive assessment of Iran's economy and believe that the nation's economic performance is satisfactory. However, many others argue that given the abundant natural resources and endowments, Iran's economy has been constantly underperforming after the Islamic revolution.

CHAPTER 9

Energy Market

A Colossal Energy Producer

As one of the founding members of the Organization of Petroleum Exporting Countries (OPEC), Iran has been a key player in the international energy market for the past 70 years. As shown in Figure 9.1, the country sits on some of the largest proven oil and gas reserves in the world and ranks among the world's top five oil and natural gas producers. Furthermore, Iran controls the Strait of Hormuz on its southeastern coast that is seen as an important route for the world energy market. An estimated 17 million barrels per day of crude oil and oil products, almost 20 percent of the global output, is transported via the Strait of Hormuz.[1] In addition to oil and gas, Iran enjoys a well-developed electricity industry by a power generation capacity of 67 gigawatts, ranked 14th in the world and 1st in the Middle East. Half of the electricity is generated by gas and combustion-based power plants while the rest is produced by hydroelectric power plants. The country enjoys a substantial aptitude in dam construction and has numerous hydroelectric projects under construction. Iran has acquired technical expertise in constructing hydraulic and gas turbines, hydroelectric, gas, and combined cycle power plants.[2] In the recent years, the nation has signed multiple contracts on building power plants in neighboring states.[3] Iran annually exports 5.5 terawatt-hours of electricity to neighboring countries including Afghanistan, Pakistan, Iraq, Turkey, Armenia, Azerbaijan, and Turkmenistan.[4] At the same time, the country is investing in alternative energy producing projects such as solar, biomass, and wind power plants to boost its electricity generation capacity to 73 gigawatts per year. In 2004, Iran opened its first wind-powered and geothermal plants. The country is able to generate 6,500 megawatts of power from wind. Solar energy is particularly promising as the country enjoys about 300 clear sunny days a year and an

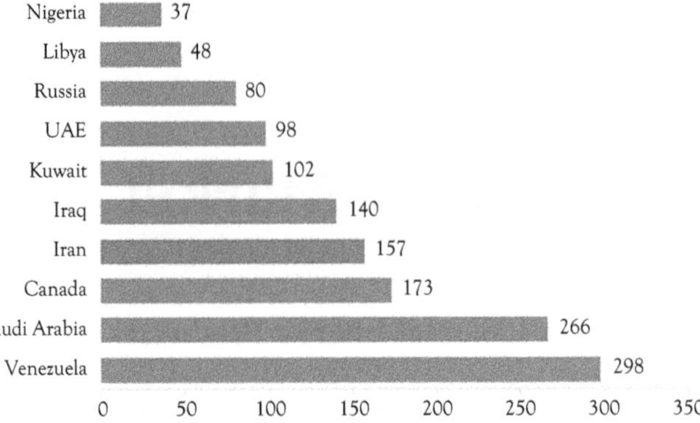

Figure 9.1 Largest proved reserve holders of crude oil, January 2014(billion barrels)

Source: EIA;[5] EIU.[6]

average of 2,200 kilowatt-hour solar radiation per square meter.[7] In 2012, Iran allocated $700 million to renewable energy projects.[8] Electricity generation from other sources like tidal power, sewage, and organic waste of domestic and industrial origin has been under assessment.[9] Iran has recoverable coal reserves of nearly 1.9 billion tons and produces about 1.3 million tons of coal annually.[10] Currently, Iran is seeking to develop an advanced nuclear program that is allegedly for civilian and energy purposes. The nuclear program provides greater energy security and may allow the country to maximize its energy export earnings.[11] For instance, the nation plans to generate 23,000 megawatt-hours of electricity through nuclear technology by 2025.[12] A combination of oil, gas, solar, wind, hydroelectric, geothermal, and nuclear sources could turn Iran into a colossal energy exporter.

Energy Consumption

With a daily consumption of 1.75 million barrels, Iran is the second-largest oil-consuming country in the Middle East after Saudi Arabia.[13] Indeed, Iran is recognized as one of the most energy intensive countries of the world with per capita energy consumption 15 times that of Japan and 10 times that of the European Union (EU). As a developing economy, Iran's energy consumption has grown by more than 50 percent over the course of the past decade.[14] The national average daily gasoline consumption hovers around 63.2 million liters. In 2010, Iran's energy consumption was estimated at 212.5 million tons of oil equivalent.[15] The consumption of electricity rose by 9.3 percent between 2010 and 2011 and it is expected to rise at about 6 percent per year for the next decade. The highest volumes of energy consumption are respectively related to residential, commercial, and industrial utilization. Oil and natural gas provide 98 percent of Iran's total energy needs but other sources are consumed occasionally. It is estimated that 87 percent of urban population and more than 30 percent of rural population have access to natural gas.[16] Energy prices are set well below the economic cost of supply and, for that reason, energy is inefficiently consumed across the country. Due to limited domestic oil refining capacity, Iran is dependent on imports of refined products, but the country's dependence on imported gasoline has been diminishing in the past five years.[17] According to estimates, the Iranian government paid $84 billion in subsidies for oil, gas, and electricity in 2008).[18] The energy subsidies have led to an excessive consumption, increasing fuel imports, and severe air pollution in large cities.[19] Thanks to government subsidies and relatively low energy prices, a lucrative cross-border industry of smuggling fuel has been developed. Fuel is being moved illegally out of the country through cities bordering Afghanistan, Pakistan, and Turkey.[20] It is estimated that between 7 to 10 million liters of petrol and diesel are smuggled out every day.[21] For the past 15 years, the Iranian government has been planning to manage the energy resources more efficiently and has made several attempts to reduce energy subsidies.[22] More recently, international sanctions have particularly targeted fuel imports and have generated further momentum for the Iranian government to restrain energy consumption.

Oil Sector: Reserves and Production

As shown in Figure 9.1, Iran is estimated to possess 157 billion barrels of proved crude oil reserves, representing nearly 10 percent of the world's crude oil reserves and 13 percent of reserves held by the OPEC.[23] Iran was the second largest producer of OPEC in 2012 by an estimated production of four million barrels of crude oil per day. Most of Iran's crude oil reserves (about 70 percent) are located onshore but some other reserves are located offshore in the Persian Gulf and the Caspian Sea. Iran shares many onshore and offshore oil fields with neighboring countries such as Azerbaijan, Turkmenistan, Iraq, Qatar, Kuwait, and Saudi Arabia.

Under the Pahlavi rule, oil production reached its highest level in the mid-1970s (6.0 million barrels per day), but it plummeted after the Islamic Revolution and the Iran–Iraq War (See Figure 9.2). In the post-war era, the oil output rose but never reached its peak of 1975. Despite the size of its oil reserves, Iran's oil production has not increased due to multiple factors. The United States and the EU sanctions, geopolitical frictions, aging infrastructure, mismanagement, old technology, and lack of new investment are some major reasons explaining the low levels of Iranian oil production.[24] In addition, the country output has been declining due to depletion of oil fields, which is estimated at 8 to 11 percent of annual production capacity.[25] It is estimated that the oil sector share in GDP has decreased from 30 to 40 percent in the 1970s to 10 to 20 percent in the recent years.[26] In 2012, a new round of sanctions imposed by the United States and the EU punitively targeted Iran's oil exports and imports, banned investment in the country's oil and gas sector and, more importantly, restricted Iran's access to the European and American sources for financial transactions.[27] Following the implementation of these harsh measures, Iran's crude

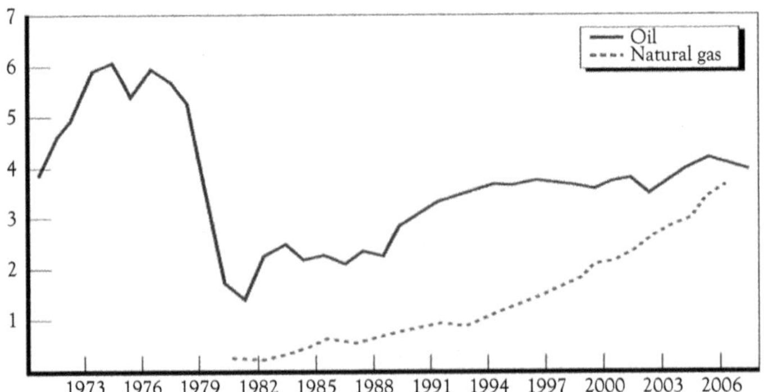

Figure 9.2 Iran's oil and natural gas production

Source: Energy Information Administration (EIA) (2007).

oil production fell significantly in 2013 and Iran dropped from being the second-largest crude producer in OPEC to the fourth after Saudi Arabia, Iraq, and the UAE.[28] According to OPEC's and other official sources, in 2013, Iran's crude oil production was estimated between 2.7 to 3.7 million barrels per day that is 25 percent lower than the production level of 4.2 million barrels per day in 2011.[29] It seems that the country's production has increased again in 2014, changing Iran's rank to the third-largest crude oil producer in OPEC.[30] The Iranian government is optimistic about Iran's potential to increase its oil output, predicting a production of 7.0 million barrels per day by 2024.[31] Currently, the main export markets for Iranian oil include Japan, China, India, and South Korea.

The oil industry is dominated by the State via the National Iranian Oil Company that suffers from grave technological and organizational inefficiencies. It is estimated that the cost of oil production in Iran is much higher than that of Saudi Arabia or other Persian Gulf states.[32] Most of Iran's oil reserves have been discovered before 1965 and the country has not had a new oil field enter into production since 2007.[33] Some new developments have been reported during the past decade, but due to the economic sanctions, multinational companies have had very restricted activity in Iran's energy sector. In the past 20 years, companies from China, Japan, France, Russia, Malaysia, and Norway have been present in the Iranian oil production.[34] Iran has sought technical assistance and investment from many multinationals such as Switzerland's energy company EGL (2006), Austria's OMV (2007), Russia's Gazprom (2008), and China National Offshore Oil Corporation (2008). Some of these deals have come under harsh criticism from the United States and have been considered as violations of the Iran Sanctions Act.[35] China Petroleum & Chemical Corporation (Sinopec), Japan's INPEX, Russia's Gazprom, and Statoil are among some major players in developing Iran's oil fields. The oil sector generally receives the bulk of domestic and foreign investment. The Iranian Constitution prohibits foreign firms from possessing equity in oil projects; therefore, the foreign companies' involvement is through buy-back agreements under which the foreign companies become entitled to the oil or gas resulted from the development projects.

Natural Gas Sector: Reserves, Development, and Production

With an estimated 17 percent of the world's proven natural gas reserves and more than one-third of OPEC's reserves, Iran has the second-largest proved natural gas resources in the world after Russia (See Figure 9.3).[36] Most of Iranian gas fields such as South Pars, Kish, North Pars, Tabnak, Forouz, and Kangan are located offshore in the Persian Gulf. South Pars is the country's largest gas field and accounts for almost 40 percent of the nation's gas reserves. Part of the South Pars basin stretches to the water borders of Iran and Qatar. This immense field has a 24-phase development plan with an estimated cost of more than $100 billion.[37] In addition to the gas fields in the Persian Gulf, Iran has significant natural gas reserves in the Caspian Sea. More recently, some new onshore and offshore reserves have been discovered; among them Khayyam, Forouz, Madar, and Sardar Jangal fields are of significant importance. Due to lack of territorial demarcation agreement among the Caspian Sea countries, exploration and production of northern fields could be very complex and litigious.

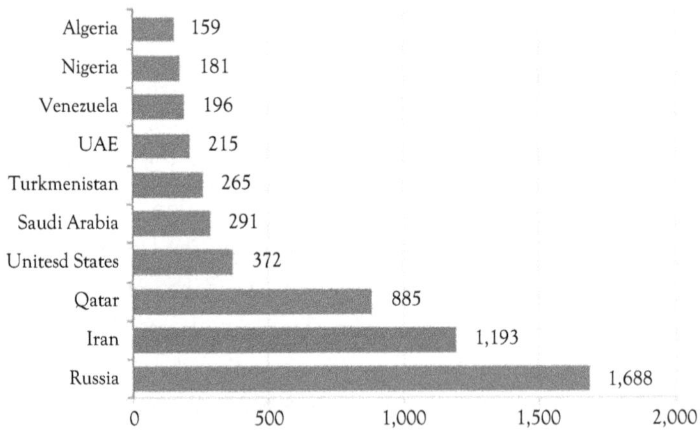

Figure 9.3 Largest proved reserve holders of natural gas, January 2014 (trillion cubic feet)

Source: Oil & Gas Journal.

Natural Gas Production

The history of gas production is much more recent in Iran and goes back to the 1980s. The natural gas is viewed as a viable substitute to oil that can diversify Iranian economy and generate substantial revenues. In line with this view, the government has been involved in developing new gas fields, building pipelines, and negotiating international agreements. For instance, Iranian government inaugurated a pipeline to Turkey in 2002 and has been negotiating similar projects with Pakistan, India, China, and Turkmenistan to export gas across Europe and Asia. In 2012, the country produced an estimated 8.2 trillion cubic feet of natural gas. According to these numbers, Iran was the third-largest gas producer after Russia and the United States, but it accounted for only 5 percent of the world gas output.[38] Currently, most of Iran's gas production is used for domestic consumption. The domestic consumption has increased to 5.5 trillion cubic feet in 2012. Furthermore, a large portion of the produced gas is injected into oil wells to boost oil recovery. Considering the high rate of oil reserves depletion, natural gas use for injection is expected to increase in the near future.[39] Considering its abundant reserves, the country could become one of world's leading natural gas exporters. Obviously, Iran's gas sector has been held back by a combination of factors including three decades of turmoil after the Islamic Revolution, geopolitical tensions, international sanctions, war in the 1980s, political instability, lack of investment, and outdated technology. Iran's natural gas production is expected to increase to 10.6 trillion cubic feet by 2020.

Natural Gas Imports and Exports

Despite its abundant gas reserves, Iran accounted for less than 1 percent of global natural gas trade in 2012.[40] Since Iran does not have the necessary infrastructure, exported and imported gas go through pipelines. The country trades only insignificant amounts of natural gas via pipelines with neighboring Turkmenistan, Armenia, Azerbaijan, and Turkey. In 2012, Iran exported 326 billion cubic feet of natural gas to Turkey and imported 188 billion cubic feet from Turkmenistan and Azerbaijan. In return,

Armenia exports electricity to Iran for the natural gas it receives. The imported gas from Turkmenistan helps Iran meet the domestic consumption especially during the winter. Armenia and Azerbaijan swap gas with Iran that account for 6 percent and 3 percent of Iran's natural gas exports respectively.[41] More than 90 percent of Iran's exports go to Turkey. It is estimated that Turkey receives approximately 20 percent of its natural gas imports from Iran.[42] As such, Iran is recognized as Turkey's second largest source of natural gas imports after Russia. While Iran and Turkey enjoy the mutual benefits of gas trade, their business relations have not been always smooth and steady. At times, the flow of gas to Turkey has been disrupted by seasonal shortages during cold weather or technical and security-related problems. Similarly, Turkey has disputed the price and the quantity of imports.[43] Furthermore, the gas pipelines have been subject to terrorist attacks and sabotage from the Kurdish rebels inside Turkey. According to the EIA, the average revenues from Iran's natural gas exports between July 2011 and June 2012 were estimated at $10.5 million per day, which is about 5 percent of the country's revenues from crude oil and condensate exports. According to the same estimates, in 2010 natural gas and crude oil accounted for 4 percent and 78 percent of Iran's total export earnings, respectively.[44] While Iran boasts of being the second largest proven gas reserves in the world, it is a net importer of natural gas.[45] The country has been pursuing the construction of a liquefaction facility to export liquefied natural gas, but the U.S. and the EU-led sanctions have hampered the financing and the acquisition of necessary technology.[46] Iran and Iraq have signed an agreement in 2013 to build regional gas pipelines transferring Iran's gas to Western Iraq. The pipeline is under construction, but the progress has been stopped by security concerns and political turmoil in Iraq and Syria. Furthermore, Iran has signed similar agreements with Oman, Pakistan, and UAE to provide them natural gas. Among them the Iran–Pakistan pipeline cost is estimated at $1.5 billion and would allow Iran to export 21.5 million cubic meters of natural gas per day to Pakistan.[47] Iran has built more than 900 kilometers of the pipeline on its soil and the next piece of the pipeline on the Pakistani side is expected to be completed by 2015.[48] The Iran–Pakistan pipeline is of tremendous importance because through this pipeline Iran can access the Indian market. Iran aims at increasing its share of global gas exports to 16 percent by exporting around 230 million cubic meters per day by 2025.[49] Different countries such as India, Bangladesh, and China, have all been invited to participate in the pipeline project, but the United States has warned Pakistan and India against cooperation with Iran. Moreover, Saudi Arabia has also offered an alternative package in which it would supply Pakistan with attractive loans and cheaper oil.[50] As a result of the pressures from the United States, India withdrew from the project in 2009,[51] but so far Pakistan has decided to resist the international pressure. According to the Turkish daily newspaper, *Today's Zaman*, following the relative détente between Iran and the world powers, the Turkish government is gradually moving to reach an agreement with Iran to build the Iran–Turkey–Europe Natural Gas Pipeline Project to transfer natural gas sourced in Iran via Turkey to Europe.[52]

Potential for the Energy Sector

With an estimated 17 percent of the world's proven natural gas reserves and approximately 10 percent of the world's crude oil reserves, Iran is an energy-rich country. Nevertheless, the political stalemate with the United States and the West has hampered Iran to capitalize on its opportunities in the energy markets.[53] Over 85 percent of Iranian natural gas reserves have not been developed yet, and despite its immense potential, Iran's exports represent only 1 percent of the global gas trade. In addition to the political standoff with the West, the resolution of disputes with the Caspian Sea countries especially with Azerbaijan and Turkmenistan over maritime borders will have significant implications for the sector and may boost Iran's oil and gas production levels. There is no commercial oil production in the Iranian part of the Caspian Sea yet and Iranian oil exploration in this area has started very recently. Due to territorial disputes, multinationals have stayed away from oil and gas exploration in the Caspian Sea. For instance, in 2001 the Iranian military forces blocked the exploration of the Alborz field in the Caspian Sea by a BP-led consortium.[54] Iran's gas production is supposed to grow substantially over the course of the next decade. There are signs that Iran is focusing on increasing the level of gas production for export purposes. More recently, after rising tensions between the EU and Russia over Ukraine, Iran has shown interest in supplying natural gas to Europe, which is very dependent on the Russian gas.[55] Likewise, Iran's oil fields have a natural decline rate estimated at 8 to 13 percent per year and constantly necessitate renovation to enhance oil recovery. According to the Iranian government's evaluation, the country should invest about 300 billion dollars over eight years in the energy sector.[56] To become a major energy exporter, Iran needs to resolve, or at least to reduce its current political tensions with the United States and EU and attract massive foreign investment in the energy sector. After three decades of political turmoil, international sanctions, and geopolitical isolation, Iran's energy sector urgently needs development and modernization. If Iran can attract sufficient level of investment, it will become a major player in the energy markets by exporting natural gas to Asia and Europe. While any significant gas export to Europe could take up to 10 years, Iran may benefit from a mounting, and probably prolonged, geo-political frictions between Russia and the West. Further sanctions on Russia may lead Iran to improve its relations with the United States and Europe and thus become an alternative energy supplier. The EU has been seeking to diversify away from Russia and has often seen Iran's natural resources as a possible alternative. At the time of this writing, Iran is negotiating its nuclear program and its relations with the West. In 2013, for the first time after the Islamic Revolution, the Iranian president had a direct phone conversation with his American counterpart. More recently, Iran and the United States along with other Western powers have been conducting intensive talks over a wide range of geopolitical matters and bilateral concerns. One may speculate that an agreement between Iran and the global powers over the controversial nuclear program will lead to opening doors to investment in the nation's energy sector.

CHAPTER 10

Nonoil Sectors

Economic Diversification: Moving Away from Oil

In the past 40 years, before and after the Islamic Revolution, Iran has been trying to diversify its economy by investing in nonoil sectors and acquiring new technologies. There are signs that Iran has reached some success as it is today a high middle-income country with a significant industrial base, a relatively well-developed science and technology infrastructure, and adequate human development.[1] The role of oil revenues in Iran's economy has been gradually declining during the past decade (2003–2012) as the country has been focusing on nonoil sectors. Likewise, the share of nonoil exports in Iran's economy has increased from 14 percent in 1992 to 24 percent in 2002 and 60 percent in 2012.[2] Export of nonoil products rose by 28 percent in 2011 to 2012 compared to the previous years and reached USD 43.7 billion. The annual nonoil exports may reach USD 60 billion in the coming years.[3] Hence, Iran may remain a middle-income country even without oil exports. According to Iran's Customs Administration, the nonoil exports cover a wide range of products and services including automotive, cement, machinery, steel, chemicals and petrochemicals, food, construction materials, and carpets. The nonoil sectors are of paramount importance because unlike oil exports, the revenues resulted from nonoil exports do not go directly to the government but rather to private or semiprivate firms, which are more likely to attract investment, create jobs, and contribute to entrepreneurship and innovation.[4] In 2012, 38.6 percent of nonoil export revenues were attributed to petrochemical, 32.2 percent to industrial, 13.1 percent to agricultural, 5.4 percent to mineral, and 3.3 percent to carpets and handicrafts.[5] The main export destinations included China, UAE, Turkey, India, Japan, South Korea, Italy, Singapore, Afghanistan, and Iraq. The government intends to develop industrial zones on the borders with

Turkey, Iraq, Turkmenistan, and Afghanistan in order to increase nonoil exports.[6]

Manufacturing

The domestic manufacturing accounts for 12 to 15 percent of Iran's GDP and consists of several industries including automotive, cement, machinery and equipment, steel, pharmaceutical, and floor coverings.

Automotive

In the past decade, Iran's automotive industry has shown an exceptionally high rate of growth. According to the International Organization of Motor Vehicle Manufacturers, in 2011, Iran produced more than 1.6 million cars and was ranked the 13th largest car producer in the world.[7] The auto industry is the second largest after oil and gas and accounts for 10 percent of GDP and 4 percent of the active workforce.[8] There are about 25 state-owned and private car makers in Iran of which two giants namely Iran Khodro, and Saipa are accounted for 94 percent of the total production.[9] In addition to car makers, Iran's automotive industry consists of approximately 1,200 companies, which are involved in production of auto parts for car makers or end users.[10] The domestic car makers have formed joint ventures with international giants such as Peugeot, Renault, and Citroen (France), Volkswagen (Germany), Nissan (Japan), Toyota (Japan), Daewoo, Hyundai, and Kia Motors (South Korea), Proton (Malaysia), and Chery (China).[11] They produce six different types of vehicles including passenger cars, four wheel drive vehicles, trucks, buses, minibuses, and pickup trucks. In 2011, around 1.6 million cars were produced and 55,000 cars were exported to other markets such as Iraq, Afghanistan, Syria, Latin America, and Ukraine. The country plans to produce at least 3 million cars and export 1 million cars by 2025.[12] Despite its importance in Iran's economy and its massive production, the export level still remains very low.[13] The low level of export may be attributed to multiple reasons such as low competitiveness, high pricing, and inadequate business and marketing strategies. The domestic automotive sector is highly dependent on many foreign suppliers, especially the

French and South Korean companies. More recently, due to international sanctions and withdrawal of many foreign companies from Iran, the car production has sharply declined. Furthermore, political turmoil and war in Iraq and Syria have resulted in the reduction of exports and associated revenues. As a consequence, Iran's car makers are under rising pressure to implement effective business strategies and adopt competitive production methods.[14]

Cement and Construction Materials

Iran has a promising capacity in producing and exporting cement, stones, and construction materials. The country has a current cement output capacity of 66 to 75 million tons, making it the world's fifth largest cement producer.[15] In 2009, the country produced some 65 million tons of cement per year and exported to 40 countries including Iraq, Azerbaijan, Turkmenistan, Afghanistan, Russia, Kazakhstan, Kuwait, Pakistan, Qatar, Turkey, the UAE, Georgia, Oman, India, and China.[16] There are more than 60 production factories in Iran as of 2012 and the cement production capacity is supposed to reach 110 million tons by 2015 to 16.[17]

Machinery

In 2008, Iran produced approximately $23 billion of industrial products and machinery.[18] The country plans to become self-sufficient in producing essential pieces of oil industry equipment. Iranian industrial companies have been carrying out projects in 27 countries including Azerbaijan, Uzbekistan, Tajikistan, Pakistan, Oman, Sudan, and Iraq.[19] The value of exported industrial and engineering services has reached over $20 billion in 2011.[20]

Steel

With a production of 16 million tons of steel per year, Iran is among the 15 major steel producers in the world.[21] According to the World Steel Association, Iran was ranked first in steel production in the Middle East in 2013. Considering the centrality of steel production in socioeconomic development, Iranian government has taken drastic measures to increase the output to 55 million tons in the next five years. Despite the significant domestic consumption, in 2013, Iran exported over $500 million of steel products. The major raw steel factories in Iran are the Mobarakeh Steel Complex with approximately 47 percent, the Khuzestan Steel Company with about 23 percent, the Isfahan Foundry with about 20 percent, and the Iran National Steel Industries Group with approximately 10 percent of the market share.[22] Overall, the prospects of Iran's steel industry seem promising as the country enjoys large and rich resources, abundant sources of energy, and adequate domestic technology.

Pharmaceutical

In 2012, Iran's health care industry was worth $28.13 billion of which the pharmaceutical market was estimated to be around $3.51 billion. The country has a strong pharmaceutical industry and according to Iran's Health Ministry, about 97 percent of Iran's required medicine is produced domestically.[23] Exports of pharmaceutical products amounted to $114 million in 2012, but the domestic pharmaceutical industry is highly dependent on the imported raw materials, machinery, and specialized drugs.[24] For instance, Iran's pharmaceutical imports were estimated at $1 billion in 2012.[25] Iran's health care market is expanding and the government plans to attain national self-sufficiency and local production of essential drugs and vaccines. Therefore, the prospects of investment and growth in Iran's pharmaceutical sector seem quite favorable.[26] Cardiovascular diseases, road accidents, cancer—particularly lung cancer— diabetes, osteoporosis, and nutritional and psychological disorders are the main health hazards and are accounted for the main health-related expenses. Furthermore, Iran enjoys a well-established medical education system and attracts a large number of medical tourists from the neighboring countries. In 2012, more than 200,000 medical tourists sought treatment in Iran and brought in over $1.5 billon.[27]

Carpets

The hand-woven carpets are an essential part of Persian history, culture, art, and business. The Persian carpets decorate the floor of every Iranian house and employ about 1.2 million weavers and merchants across the country. Thanks to their artistic designs and high quality, Iranian carpets are among the top Iranian traditional manufacturing items. Iran controls almost 30 percent of the world carpet market and in 2011 the country exported more than $560 million worth of hand woven carpets.[28] It is estimated that around 70 percent of Iranian-made carpets are exported to more than 50 countries.[29] In the past 20 years, the Iranian carpet industry has faced fierce competition from other countries such as China, Pakistan, and Turkey imitating the original Persian designs at a cheaper price. Furthermore, international sanctions coupled with rising costs of labor in Iran have put significant pressure on the industry. Yet, the Persian carpets still enjoy a good reputation and Iranian exporters are optimistic that the country will remain the world's leading exporter of hand-woven carpets for the foreseeable future.

Telecom and Information Technology

Iran's telecommunications sector is highly regulated and is dominated by the state-owned Telecommunication Company of Iran. There were 1,200 registered information technology companies in 2002. The telecommunication sector accounted for 1.5 percent of GDP in 2002. There is insufficient data about the export of telecommunication services, but Iran is involved in exporting domestically made products and software to several countries. Major domestic firms involved in software production include Sena Soft, Dadeh-Pardazi, Iran Argham, Kafa System Information Network, Iran System, and Puya.[30] Software exports were estimated to be over $400 million in 2013.[31] Landline and mobile phone penetration rate is very high by regional standards.[32] For instance, in 2012, Iran had more than one mobile phone per inhabitant.[33] The country's mobile phone segment is still growing, and there is a potential for growth particularly in broadband Internet and software development.[34] In 2012, there were 43 million Internet users in Iran ranking the country first in the Middle East.[35] Considering the socioeconomic and demographic variables such as GDP per capita, literacy (over 80 percent), population size, and median age, the prospects of Iran's telecommunications sector seem very promising. Almost all cities, small towns, and villages have full

Internet access. In the recent years, the government has been computerizing administrative and commercial services. The banks, schools, colleges, hospitals, supermarkets, and small businesses have been adopting the latest telecommunication platforms. Most importantly, Iranian consumers are quite tech-savvy and are increasingly demanding new products, innovative services, convenient software, and more reliable networks.

Agriculture and Food

Agriculture sector accounts for 10 percent of Iran's economy and 21 percent of nonoil exports.[36] It is estimated that 80 percent of Iran's consumed food is domestically produced. With an average rainfall of 240 millimeters per year, Iran is considered a dry land. Approximately, 90 percent of its territory is classed as arid and semiarid. Only one-third of Iran's total area is suited for farming. The western and northwestern provinces have the most fertile soil and enough water resources. Around 21.5 percent of the population live in rural areas and are directly engaged in agriculture.[37] Farms are small, generally less than 25 acres, and are not economically viable. Many farms are smaller than 10 hectares and do not benefit from economies of scale. Furthermore, around two-thirds of cultivable land is not in use and the majority of farms operate far below full capacity. As a result, the farms have low yields, and poverty in rural areas is very common. Wheat, rice, and barley are grown on 70 percent of cultivated land, with wheat accounting for over half of the total crop production. Iran is a net importer of rice, importing around 450,000 tons per year. Other important crops include potatoes, dates, figs, pistachios, walnuts, almonds, cotton, sugarcane, sugar beet, tea, and tobacco. Main produces are wheat, milk, fruits, nuts, potatoes, tomatoes, rice, barley, and grapes. It is estimated that in 2011–2012, Iran exported $5.1 billion and imported $9.7 billion of agricultural products.[38] During 2012 to 2013, the government invested about $12.2 billion to stimulate agriculture sector. The objective of the government has been self-sufficiency in major crops such as wheat and sugar.[39] The country was ranked the 11th producer of wheat in the world in 2011. Pistachio and saffron are the two top agricultural exports. According to the World Food and Agriculture Organization (FAO), Iran was marked as the top pistachio producer with an annual production of 300,000 metric tons.[40] Both pistachio and saffron producers have been under growing pressure from more technologically advanced countries such as the United States and Spain. Indeed, while Iran is recognized as the top producer and exporter of pistachio and saffron, it suffers from low productivity and competitiveness. The producers have been planning for raising value of the pistachio and saffron exports by increasing the output, finding new markets, and improving packaging and marketing strategies. The processed and packaged food products have been growing quickly in the recent years as a large number of small and medium-sized businesses have entered the industry. Similarly, the Iranian dairy industry is expanding as the investment is being increased. The exports of dairy products were estimated at $500 million in 2012 and are expected to rise in the coming years.[41] With a diverse climate and an annual harvest of about 20 million tons, Iran is also a major fruit producer in the world.[42] Main produced fruits include different types of citrus, apples, grapes, dates, and peaches. The country is one of the largest producers of dates with an annual production of more than one million tons in more than 40 varieties.[43] Sheep are the primary livestock with smaller numbers of goats, cattle, donkeys, horses, and water buffalo.[44] According to the FAO of the United Nations, Iran is ranked 33rd in fishery output. Over 200,000 individuals work in the fishery sector and output was estimated at 735,000 tons with the exports around $210 million in 2012.[45] Similarly, the production of meat is estimated at over 2.5 million tons per year that is enough to satisfy the domestic demand.[46] Overall, it seems that the agriculture sector has suffered from lack of public and private investment, droughts in the past 10 years, poor quality seeds, and outdated farming techniques.[47] Therefore, the food and agriculture industries offer many business opportunities in water and soil management, advanced farming, and animal husbandry.

Mining

Iran is ranked among the 20 major mineral-rich countries of the world;[48] it holds 68 types of minerals, 37 billion tons of proven reserves, and more than 57 billion tons of potential reserves.[49] In 2011, Iran's mineral reserves were valued at more than $770 billion.[50] The country is one of the major producers of zinc, lead, cobalt, aluminum, manganese and copper in the world and exports its mineral products to 159 countries. The country holds the world's largest zinc reserves, the 2nd largest copper reserves, the 9th largest Iron reserves, the 10th largest uranium reserves, and the 11th largest lead reserves. While Iran holds more than 7 percent of the world's total mineral reserves, the mining industry contributes only 0.6 percent to the national economy.[51] Many factors contribute to the underdevelopment of mining industry including lack of foreign investment, obsolete technology, legal barriers, and government intervention. Indeed, the government owns and controls 90 percent of all mines and related industries.[52] The country plans to increase mining production by attracting investment and modernizing technology. The prospects of Iran's mining sector seem very favorable as it benefits from many advantages including the abundant metal and nonmetal resources, existence of supporting and related industries, sizeable domestic consumption market, and relatively well-developed transportation networks across the country.

Transportation

Transport sector accounts for 10 percent of Iran's GDP.[53] The country has a network of 140,200 kilometers (87,120 miles) of roads, of which 49,440 kilometers (30,722 miles) are paved. Some major highway networks run across the country and connect major cities. Many private companies provide bus service between large and small cities. The Islamic Republic of Iran Railways is the national state-owned railway company of Iran and manages all the passenger trains and some international trains. The major ports are on the Persian Gulf or the Caspian Sea coasts and include Assaluyeh, Bandar Abbas, Bandar Imam, Khomeini, Bandar Anzali, Bandar Mahshahr, Bandar Shahid Rejaie, Sirri Island, and Khorramshahr. Imported goods are transported throughout the country by trucks and freight trains. The Tehran–Bandar Abbas railroad that opened in 1995 connects Bandar Abbas to the railroad system of Central Asia via Tehran and Mashhad. Iran's aviation is relatively well-developed and dozens of cities have airports that serve passenger and cargo planes. Tehran has a subway system (metro) and many other cities including Mashhad, Shiraz, Tabriz, Ahwaz, and Isfahan are in the process of constructing underground mass transit rail lines. The government is planning to carry out several projects including highways, arterial and rural roads, railroads, ports, and airport facilities. Iran is considering a land transport development plan to establish a quick and affordable network between the north and south. The construction of North Free Way, which would connect Tehran to the Caspian region and Qom to Mashhad, are other road building projects.[54] The expansion of the railway system to major ports is another pressing priority. Similarly, the country aims at developing the logistic advantages in the maritime transport. In the aviation sector, the country needs to make huge investments to renovate the airports and purchase new aircrafts. Despite the old aviation system, the number of domestic and international passengers at Iran's airports has been increasing in the past five years and has reached to 40.1 million persons in 2010 to 2011.[55]

Tourism

Iran's natural environment is highly diverse and offers various landscapes and climates. The country's historical and archeological sites represent significant cultural attractions. In addition, the country offers a promising prospect for attracting a large number of health-related and medical tourists. Before the Islamic revolution (1979), Iran was considered a major touristic destination and attracted a large number of visitors. The things changed shortly after the revolution and particularly during the Iran–Iraq War in the 1980s as Iran's tourism sector substantially declined. In the recent years, there have been timid improvements in the tourism industry. The number of foreign tourists who visited Iran was estimated at 3.2 million in 2011–2012, contributing more than $2 billion to the national economy.[56] The majority of foreign visitors to Iran consist of religious pilgrims, Iranian diaspora, and businessmen.[57] The most visited cities in Iran include Tehran, Mashhad, Yazd, Isfahan, Shiraz, Tabriz, and Kish Island.[58] The tourism sector provides an appropriate option for Iran to create jobs and diversify its economy. The government aims at increasing the number of tourists to 20 million by 2025. To attain this objective, the country needs to make huge investments in tourism infrastructure and services including hotels, airlines, airports, marketing and promotion, travel agencies, shopping centers, and recreation facilities.

Residential Construction and Urban Infrastructure

The residential construction is one the most attractive sectors to the private entrepreneurs and investors. Indeed, the residential construction is among the few sectors of economy that is somewhat immune to government intervention. The share of private investment in the housing sector is estimated to be around 98 percent. After the Iran–Iraq War and particularly in the past decade, the residential construction has attracted huge investments and has grown significantly. The house prices have been increasing at around 20 percent per year over the past two decades.[59] The average price of a housing unit in urban areas is estimated to be about 10 times the annual income of an urban household.[60] To create more stability in the housing market, in 2011, the government implemented a national electronic system for tracking real estate transactions. According to the Central Bank of Iran, almost 70 percent of the population own homes or dispose of sufficient amounts that they can invest in the housing market.[61] Considering Iran's demographical trends, the housing sector is supposed to continue its phenomenal growth in the foreseeable future. It is estimated that every year there is a need for 750,000 additional housing units as the youth reach the marriage age.[62] What's more, some old dwellings need to be renovated or replaced by earthquake-resistant buildings. Furthermore, Iran has been embarking on an accelerated urbanization for more than six decades and more than 70 percent of its population resides in urban areas. The massive urbanization requires large investments in infrastructure, public services, urban transport, water supply, traffic management, sewage system, environment protection, waste management, and other associated projects. The Iranian house builders are keen on adopting new construction techniques and materials to enhance the quality and reduce the cost of construction. Iran has been seeking to attract foreign investment in the housing sector. More recently, the country has started some cooperation with Turkish companies for training experts, producing construction materials and applying new technologies.[63]

Retail

The prospects of retail sector in Iran seem particularly favorable as the country enjoys a predominantly young, urban, and middle class population. Due to international sanctions, the backbone of Iran's retail sector and distribution system is controlled by traditional bazaar merchants and some state-supported companies. The current retail and distribution system relies on outdated technologies and procedures and is mostly inefficient and unproductive. In the recent years some large supermarkets have been emerging in Tehran and other large cities, but their operations have remained very limited. In view of its size and its projected growth, Iran's retail sector seems an attractive target for modern and experienced retailers.

Petrochemical

Iran's strategy has been to create value-added petrochemical products for export instead of selling crude oil. For that reason, the petrochemical industry has been the focus of the Iranian government in the past 20 years. Iran's oil and gas endowments offer a strong competitive advantage to petrochemical industry. Capitalizing on this advantage, Iran has built some of the largest petrochemical complexes in the world.[64] At present, the petrochemical industry accounts for about 35 percent of nonoil exports and has a production capacity of 55 million tons per year. Methanol, polyethylene, butadiene, ethylene dichloride, and ethylene are the main exported petrochemical products. The country exported a total of 18.2 million tons of petrochemicals and polymer products estimated at $14.2 billion in 2011. The petrochemical industry is expected to grow significantly in the near future and production may reach 100 million tons by 2015.[65] The current investment opportunities in Iran's petrochemical industry are estimated to be about $80 billion in both upstream and downstream activities.[66]

Prospects

Since the 1960s, Iran has been resolute to diversify the structure of its economy by placing emphasis on development of nonoil sectors. Relying on the oil revenues, the government has been developing appropriate infrastructure in the country and has taken drastic measures to boost nonoil exports particularly in petrochemicals, manufacturing, and agriculture sectors. The reduction of oil revenues, international sanctions, and the rising number of young and educated job seekers are the main motives of such emphasis on nonoil sectors. It seems that the growth of Iran's nonoil sector will be accelerated in the coming years, as the country is pushing forward multiple privatization programs and subsidy reforms and is introducing attractive incentives to entrepreneurs and investors. Manufacturing industries, such as automotive, pharmaceutical, and consumer electronics, have been developed mainly through licensing contracts and reverse engineering. While Iran has shown some success in developing nonoil sectors, its overall achievement has been substandard in many industries such as car manufacturing and petrochemicals. Iran's manufacturing exports are very limited and consist of a few products. Except for mining and metals, the manufactured products lack technological improvements and cannot compete on international markets.[67] Iran has built a significant technological capacity by building research institutes, and training a large number of scientists and engineers, but according to the United Nations Development Program, the country has a very low proportion of technology-based exports, estimated at around 2 percent of the total exports.[68] The research centers and universities are generally government owned and are disconnected from the consumer market. Furthermore, entrepreneurship is not advanced mainly because business associations and consumer groups are not well represented and do not play an active role in production. That may explain why the small and medium enterprises (SMEs) play only a small role in the national economy. International isolation, trade sanctions, lack of innovation, the gap between consumers and producers, the complex system of licenses and subsidies, and inadequate regulatory system can be considered as some of the main causes of Iran's poor performance in developing and commercializing nonoil products. While opening the Iranian business environment to foreigners may create serious challenges to domestic businesses, it could bring in new ideas, technologies, products, processes, and management styles and push the domestic players to improve their products and services.[68]

CHAPTER 11

Business Environment and Management Practices

Open for Business?

While Iran represents a sizeable economy, the foreign direct investment (FDI) in the country has been very insignificant over the past decades. The World Bank data shows that inflows of FDI reached $909 million by 1978 but subsequently fell to $164 million in 1979 and $80 million in 1980.[1] In 2007, the inflow of FDI in Iran hovered over $754 million, which is a fraction of neighboring economies such as Turkey and Saudi Arabia.[2] Iran has suffered from a significant domestic capital flight mainly to the UAE and Turkey. What is more, Iran's GDP has contracted by 25 percent in the past three years from 2011 to 2013 mainly due to international sanctions. In addition to the international sanctions, political frictions with the West, inefficient regulatory system, country risk, and lack of support from the government are among the major obstacles to FDI in Iran. To overcome the United States economic sanctions, Iran has been seeking investment from emerging and developing countries such as China, Russia, India, Malaysia, and Turkey. More recently and particularly after the presidential elections of 2013, Iran has moved to abandon its isolationist policies by letting foreign investors enter the country. In his first appearance at the World Economic Forum (WEF) in 2013, Iran's new president, Hassan Rouhani, invited world policy makers and business leaders to invest in Iran and take advantage of the business opportunities of his home country.[3] The Rouhani administration has clearly taken a probusiness stand and has been quickly reforming economic policies in the country.[4] While contentions over the Iranian nuclear dossier are not fully resolved, it seems that foreign companies are planning for the time when international sanctions are lifted or relieved. In the same vein, the International Monetary Fund and the World Bank assess that Iran's economy will expand with an estimated growth rate of 1.3 percent and 1.98 percent in 2014 and 2015, respectively. It seems that these estimates take into account the effects of relaxation of existing sanctions, or at least, do not expect new punitive measures. Any peaceful resolution to Iran's nuclear program will have huge business implications. In the past two decades, even despite the imposed economic sanctions, American and European companies have been seeking business opportunities in Iran through their intermediaries.[5] The business opportunities in the country are abundant and include a wide range of industries and sectors such as oil, gas, automotive, agriculture, food processing, minerals, construction, education, manufacturing, and tourism.[6] According to the *Wall Street Journal*, energy companies such as Total, Royal Dutch Shell and ENI, car makers such as Peugeot and Renault, and financial firms such as Deutsche Bank and Russia's Renaissance Capital Ltd. are among those firms that are considering investment in Iran.[7] Reportedly, Boeing has made its first sale to Iran after the Islamic Revolution of 1979 and managers from Peugeot and Total have been visiting Tehran on many occasions. As the French Finance Minister Pierre Moscovici has declared, France will have significant commercial opportunities in Iran if sanctions are lifted.[8]

Ease of Doing Business and Economic Openness

There is no secret that doing business in Iran is difficult. According to the World Bank reports, Iran is ranked 152 out of 189 countries in the Ease of Doing Business in 2013 and 2014.[9] This ranking is an effective way to understand the business environment in a country. The ranking is based on many criteria; for example starting a business, dealing with construction permits, getting electricity, registering property, getting credit, protecting investors, paying taxes, trading across borders, enforcing contracts, and resolving insolvency (See Table 11.1). This approach does not measure all aspects of the business environment that are important to businesses, but a high ranking generally indicates that the government has created an adequate regulatory environment conducive to operating a business.[10] According to the World Bank report, the overall environment of doing business in Iran does not seem attractive. As shown in

Table 11.1 The Ease of Doing Business (DB) in 2013 and 2014

Criteria	DB 2014 rank	DB 2013 rank	Change in rank
Starting a business	107	101	−6
Dealing with construction permits	169	171	2
Getting Electricity	169	166	−3
Registering Property	168	168	No change
Getting Credit	86	82	−4
Protecting Investors	147	147	No change
Paying Taxes	139	138	−1
Trading Across Borders	153	154	1
Enforcing Contracts	51	52	1
Resolving Insolvency	129	129	No change

Source: World Bank's Doing Business (2014).

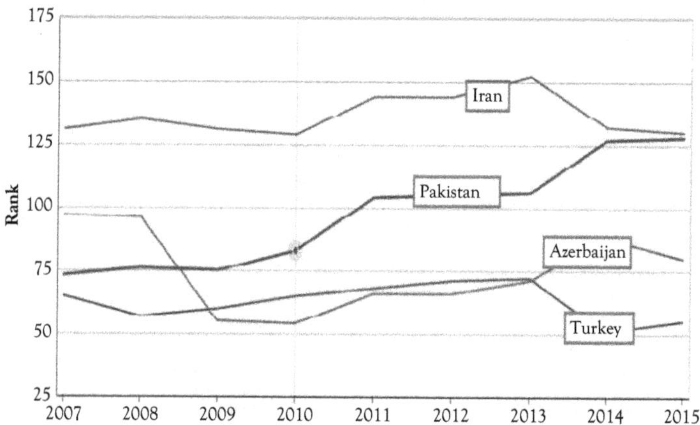

Figure 11.1 The Ease of DB in Iran and neighboring countries

Source: World Bank Doing Business (2015).

Figure 11.1, in comparison with neighboring countries such as Turkey, Pakistan, and Azerbaijan, the Iranian business environment is not very welcoming. The government has taken some measures to streamline the business activities, but the entrepreneurs still face various hurdles such as bureaucratic red tapes, bothersome regulations, and corrupt business behaviors. After taking office in 2013, President Rouhani has been advocating a more business-friendly attitude, but the effects of such reforms may take a few years to be felt by businesses.[11]

Another effective way to evaluate Iran's business climate is to rely on the Enabling Trade Index (ETI) developed and measured by the WEF. The ETI is a comparative measure of international trade liberalization and is composed of four subindexes: (1) the market access subindex, (2) the border administration subindex, (3) the transport and communications infrastructure subindex, and (4) the business environment subindex.[12] According to the Global Enabling Trade Report (2014) Iran is ranked 131 out of 138 countries that means the national business environment is extremely unsupportive of trade. As shown in Figure 11.2, Iran lags behind the Middle Eastern and North African countries in all

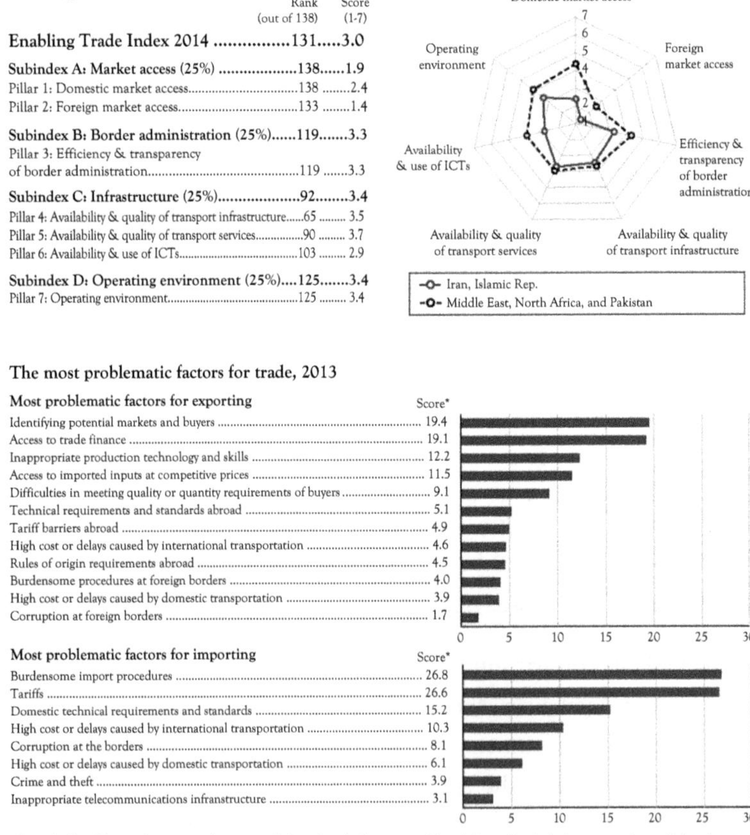

Figure 11.2 Iran's ETI in 2014

Source: The Global Enabling Trade Report (2014).

aspects of the ETI, particularly with respect to foreign market access. While the international sanctions have been pinching Iran's economy, the undesirable effects of mismanagement and poor planning should not be underestimated. According to the Global Enabling Trade Report (2014), identifying potential markets and buyers, access to trade finance, inappropriate production technology and skills, access to imported inputs at competitive prices have been recognized as the most problematic factors for Iran's trade in 2013. Likewise, burdensome import procedures, tariffs, domestic technical requirements, and standards are considered as the most problematic factors for importing. Other alternative measures of trade and economic openness developed by the Fraser Institute and Heritage Foundation point to similar results. For example, according to the Heritage Foundation's trade freedom scale, Iran is ranked 178 out of 181 countries in 2013.[13] On the basis of this ranking, Iran is ranked last out of 15 countries in the Middle East and North African region, and its score is far below the world and regional averages. Lack of economic freedom and heavy state interference in economic activities may explain the stagnation and absence of trade, investment, and entrepreneurship.[14]

Privatization

Shortly after the Islamic revolution (1979) the new government took some drastic measures to gain control over major enterprises and institutions through forceful nationalization and expropriation. The banks, insurance companies, car makers, industrial firms, transport and telecommunication corporations, large and medium-sized business, and educational institutions came under direct control of the state. Furthermore, the new government confiscated the assets of many individuals who were associated with the Pahalavi regime. Over time, the state-controlled institutions and enterprises suffered from unproductivity and became dependent on the government subsidies to run their operations. A decade later in the 1990s after the end of war with Iraq, economic liberalization in general and privatization in particular became attractive economic orientations once again. During this time, the government was seeking to stimulate economic growth and improve the efficiency of large organizations by reducing the government intervention in economic activities. The first

Socioeconomic and Cultural Development Plan of the Islamic Republic of Iran that was prepared in 1990 advised the sale of some state-owned enterprises to the private sector and urged the government to reduce its control over production and economic activities. Accordingly, the government began to transfer ownership of many enterprises to the private sector through Tehran Stock Exchange, direct negotiation with the prospect buyers, and public auctions. Privatization through direct negotiation has been criticized for the lack of transparency and conflicts of interests.

A high degree of government intervention in economic activities has been linked to budget deficits, inflation, disturbance in optimal resource allocations, and unrealistic prices.[15] As such, the successful execution of privatization in a country should result in greater efficiency and profitability, improvement of the firms' performance, and the quality of their goods and services.[16] Contrary to arguments that privatization increases efficiency and stimulates economic growth, multiple empirical studies show that in the case of Iran, privatization did not lead to any significant effects on the firms' productivity, profitability, and efficiency.[17] Despite its lofty aspiration, it is widely believed that the privatization process in Iran has not been very successful in attaining its goals. Instable economic policies, lack of appropriate legal frameworks, and above all, corruption and lack of transparency can be considered as major causes of the privatization failure in Iran.

Small and Medium-Sized Businesses

Despite the high involvement of the government in economic activities, majority of Iranian businesses, particularly in manufacturing sector, remain small (less than 50 employees) or medium-sized (50 to 249 employees). Small and medium-sized businesses (SMB) are accounted for about 60 percent of employment in the industrial sector. According to the Statistical Yearbook of Iran (1996–97), it is estimated that approximately 98 percent of all businesses are microenterprises with less than 10 employees. This is an astonishing number because it shows the absence of medium-sized enterprises, which amount to only 0.1 percent of the total number of enterprises. Obviously, the microbusinesses lack the necessary technological, financial, and managerial resources to become competitive on the international or regional markets. Furthermore, the microbusinesses cannot benefit from the economies of scale to reduce their prices and for that reason remain often uncompetitive. It has been recognized that those medium-sized businesses with 50 to 250 employees are usually more likely to get involved in international business activities. While licenses can be obtained by presenting a business plan, the lack of supportive environment and obstacles to raising capital and technology result in low growth of small business start-ups. As most of the start-up businesses are very small and rely on less than 10 employees, they often face the risk of bankruptcy and permanent shutdown. In the 1990s thanks to the postwar reconstruction and a boom in urban population, there was a quick and significant jump in the demand for various consumer products and services. These sociodemographic trends in conjunction with economic liberalization policies created favorable opportunities for Iran's SMBs in the 1990s and the 2000s. Thanks to growing domestic consumption, Iran's large industrial enterprises mainly car makers such as Iran-Khodro and Saipa outsourced the production of their components to SMBs. Furthermore, some SMBs particularly in food processing, textile, and furniture sectors have been involved in distribution, maintenance, and customer support activities of large enterprises. According to the Ministry of Industries' projections,[18] the share of the industrial SMBs in Iran's exports could reach $56 billion by the year 2020. As the reliance of Iran' economy on oil revenues has been declining in the past two decades, the role of SMBs in creating revenues is becoming increasingly essential. It should be noted that for these projections to happen, Iran should put in place adequate policies to increase the economic openness. It seems that in the recent years the growth and profitability of SMBs have been hampered by the overall Iranian business conditions notably international sanctions, capital shortage, and obsolete technology. Furthermore, the growth of Iran's SMBs has been hampered by their low-quality standards and high prices as customers have often opted to consume imported goods. Another threat to the Iranian SMBs comes from increased competition of emerging countries mainly China. The SMBs are generally suffering from low productivity in comparison with other developing countries and for that reason cannot reduce the price of their products. For instance, the labor productivity rate for Iran is much lower than those for emerging countries such as Malaysia, China, and South Korea. In general, the SMBs are motivated by short-termism and quick profits and neglect the long-term reputation of their brands. For that reason, their products do not often meet international quality standards and some even fall short of reaching national standards that are relatively lenient. Low quality is one of the most important factors hindering the competitiveness of SMBs on the international and domestic markets and no effective quality assurance mechanisms and policies have been implemented in the country. Many Iranian micro or small businesses operating in traditional sectors such as furniture, garment, and food have been under increasing pressures of global competition. Many factors may explain the low level of SMBs success and growth, but among them the lack of an entrepreneurial culture, adverse business environment, red tape and complex regulations, and lack of supportive government policies seem notably significant. Furthermore, entrepreneurship receives very little attention in Iran's educational system and the youth are not equipped with the skills and knowledge necessary for running a small business.

Banking and Financial System

After the Islamic Revolution (1979), all banks in Iran came in the possession of the government. Like other state-owned enterprises, the banks were mismanaged and suffered from grave inefficiencies. In the 1990s, after the implementation of privatization plan, some private or semiprivate banks and credit unions started working alongside the state-owned banks. Currently, there are about 10 state-owned and 20 private commercial banks and credit unions operating across the country. The state-owned banks are among the largest Islamic banks in the world and retain a considerable market share. As of 2011, the state-owned and private banks controlled 80 to 90 percent and 20 to 10 percent, respectively of the country's market share.[19] In 2009, Iranian banks accounted for about 40 percent of the total assets of the world's top 100 Islamic banks. Three of the leading four Islamic banks are Iranian, namely, Bank Melli Iran with assets of $45.5 billion, Bank Mellat with assets of $39.7 billion, and Bank Saderat Iran with assets of $39.3 billion.[20] Commercial banks are involved in operations related to checking and savings deposits and term investment deposits. They may use term investment deposits in business activities such as joint ventures, direct investments, and limited trade partnerships. Furthermore, they are involved in banking operations with state-owned institutions, government-affiliated organizations, and public corporations. The commercial banks are marked by an extensive network of local branches covering all provinces and cities. In 2004, there were about 14,000 commercial bank branches across the country.[21] Iran's banking system includes some banks specialized in certain sectors such as Bank of Industry and Mines, Export Promotion Bank, Housing Bank, and Agriculture Bank. Among these specialized banks, the Bank of Industry and Mines is the main provider of financing to SMB. Iran's banks are famous for their high interest rates on term deposits and investments. For instance, the annual interest rates in state-owned and private banks for the period between March 2011 and March 2012 (Iranian year 1390) were hovering between 12.5 percent for one-year and 17.5 percent for four-year investments. While these interest rates seem highly exaggerated by the Western standards, they seem quite normal in a country marked by high annual inflation rates soaring between 15 to 30 percent. In the past decades, the banks have been paying 6 to 15 percent on deposits and charging about 20 to 27 percent on loans. In addition to term deposits, the Participation Papers (mosharekat) are very popular in Iran's banking system. The Participation Papers are short-term bonds (from one to three years maturity) and have the same economic characteristics as fixed-rate conventional corporate bonds. More recently, they can be traded in an OTC fixed income market. Participation Papers are used to finance major projects and the profit must be calculated and distributed to the shareholders at the end of the project. During that time, dividend or interest is paid. The Participation Papers generally pay coupon rates of around 15 to 18 percent, which are 2 to 3 percent above bank rates, and due to their popularity are sold out shortly after their offering. All profits and awards accrued to Participation Papers are tax exempt. Many state-owned or private enterprises or organizations, such as Oil Ministry, Agriculture Bank, and Tehran Municipality, have issued hundreds of millions of dollars in Participation Papers. The interest rates charged for participation loans depend on the profitability of the project for which financing is required. In addition to Participation Papers, Sukuk is another fixed income instrument in Islamic banking that is similar to an asset-backed debt instrument. Iranian state-owned or private businesses such as Mahan Airlines and Saman Bank have used this instrument to raise more than $100 million.[22]

The Iranian banking system hinges on Islamic finance principles and has been striving to offer interest-free financial instruments. While the Islamic financial system offers some quickness in financing arrangements, due to its participatory nature, it involves more detailed financial disclosure than non-Islamic systems and requires client awareness of the banks' risks, losses, and gains. Not all banks make their financial statements available and many offer results that are out of date. On the basis of their balance sheets, most of the Iranian banks are showing strong results in terms of high profits and quite low operating costs. However, a closer look at their assets reveals that many Iranian banks are suffering from bad debt. For instance, the amount of nonperforming loans in the banking system was estimated to be around $50 billion in 2010. The share of nonperforming loans in the Iranian banking system has risen from 10 percent in 2004 to 25 percent in 2010. The rapid devaluation of rial (Iran's currency) between 2010 and 2012 pushed many depositors to withdraw their funds from their rial-denominated accounts to convert their money to hard currencies, gold, and other assets. As a consequence, many banks have suffered from massive cash withdrawals. Furthermore, the international sanctions have been crippling the Iranian banking system in the past five years (2011–2014) and have made international transactions impossible or extremely difficult. What is more, confidence in the banking system has been severely damaged as many cases of corruption, embezzlement, and fraud have been revealed. In September 2011, the news about a colossal fraud of $2.6 billion in Iran's largest banks such as Bank Melli and Bank Tejarat shook the highest levels of Iranian banking system. Despite all these issues, Iranian banks are operating in a sizeable and growing economy and have continued to enjoy huge margins.

As the economy is dominated by the state intervention, the demand for investment and financing remains very limited. A source of problem is that bank loans and facilities are granted mainly to the large and influential enterprises and smaller borrowers remain largely at a disadvantage.

This can generate serious hurdles for SMB to raise capital and finance their operations and expansion projects. In the recent years, the banks have modernized their operations and have adopted electronic payment equipment and systems. Due to international sanctions, the giant multinationals such as Visa and MasterCard are not present in Iran, but the local banks have been issuing more than 200 million banking cards including debit, credit, gift, and prepaid cards.

The Tehran Stock Exchange

The Tehran Stock Exchange was founded in 1967 and witnessed a solid growth in its first decade of operation thanks to the country's political stability, rapid industrialization, and higher than average economic growth. After the revolution (1979), and particularly during war with Iraq from 1980 to 1988, the Exchange activities were substantially reduced and market capitalization fell to about $149 million. In the postwar period, the Tehran Stock Exchange received attention and with the privatization programs of the 1990s experienced a robust growth. Indeed, the government used the Tehran Stock Exchange as an instrument to transfer the shares of many state-owned enterprises to the private sector. Therefore, the number of listed companies increased from 56 in 1982 to 306 in 2000.[23] Currently, the Tehran Stock Exchange is the second-largest in the Middle East, with a capitalization of about $150 billion.[24] Iran's economy is much more diversified than neighboring countries' and offers companies operating in more than 35 industries including automotive, food, petrochemical, steel and industrial, oil and gas, copper, banking and insurance, and petrochemicals. As more state-owned firms are being privatized, individual investors are allowed to buy the traded shares on the Tehran Stock Exchange. About eight million Iranians own shares and 500,000 trade actively.[25] Regardless of the introduction of supporting regulations, foreign investment remains insignificant as foreigners own only 0.1 percent of listed companies' shares. In addition to ordinary investors, pension funds and institutional investors are active market participants. Despite the international sanctions and Iran's political standoff with the West, the Tehran Stock Exchange has consistently shown robust performance over the course of the past decade. Indeed, the Tehran Stock

Exchange has been one of the world's best performing stock exchanges in the world between 2002 and 2013. The Tehran Stock Exchange Index has grown more than 500 percent in the last five years and despite some occasional corrections, the trend has been consistently upward.[26] This rate of return is particularly astonishing because it does not correspond to the economic deterioration, soaring inflation, and high employment on the ground. The phenomenal growth might be due to a bubble that can burst sooner or later, but there are many other explanations. One alternative explanation for this amazing growth is the impact of privatization and transfer of state-owned shares to investors. It is argued that the entry of privatized state-owned enterprises to the Tehran Exchange increases the market capitalization and volume of trading and thus has a positive effect on the Index. Growing confidence in the Tehran Stock Exchange, entry of new investors, the intrinsic high value of many listed companies, and depreciation of Iran's currency are other factors that may explain the robust growth of the Index.[27] According to the Central Bank of Iran, almost 70 percent of Iranians own homes and possess large amounts of idle capital that they have invested in gold, real estate, vehicles, and foreign currencies. If Iran's economy improves, these idle capitals are very likely to be directed towards equities.[28] Furthermore, there are huge amounts of capital held by Iranian expatriates abroad, estimated at $1.3 trillion.[29] Upon the improvement of Iran's political and economic conditions, Iranian expatriates may invest part of their assets in Iran's economy and particularly in the Tehran Stock Exchange. Foreign investors are almost absent from Iran's equity market for some obvious reasons such as international sanctions and difficulty to transfer funds, but once the sanctions are lifted and geopolitical tensions are defused, they can rush into Iran and push the Tehran Exchange Index even higher. Considering all the potential internal and external flows of fresh capital into the Iranian equity market, the Tehran Stock Exchange could offer attractive investment opportunities. More recently, the Tehran Stock Exchange has initiated a modernization program to enhance market transparency and attract more domestic and foreign investors. With the new trading platforms, investors can conveniently make intraday trades through a relatively large number of accredited brokerage houses. The exchange has the capacity to handle as many as 150,000 transactions per day.[30] The

Exchange trading system offers details of past trading activities including prices, volumes traded, and outstanding buy and sell orders, so the investors can take informed decisions. While the Tehran Stock Exchange offers automated trading platforms and online real-time data, there are some concerns about the lack of transparency and sudden suspension of listed shares. Another problem is that only a limited number of independent private companies can benefit from using the Tehran Stock Exchange to raise capital and finance their expansion.

Corrupt Business Behavior

Iran is still a traditional country in which interpersonal connections and informal channels seem practical, whereas formal systems, official institutions, and procedures are considered less efficient and sometimes troublesome. As a result, the Iranian society tends to operate rather on the basis of personal relationships among people than on the basis of impersonal and dehumanized institutions. The use of informal channels is often associated with bending rules and taking advantages to which one is not formally entitled. The popular Persian term for this practice is *partibazi,* which is quite common in Iranian organizations. Those who receive a service, an advantage, or a special treatment via *partibazi* may choose to reciprocate indirectly or directly. The indirect approach involves compensating favor-givers by similar services, advantages, and special treatments. However, the direct approach involves paying bribes or commissions. Depending on the circumstances, this practice is called *pourcaantage, raante, commission* (from French *pourcentage, rente, commission*) or *pool-chai* (from Persian, meaning tea expenses). As a general rule, when *partibazi* does not imply any bribe or cash, it is not seen as a corrupt behavior. Favoritism may be regarded even as a positive or humane act toward friends, family, and acquaintance.

The Corruption Perception Index (CPI) developed by the Transparency International is a standard measure of corruption that is based on an aggregation of multiple surveys of public and expert opinion. The CPI offers scores for nearly 170 countries on an annual basis. According to the Transparency International, the CPI is "a composite index drawing on 14 different polls and surveys from seven independent institutions carried out among business people and country analysts, including surveys of residents, both local and expatriate."[31] Based on the Transparency International reports, Iran was ranked 144th out of 175 countries in 2013, 133rd out of 174 countries in 2012, and 120th out of 182 countries in 2011. In view of these results, Iran is recognized as a relatively corrupt country comparable to the Central African Republic, Nigeria, Papua New Guinea, and Ukraine. These rankings confirm the facts on the ground, as in the past 10 years (2005–2014) Iran has been witnessing many cases of corruption and fraud at the highest level of government. In 2005, President Ahmadinejad took office seemingly by vowing to fight corruption at all levels of government, but ironically during his tenure the government transparency vastly deteriorated, and bribery, embezzlement, and misuse of public office became a common practice. In September 2011, the news of Iran's largest embezzlement astonished citizens as many state's banks and high ranking government officials including a close aide to President Ahmadinejad were allegedly involved in a $2.6 billion fraud. Despite their moral and Islamic rhetoric, a large number of government officials are well known for involvement in corrupt business behavior including bribery, embezzlement, and misappropriation. What is more, Iran's judicial system is highly influenced by political forces and lacks transparency and decisiveness.[32] The fact that many important positions in the economy are occupied by personalities or organizations connected to the powerful Revolutionary Guard may explain the prevalence of embezzlement.

Labor Market and Working Conditions

Iran's population experienced an extensive growth during the 1980s at an average annual rate of 3.9 percent. Since then the population growth has been declining drastically and currently Iran has the slowest rates of population growth among all the Middle Eastern countries. Those children born in the 1980s have been entering the labor market in the recent years. It is estimated that around 800,000 young people enter the labor market each year.[33] In addition to the population growth, young women are increasingly more educated and therefore are added to the number of new job seekers. The female participation in the labor market was negatively affected by the Islamic Revolution in the 1980s, but rose substantially in the 1990s and is projected to rise in the coming years.[34] The bulk of unemployed people belong to the age group of 20 to 29.[35] The new job seekers are mainly more educated than their predecessors and naturally have higher expectations. High schools focus on preparing students for college and generally do not provide the students with the required skills for a profession. The youth spend a long period of time, sometimes a few years, for the university entrance preparation. In general, Iran's labor force is engaged in manufacturing, construction, agriculture, services, transportation, communication, and finance. Working conditions depend on the sector and the nature of business activity. In public sector the working conditions are better, work stress is lower, and employment security is higher. While the private sector jobs are less stable and more demanding, however, they may offer more generous salaries. Iran's labor laws touch on all labor issues such as hiring, compensation, severance, unemployment insurance, minimum standards, and dismissal. Due to their inflexibility, the Iranian labor laws tend to be rather employee-friendly, and to some extent, discourage the employers from hiring new applicants. A typical working day starts at 8:00 AM and ends at 4:00 PM. The work week in Iran consists of 44 hours from Saturday to Wednesday and half days on Thursday and Friday is a public holiday in the country. In addition, there are roughly 25 days in a year as official holidays.[36]

Women in Workplace

Men are still considered as the family breadwinners and are responsible for their household expenses. For that reason, the women unemployment rate is higher and women generally have lower incomes than their men counterparts.[37] Nevertheless, the habitual image in the west of Iran being repressive towards women is not appropriate.[38] Iranian women may hold offices and conduct business and there is nothing to prevent them from doing so, on the condition that they do not violate the codes of conduct as prescribed by the government.[39] Women are mainly working in such sectors as education, health care, and government offices. In rural areas, many women participate in agricultural activities or contribute to the family income by knotting carpets.[40] While employed women contribute to their household well-being, it is common for them to spend their income shopping for themselves or saving the money for their future needs. Over the course of the past 15 years, many of the women's restrictions have been gradually relaxed and women are present in most occupations of their choice including managerial and professional positions.[41] In 2005, except for technical and engineering studies, women outnumbered men in all academic disciplines.[42] It may seem paradoxical, but imposing the Islamic dress (*hijab*) has led to growing presence of women in all spheres of the society. One may suggest that as the Islamic dress (*hijab*) is in conformity with the Iranian conservative culture, it provides traditional women especially those working in rural areas with more flexibility. In 2004, women accounted for 33 percent of the country's labor force.[43] In the same year, approximately 13 percent of senior officials, legislators, and managers were female.[44] These numbers are very promising, because they are the highest in the Middle East and indicate a steady progress after the Islamic Revolution.

Human Resources Management

Selection and Staffing

Large organizations advertise job vacancies and conduct professional interviews to select the best candidates, but the results of their selection are generally affected by connections and favoritism.[45] It is quite common to see someone who has been employed as a favor towards a family member, acquaintance, or colleague.[46] Among different selection criteria, education and university diploma receive a good deal of attention even if they are not directly related to the job requirements. Other important criteria in the selection process may include professional experience, technical skills, and personal conduct of the candidate in his previous positions.[47] In general, the state-owned organizations pay attention to the candidates' compliance with Islamic and revolutionary values and behaviors. Only those who conform to the widely-accepted Islamic and revolutionary guidelines are selected by the state-owned organizations and government agencies. The government employers often require an entrance exam, interviews, and intrusive background checks, which might look into the candidate's family background and their commitment to religious beliefs and practices.[48] Checking the candidates' political conformity is often a separate procedure that takes long time and might be evaluated by those who are not concerned about candidates' professional capabilities. Such restrictions have underprivileged skillful workforce for more than three decades and have resulted in increasing inefficiency particularly in public sector and state-owned companies. In large organizations, the criteria for promotion are based on a wide range of behaviors that are not connected to performance or professional capabilities.[49] Nevertheless, the selection process in the private sector could be quite different. In most of private businesses, professional experience, qualification, technical skills, education, and fluency in English and other languages are considered the key success factors.

Training and Development and Performance Appraisal

Job seekers are abundant, young, and well-educated but often do not meet the job market requirements. The mismatch between the job seekers' qualifications and job requirements may be attributed to the Iranian education system that emphasizes theoretical aspects. The typical Iranian worker has a good base of theoretical education that may not be useful for potential employers. Furthermore, there is a constant pressure from family and society to study in such fields as engineering or medicine, but many graduates end up working in entirely different jobs.[50] Large organizations often have training centers to enhance employees' competence. The training programs cover a wide range of topics such as technical, managerial, and clerical skills. While most of the organizations recognize the importance of training and development programs, they do not take enough time for planning and preparation. Appraisal is not a common practice in Iranian organizations and those managers involved in appraisal performance hardly rely on systematic methods. An important issue in the appraisal process is the extent to which criticism is accepted. In traditional cultures such as that of Iran, people attach too much importance to interpersonal relations and negative feedback can bring about many problems for both, managers and subordinates.[51]

Compensation

The compensation policies in large organizations or government agencies are not closely related to performance as the preference for fixed pay is very widespread.[52] By contrast, variable pay is used mainly in young and small enterprises that are concerned about their productivity and growth.[53] Many Iranian organizations regard seniority as the major criterion for pay increase and promotion. This orientation is in conformity with the traditional cultural values cherishing past experience and elderly people. Indeed, seniors are often viewed as savvy, experienced, and knowledgeable.[54] Another criterion for pay increase is the level of education. People with higher levels of education get more chances not only in recruitment but also in promotion. In addition, there is considerable difference between compensation packages intended for people working at the top of an organization and those working at entry levels. All active personnel qualify for pension plans that vary depending on the length of their employment, their contribution, and the nature of their work. In general such pension plans disburse monthly payments to men at age 65 and to women at age 60; however, employees working under difficult conditions and in physically demanding environments may be eligible for early retirement.

Leadership

Culturally, Iran is ranked high in the hierarchical distance.[55] The effects of high hierarchical distance in organizational behavior and leadership appear as top-down management, authoritarian decision-making, and hierarchical structure of reward systems.[56] Furthermore, high hierarchical distance and family-orientation of the Iranian culture encourage a paternalistic management or leadership style. Paternalistic management can be considered as an authoritarian fatherliness in which the responsibility of managers extends into private lives of their employees.[57] Paternalistic managers consider it their function to protect and solve personal or familial difficulties of their employees both inside and outside of the organization.[58] For instance, it has been reported that Iranian employees expected superiors to help them in a variety of issues such as financial problems, wedding expenses, purchasing of new homes, illness in the family, education of children, and even marital disputes.[59]

CHAPTER 12

Consumers and Consumption

Revolution, Consumption, and Consumerism

The Islamic Revolution of 1979 was mainly a reaction to the rapid pace of Westernization under the Pahlavi rule. Therefore, the revolutionaries denounced the Western life style and all associating behaviors particularly materialism and consumerism. On the one hand, they were inspired by spiritual values and called for a modest life style. On the other hand, they vehemently advocated the economic independence and self-sufficiency. As a result, the early years of the Islamic Revolution from 1979 to 1990 were marked by an emphasis on consuming domestic products and avoiding luxurious foreign and Western brands. This trend was intensified by war with Iraq in the 1980s, the subsequent falling oil revenues and financial hardship, and the need for a frugal life style. After the war with Iraq, the government of President Rafsanjani took drastic reforms to rebuild the country and modernize the economy.[1] These reforms continued under Khatami presidency from 1997 to 2005 and resulted in a more hospitable environment for business activities, privatization, and economic liberalization. The Islamic Republic gradually distanced itself from the strict populist economic discourse and implicitly accepted the importance of business and free market economy. After 1990, foreign investment was attracted; a large number of small and medium-sized businesses started up, and massive amounts of foreign and Western products were imported to the domestic market. While the early revolutionaries emphasized the importance of a frugal life style, the second generation in the 1990s tried to reconcile to the Islamic values with business activity and the associated phenomena such as consumerism, capitalism, profit orientation, and the rule of supply and demand in the marketplace.

Consumer Behavior

As members of a collectivist and hierarchical culture, Iranian consumers are marked by status consciousness. They attach importance to product brand, image, and fashion. For them the brand and image of their possession are the main components of their social identity that reveal who they are, what they do, and where they come from. As prestige-seeking consumers, they are often concerned about what others think of them and tend to purchase expensive brands.[2] Many consumers are influenced by their peers and those with whom they want to be associated.[3] Not surprisingly, the opinions of friends and peers play an important role in shaping their consumption behavior. Torn between new trends and their identity, Iranian consumers are seemingly reconciling traditional and religious tenets with modern, materialistic, and hedonistic values of consumerism. Hedonic shopping reflects the experiential values that include fantasy, arousal, sensory stimulation, enjoyment, pleasure, curiosity, and escapism.[4] The youth are particularly keen on experiencing new trends and are attracted by luxury, fancy, and high-tech products. Since family and interpersonal relationships are very important in Iran, consumers spend considerable amount of time and money to buy and exchange gifts. Furthermore, household size is still larger than the Western countries and the averages of spending per purchase particularly in food and general staples are relatively higher. Shopping malls (passage) are very popular in urban centers and vary in size, construction, and layout. In addition to shopping, the malls are considered as ideal meeting places for the youth to socialize, have fun, and eat or drink together. Major purchase decisions especially those about furniture and appliances are often taken within the family. Women are increasingly playing important roles in both major and daily purchase decisions. The use of Internet, mobile phones, and social media is widespread and is gradually replacing the traditional forms of media mainly newspapers and catalogs. Meanwhile, radio, television, and banners are still popular. Iranians are well-known for their extraordinary sense of humor and linguistic subtleties that may be used by marketers to capture their attention.[5]

Market Potential and Consumption

Iran is a sizeable market of 80 million consumers with a purchasing power parity of more than $12,000 classified as an upper middle income country.[6] With a Gini Index of 44.5 in 2006, it is evident that the income inequality is high in the country and there is a significant gap between the rich and the poor.[7] Traveling across the country, one may observe that large portions of the population are living under a decent level of disposable income, particularly those living in villages and small towns. Nevertheless, Iran has a large well-educated and urban middle class that can afford a wide range of consumer products.[8] During the 2000s, Iran's economy grew significantly as a result of high oil prices leading to increased incomes and expenditures. Since 2010 the country has been facing some harsh international sanctions that have negatively affected the economy, resulted in double-digit inflation, and by consequence, have reduced the purchasing power of consumers. More recently, the value of rial (Iranian national currency) has dramatically fallen and the purchasing power of consumers has been severely eroded. Thus, consumers are saving less and spending more and some imported products have become extremely expensive for average Iranians. Some families have been relying on their savings to mitigate the effects of the past years' vertiginous inflation. Many others have sought a second job in the informal sector to support their families.

Iran's fertility rate has been slowing radically, but with a median age of 27.1 years in 2010, Iran is still considered a young country where almost 50 percent of the population is under the age of 27. An average Iranian family consists of four persons. In general, large households are found in rural areas or poor urban neighborhoods. As a modernizing society, the urban Iranians are gradually moving away from traditional life style, tend to have smaller families with one or two children, and generally reside in apartments with one or two bedrooms.[9] Most young couples are professionals with both men and women working outside of the home and have busy life styles. Thanks to educational attainment and urbanization, the new generations of Iranian consumers are more sophisticated than their parents and seek the highest quality products and services. Urban middle class Iranians are much larger than other Middle Eastern countries and constitute the bulk of the country's consumers. They consume a wide range of nationally and internationally made products such as appliances, electronics and computers, vehicles, clothing, food, and accessories. With changes in their traditional long-term orientation, Iranians are spending more than their parents and are becoming more hedonistic consumers. Middle class women are often professional and play an important role in purchasing decisions, but men are still breadwinners and enjoy higher levels of income. As head of household, the men are responsible for major family expenses. Many professional women prefer to spend their income at their own discretionary shopping such as clothing, cosmetics, kitchen appliances, and jewelry. While shopping is done by both men and women, the latter have more influence in the purchase decisions related to food, furniture, and appliances. Nearly all shopping is done by cash or certified checks as credit cards are not very common in Iran. For that reason, many customers tend to postpone their shopping until the end of month when their salaries are paid.

Like other collectivistic cultures, socialization with friends and family receives a good deal of attention in Iran. The family gatherings are often occasions to enjoy a meal together and exchange gifts. Culturally speaking, Iranians are very status conscious and consider appearances and fashion very important, especially if the consumption takes place in the presence of others. Showing off the most recent fashion trends or expensive brands is a sign of wealth and social status in Iran. The European trends in clothing and beauty products and cosmetics are in great demand, especially among young girls.[10] As mentioned previously, the socioeconomic inequality is significant and only a small fraction of households are able to afford expensive and luxury products. Consumers have a great admiration for famous brands and those who can afford the luxurious lifestyles boast of their high social status.

Retail and Distribution

Small shops dominate the Iranian marketplace and the quality of products and services vary hugely from one business to another across the country. Some large department stores and Western-style supermarkets were selling merchandises before the Islamic Revolution of 1979, but during the 1980s they practically closed down or downsized. Since 2000, modern supermarkets and shopping malls have become popular in Tehran and other major cities like Isfahan, Tabriz, Shiraz, and Mashhad. The new supermarkets are particularly practical for middle class professional young families who have busy lifestyles and intend to save on time and money.[11] Since the department stores are well decorated and display large quantities of products, they effectively attract Iranian customers and result in higher volumes of sales. Furthermore, the modern supermarkets are attractive to many middle class Iranians who have enough disposable income and seek a wide variety of products in one place. Haggling is widespread in Iran and leads to some discount that could range between 10 to 25 percent of initial price, but the department stores and modern retailers do not permit such practice. In addition to supermarkets, shopping malls are popular places that are used for recreational purposes where people can spend some time with friends and share a meal or drink. People often consider shopping in supermarkets or malls as a family activity where all members including children play a role in consumption behavior. In large cities, shops are open until late at night and shopping is done mainly in the afternoons or evenings. With the advent of Internet and new telecommunication technologies, e-commerce and online shops are gaining popularity. While electronic payments and new banking services have become common, it seems that the Iranian consumers are not completely prepared for online shopping and still prefer brick-and-mortar stores.

Promotion and Communication

As discussed in the previous chapters, Iranian culture is marked by traits such as collectivism, polychronic orientation, and high-context communication. In such a culture, people prefer to socialize, share information with each other, build interpersonal relations, and communicate orally. Socialization and gathering represent appropriate occasions for spreading word-of-mouth and making recommendation about the consumption experience. With the advent of new technologies, the processes of communication and socialization are undergoing significant transformations. Mobile phones are becoming very popular and affordable in the country and are used by a large majority of the population. Like other products, smartphones come in many shapes and brands and often indicate the social status of their users. In addition to phone conversations, short text messages are very common and are used for business or fun. In the recent years, some businesses are using Short Message Services for advertisement. Other technological advancements like Internet and satellite TV are often used for advertisement and play important roles in shaping the consumer decisions. The Iranian government considers satellite TV illegal and enforces Internet censorship, but the younger generation is mostly tech savvy and is able to overcome these barriers easily. Internet penetration in Iran has grown drastically in the past 10 years and has reached 53 percent of the population in 2012 (42 million users). It is estimated that more than 40 percent of the population watch satellite TV channels that broadcast from abroad in Farsi or English. The luxuriant advertisements and products shown via satellite TV channels are particularly tempting to a population that has been under political pressure and international sanctions in the past three decades.[12] Social networking sites such as Facebook, Google+, and Twitter are very popular among the youth and more recently are being used for advertisement and business purposes. Despite prohibition and censorship, it is estimated that more than 50 percent of Iranians regularly use Facebook.[13] As a consequence of these technologies and devices, Iranian consumers are becoming aware of the latest trends, are targeted by more sophisticated marketing campaigns, and increasingly are tempted to change their consumption patterns.

Since the 1990s, marketing activities have grown tremendously and many businesses are relying on experts to conduct consumer research and carry out advertising campaigns. It seems that businesses are gradually becoming more sensitive to consumers' needs and wants. They are finally shifting from their traditional push marketing to pull marketing techniques. Iran state-run TV and radio stations, newspapers, magazines, and other forms of printed media contain commercial advertisement, particularly for Iranian-made products. Similarly, Iranian cities and highways are decorated with many large billboards showing domestic and foreign brands targeting middle-class consumers. Printed media such as newspapers and magazines are often used to promote certain products. As a general rule, the marketing campaigns aim at the middle class consumers in Tehran and large urban centers such as Isfahan, Shiraz, Tabriz, and Mashhad that are believed to have consumers with higher levels of disposable income.[14] The contents and forms of commercials are generally adapted to the Iranian culture and customs, emphasizing values such as family, status, nationalism, functionality, and collective well-being. As a general decree, sexuality and nudity are not allowed in marketing messages. Furthermore, the commercial advertisement in the Iranian official outlets such as billboards, state-run TV and radio stations are required to observe the strict Islamic Republic's rules and guidelines.

Products, Consumption, and Expenditures

Despite economic sanctions, the Iranian market is currently flooded with all types of imported products such as machinery, luxury cars, appliances, computers, electronics, clothes, cosmetics, foods, beverages, and cigarettes. Many American brands and products such as Apple, Dell, Pepsi, Coke, Kodak, GE, Nike, and Levi's are found in the Iranian marketplace. The American products are imported generally via UAE and Turkey. Iranian consumers attach a great deal of importance to brands and pay a premium for those products originating in the United States, Germany, and Japan.[15] The products, especially appliances, from European and Japanese manufacturers are preferred, while Korean and Chinese brands receive less consideration. In the recent years, Iranian markets have been saturated with Chinese products mainly due to their low prices. Middle class and low income Iranians who constitute a large portion of the population demand cheap and functional products such as clothing, appliances, vehicles, and furniture that are often supplied by Chinese manufacturers. Other Asian products, especially South Korean brands such as Samsung and LG Electronics are present in the Iranian marketplace and enjoy a large market share. In some cases, large European or Asian multinationals like Nestlé, Nokia, and Samsung have created joint ventures or alliances with local businesses and aggressively advertise their products. Domestically made products, particularly packaged drinks, sweets, and snacks are very popular and are advertised on the state-run TV. Iran has not signed the international treaty for the protection of intellectual property, and consequently the Iranian market is full of a wide range of counterfeit products including electronics, software, books, and music and entertainment disks.

Housing

Real estate occupies an important place in the Iranian society. It is estimated that almost 120 industrial activities are related to the real estate sector and almost 50 percent of the final goods are consumed in home construction.[16] While the rate of home ownership is estimated at 65 to 70 percent, some authorities have warned of a housing crisis especially for the younger families.[17] Over the past decades, accelerated urbanization and the government policies have resulted in an astonishing increase in the cost of living in urban areas. It is estimated that relative to income, housing costs for Iranian urban residents are among the highest in the world.[18] The average housing price at 70 square meters was estimated around $120,000 in Tehran in 2013. What is more, home purchases are done mainly in cash and even when financing is available, the financial institutions provide mortgages up to 20 percent of the home value. Many young couples receive financial help from their parents to make their first home purchase. According to the Statistical Center of Iran, 55 percent of household income is devoted to rents in Tehran. Considering the paramount importance of housing, a large number of construction and renovation materials and products such as cement, steel, bricks, wood, flooring, and complex structures are in high demand. At homes, the floors are covered with carpets that could be very expensive. Increasingly, some families are using factory-woven carpets as cheaper substitutes to expensive handmade Persian rugs.

Food

After housing, food ranks as the second largest household expenditure. Iran's food consumption market was estimated at $77 billion in 2012.[19] Due to significant socioeconomic development in the past 30 years, hunger and malnutrition have been generally reduced. Nevertheless, the food prices have been soaring and many families had to cut on their daily calories. The reliance on food imports has increased the country's vulnerability to global forces, particularly price volatilities and geopolitical issues. Iranians mainly consume rice, meat, poultry, dairy products, and vegetables. Like many other developing countries, a nutrition transit is happening as the traditional diet based on a combination of wheat, fruits, and vegetables is being replaced by consumption of processed or fast food, sugar, salt, and fat. As a result of these transitions, 55 percent of women and 38 percent of men in Iran are considered overweight.[20] Despite the hike in food prices, eating out remains popular especially among young middle class Iranians as it offers pleasant occasions for socialization with friends and family. The demand for food is growing and new products are constantly introduced. Iranian consumers are becoming increasingly conscious about their health and for that reason they take into consideration the health benefits of food products. Busier lifestyles in large cities contribute to attractiveness of numerous canned, frozen, and ready-to-eat meals, jams, and pickles. Many of these products are produced by domestic companies and are widely advertised on TV and radio stations, newspapers, and billboards. Wealthier consumers may afford fancy imported food products, beverages, chocolates, cookies, and cans that are generally more expensive. Most of the Iranians buy their foodstuff from small grocery stores, but in large cities there are some chain supermarkets that offer a wide selection of domestic and imported items. It seems that gradually Iranian consumers, especially in large cities, are changing their shopping habits and are embracing modern supermarkets. The consumption of alcoholic drinks is officially forbidden, but some alcoholic drinks are smuggled and consumed. Many domestic factories produce soft drinks, soda, juices, bottled water, and nonalcoholic beer. The national dish is *chelo-kabab* consisting of steam-cooked white rice (*chelo*) and some varieties of minced or spiced meat on skewers cooked over fire (*kabab*). Chelo-kabab is served with other accompaniments such as grilled tomatoes, butter, bread, yogurt, and powdered sumac. Almost all restaurants offer this popular dish throughout the country. Alongside traditional cuisine, there are many restaurants offering pizza, pasta, hamburger, and fried chicken. Since the American fast food franchisees are not present in the country, some local restaurants have imitated their products and even their logos.

Transport

It is estimated that more than one million people work in the transportation sector accounting for 9 percent of the GDP. In the past three years, the prices of fuel, and by extension, the cost of transport have been increasing. Much of transport in Iran is done via roads by buses, taxis, and private cars. The number of vehicles has grown significantly in the past 10 years. In Tehran alone, the number of cars is estimated at eight million. The Tehran subway system (Metro) consists of four operational lines and carries 2 million passengers a day. The country has a well-developed network of highways and roads linking villages, towns, and large cities. Nevertheless, the road safety is very low and every year almost 38,000 people die or get injured in car accidents. Iran has a national railway system of 12,998 kilometers with a ridership of 21 million passengers per year connecting far flung cities to Tehran and other large cities. Three major airlines namely Iran Air, Mahan, and Aseman offer national and international flights to destinations in Asia and Europe and to more than 35 destinations within Iran. While the air transport is relatively developed, the U.S. led sanctions have seriously undermined the Iranian airlines as they cannot procure spare plane parts.

Telecommunication

Spending on telecommunication includes a wide range of products and services such as mobile phones, computers, laptops, tablets, e-readers, satellite receivers, and telephone land lines. In the past 10 years, spending on communications particularly on the Internet and mobile phones has grown drastically. The country reached more than one mobile phone per inhabitant in 2012. While Iran has done very well in connecting people via telephone, it is well behind other neighboring countries in the number of Internet users.[21] More recently, schools encourage students to use Internet resources. Social networking websites such as Facebook and Twitter are very popular among the younger generations. In addition to talking, mobile phones are used for sharing photos, music, and video files. There is a strong demand for satellite TV mainly because of a harsh censorship of the news and media in the country. Satellite dishes can be seen on many rooftops or on balconies.

Education

Education accounts for almost 2 percent of consumers' expenditure, which is well above the Middle East average. Despite the existence of state funded public schools, the number of private schools has grown sharply in the recent years. The private schools generally offer smaller classes and better services and are preferred by middle-class Iranians. State-run universities are free but their capacity is limited and their entrance remains very competitive. Many students have to enroll in private universities that require tuition fees. Spending on higher education has grown fast in the past 15 years as a large number of families are sending their kids to college in preparation for a better future. In 2008, Iran had over 3.5 million students enrolled in both state-run and private universities.[22] Education expenditures are related to a wide variety of services offered by day care centers, elementary and high schools, language institutes, college preparation departments, professional training institutes, and public or private colleges and universities.

Clothing and Footwear

Clothing and footwear are considered as other significant family expenditures. According to Thompson Reuters report, Iran has the second biggest global market for Muslim clothing after Turkey, valued at $20.5 billion in 2012.[23] The Iranian garments market is flooded with varieties of domestic and imported products. In the recent years, the cheap imports from China have replaced the Iranian-made clothing and footwear. Shopping for clothing peaks in the last weeks of winter from February to March in preparation for the Persian New Year (*Nowrouz*), which falls on the first day of spring (March 20th). Many exhibitions and markets are held at the end of Iranian New Year, a few days or weeks before the *Nowrouz* holiday. All people, particularly children, are expected to wear new clothing and shoes during *Nowrouz* celebrations. Employees receive the end-of-year bonuses and allowances that are spent mainly on clothing or food. Iranian consumers generally prefer European fashion brands and many upper class consumers make shopping trips to Dubai, Turkey, and Malaysia to purchase high quality clothing brands. Others may travel to the Iranian free trade zones such as Kish and Qeshm islands to purchase foreign made clothing.

Gold and Jewelry

Spending on gold and jewelry is very common as many Iranians consider gold as a reliable investment and ornament. Thanks to limited investment opportunities, Iran has been a major gold consuming country in the recent years.[24] With high inflation rates hovering around 15 to 25 percent per year, gold has become a performing asset. In addition to investment, wedding celebrations involve the exchange of gold and jewelry gifts. After all, a wedding without gold is meaningless. Jewelry and gold shops are seen in all cities and neighborhoods and offer a combination of traditional and European designs made with 18 carat gold and decorated with precious stones.

Health care and Pharmaceutical

Iran's health care industry was estimated to be around $28.13 billion in 2012.[25] Almost 7 percent of consumer expenditure is devoted to health-related products and services. This number represents almost 9 percent of GDP in 2008, which is higher than that of other Middle Eastern countries.[26] Cardiovascular diseases, road accidents, and different types of cancers are the major causes of death and injury and respectively account for 45, 18, and 14 percent of deaths. Furthermore, diabetes, osteoporosis, and nutritional and psychological disorders are on the rise. Drug addiction problems affect 3 to 5 percent of the population.[27] With an aging population, it is estimated that the demand for health care services will increase in the next two decades. Large cities and urban centers enjoy developed clinics and hospitals, but the small towns and villages suffer from lack of adequate health care services. Therefore, many Iranian patients from small towns refer to hospitals and clinics in Tehran and other provincial capitals. The national average of consumption of medicines is higher than normal and it seems that Iranians consume a lot of over-the-counter medications. Iran enjoys a well-developed pharmaceutical industry, but many critical drugs are imported. With the Western sanctions, Iran has been importing Indian and Chinese medications that are generally of lower quality. Iran's pharmaceutical market was estimated at $3.26 billion in 2011. In addition to medicine, the demand for vitamins, food supplements, and slimming products is growing as consumers are becoming more sensitive to their aesthetics. Indeed, appearance is very important to Iranian consumers, particularly to women. For that reason, the country is ranked sixth in the consumption of cosmetics and beauty products in the world. Ironically, despite having to wear the hijab in public, Iranian women pay a good deal of attention to their appearance and meticulously take care of their hair. The demand for all sorts of cosmetics, perfumes, and hair care and skin care products is strong and is estimated to increase over time.

Leisure and Recreation

In tandem with other expenses, spending on leisure and recreation is growing. Most of the outdoor activities are done in groups with friends or family. Among indoor activities, reading books and watching TV and films are very popular. Films, CDs, computer games, and some foreign books are sold as pirated or copied products. In Tehran and other large cities, cinemas, theatres, and music concerts are popular. Due to the Islamic codes of conduct imposed after the revolution, most people prefer to organize their gatherings and celebrations in homes or private gardens. Every year many Iranians travel across the country to visit other regions and enjoy differences in landscape, climate, and cultural heritage. Some holy cities like Mashhad and Qom attract millions of pilgrims. Isfahan, Shiraz, and Tabriz are home to numerous cultural and historical attractions and receive large number of tourists each year. Every weekend, the Caspian Sea coastal cities are vacation destinations of many Tehranis who are impatient to escape the air pollution and traffic jams of the capital. The southern regions and Khuzestan are preferred in winter times and during Nowrouz holiday. The upper class Iranians can afford to visit foreign destinations. In the recent years, Dubai, Mecca, Turkey, Armenia, Azerbaijan, Malaysia, Singapore, and Thailand have been popular foreign destinations.

E-commerce and Online Shopping

E-commerce is quite young and undeveloped in Iran and according to unofficial estimations, it represents only about 0.7 percent of the GDP. This number is much lower than in neighboring countries such as Turkey and the UAE.[28] Despite its underdevelopment, e-commerce may have a promising future in Iran. The country enjoys a large number of Internet users estimated at about 35 to 45 million and is the second largest in the region after Turkey. Iran has high Internet and mobile phone penetration rates estimated at about 55 and 126 percent, respectively. More importantly, the number of Internet users has reportedly doubled every year since 2005 and the number of broadband connections has been growing exponentially in the recent years.[29] Majority of the Internet users are urban, young, educated, tech-savvy, and middle-class citizens who have higher than average income and are fascinated by Internet, smartphones, and technology. The fixed broadband Internet connection is very affordable and Internet advertising is generally cheaper than other media and outlets. Iranian consumers traditionally have been skeptical about online shopping, but the new generations are more likely to consider the benefits of e-commerce. For instance, online shoppers have easy access to wider selections of products, can easily compare prices, and may avoid the hassles of shopping, such as transport, traffic, and parking-related problems.

Obviously, there are huge obstacles to e-commerce development in Iran. In addition to international sanctions and isolation, Internet censorship implies that Iranian businesses are, at least formally, banned from advertising on outlets such as YouTube, Twitter, Facebook, Yahoo!, and Google. While the Internet infrastructure and telecommunication services are quite satisfactory, due to ideological and political reasons, numerous websites or services are restricted, and occasionally, Internet speeds are kept low on purpose. Bureaucratic complexities and obtaining operating licenses for online retailers make the e-commerce operations even more difficult. The new administration of President Rohani has tried to lift some of the harsh restrictions and reduce Internet censorship. More recently, the introduction of mobile 3G and 4G has been approved by the government and Internet providers have been allowed to increase bandwidth to 10 megabits a second for domestic customers.[30] While the international sanctions and Internet censorship have created considerable hurdles to e-commerce, ironically they have brought golden opportunities for Iranian startups to gain market shares in the absence of tech giants such as Amazon and eBay. It is estimated that there are about 15,000 Iranian online shopping websites. In the past years, numerous Iranian e-commerce retailers like Digikala, Takhfifan, eSam, Kadochi, Sheypoor, and Persian Luxury have witnessed amazing growth rates. Reportedly, half of Internet users in Iran have made an online purchase and online retailers are receiving half of the Internet traffic.[31] Due to international sanctions, Iranian consumers and businesses do not have access to services offered by Visa, MasterCard, and PayPal. More recently, domestically-designed services have emerged to increase public trust in online payments. For instance, ZarinPal, the Iranian PayPal substitute, is offering security and convenience to Iranian e-commerce.

CHAPTER 13

Cultural Traits

A Constant Tension Between Nationalist and Islamist Identities

Iranian culture is especially complicated because it is a constant tension between nationalist and Islamic identities. The nationalist aspect of Iranian culture is related to the Ancient Persian civilization and Zoroastrian heritage that date 3000 to 2000 BC but are still prevalent in the society. On the other hand, the Islamic and subsequently Shia aspects are relatively younger and date the 7th and 16th centuries. Historically, the Persian and Islamic elements have been in constant interaction and have evolved together. After the Islamic conquest of Iran in the seventh century, many aspects of Iranian culture were affected by Islamic teachings. Reciprocally, the original version of Islam was highly enriched by the Persian culture and civilization. Some scholars go further and claim that much of the greatness of Islamic civilization stems from the Persian culture and its inputs, especially during the Abbasids dynasties in Mesopotamia or the current Iraq.[1] The Iranian social psyche is marked by a twist between Iranian and Islamic identities. On the one hand, Iranians consider themselves Muslim and share many values, customs, and traditions with other Islamic nations; on the other hand, they attach a great importance to their ancient Persian identity and distinguish themselves from the rest of the Muslim community. Which one should prevail? This is a controversial question that has been addressed in different ways. Seculars and ultranationalists attach importance to the Persian culture and civilization. Their radical supporters argue that the ancient Persian culture is a model for a strong, independent, and successful Iran. They qualify the Arab-Islamic conquest as a disturbing event that brought about cultural and political decline. In contrast, the Islamists, clerics, and religious leaders consider that Islam and Iran are narrowly intertwined. They highlight the importance of Islamic identity and emphasize the benefits of Islam for the country. They are proud of Islamic ear and maintain that Iran's greatest scientific, philosophical, and literary achievements appeared after the Islamic conquest. The tension between Islamic and nationalistic dimensions can be observed very clearly in Iran's main language Farsi. While Farsi (Persian) is essentially an Indo-European language, it has been enriched by many Arabic or Islamic words. Interestingly, over the course of history, Iranians have struggled to preserve their grammatically distinct language, although they have accepted and digested a lot of Arabic words. The blend of Persian and Islamic elements can be found in many aspects of Iranian society including architecture, calligraphy, literature, education, economy, and urbanism.

Iranian Nationalism

Few nations in the world have been able to preserve their cultural distinction as well as Iranians.[2] According to the 2000 World Values Survey, Iranians are ranked as *strongly nationalistic*.[3] As an ancient civilization on the Eurasian crossroads, Iran has long fostered both ambitions of primacy and a sense of cultural superiority.[4] Indeed, despite all the criticism that they make of their society, the Iranian people remain fervent nationalists who yearn for recognition and believe that their country deserves a higher place on the world stage.[5] The development of Iranian nationalism has been associated with its historical experience as a vast empire witnessing foreign invasions and the Western imperial interference particularly in the past two centuries. While Iran has never been formally colonialized, every Iranian leader has felt the vital need to protect the Iranian identity and fight against foreign influence.[6] Nationalism is a recurrent theme in Iran's culture, politics, literature, art, music, and cinema. While Iranians are Muslims, they consider themselves different from the neighboring countries due to their linguistic, racial, and religious differences. As such, there is a sense of national solitude, as Iran has difficulty to find natural affinities with other Muslim or neighboring countries. Furthermore, most Iranians view themselves primarily as the descendants of the Persian civilization and take great pride in their historical and cultural achievements.[7] Even, the pious Iranian Muslims maintain that Islam hugely benefited from the Persian culture to achieve its cultural, scientific, and artistic glory.[8] Since Iran is such a multiethnic and multilinguistic country, sometimes it is very difficult to delineate one single national identity. From one perspective, the Iranian national identity is inclusive and comprises all the Iranian ethnic groups such as Persian, Azeri, Kurd, Arab, Lur, and Turkmen. However, there is another exclusive perspective that limits the Iranian national identity to Shia Persian speakers. This exclusive national identity has led to assimilating large numbers of ethnic minorities into the Persian culture under the Pahlavi and the Islamic Republic regimes.

A Traditional and Collectivist Culture

According to the World Value Survey, Iran is categorized as a traditional culture emphasizing values and ideals such as the importance of parent–child ties, deference to authority, seniority, and absolute moral standards.[9] While these traditional values and behaviors are in conformity with Islamic and Shia teachings, some date back to ancient times and are common among most of the Eastern societies, notably India and China.[10] The traditional values are particularly rampant among the lower and uneducated classes whereas they seem to be fading in the upper classes and Westernized families. Very similar to many Eastern and traditional cultures, in Iran the elderly people are much respected. The youth are supposed to treat their elders politely and consult with them about important life decisions such as education, marriage, and investment. Furthermore, the youth are expected to refrain from drinking alcohol or smoking cigarettes in the presence of their elderly parents. While arranged marriages are not very common in Iran,[11] the seniors, especially grandmothers and aunts, still play an important role in finding suitable wives or husbands for the young in the family. It is common for the youth to seek moral and financial help from their parents, aunts, or uncles in matters concerning marriage. Like other traditional cultures, the gender gap is quite high, but the urban and upper level classes generally treat both sexes as equal at home and in the workplace. Not surprisingly, male children are still preferred especially in the poor or rural families that rely on their sons as a source of financial and moral support. In 2013, a United Nations report ranked Iran 107 out of 148 countries on the Gender Inequality Index that measures reproductive health, empowerment, and economic activity of women. Over the course of the past 20 years, women literacy and school enrollment rates have improved and currently women constitute 65 percent of university students.[12] Similarly, the gender gap has been declining in Iran as more women have shown presence in the educational institutions and job market.

A very fundamental issue in every society is the priority given to the interests of individuals versus those of groups. In an individualistic society, beliefs and behaviors are determined mainly by the individuals; whereas in a collectivist society, the attitudes and behaviors are shaped by loyalty toward one's group.[13] In that sense, Iranian culture is marked by a high degree of collectivism as one's identity is shaped mainly by the group's interests and private life is often invaded by others. Collectivism may have its antecedents in resource scarcity and the presence of large and extended families that were quite prevalent in Iran until the 1970s.[14] We may suggest that under difficult circumstances people tend to embrace collectivism as their survival depends on communal efforts. By contrast, when living conditions are more comfortable, people can survive individualistically and conduct their lives on their own.[15] The collectivist orientation of Iranian culture is confirmed with the centrality of the family. As a collectivist culture, Iranians view the family relations more important than other social arrangements. One can see that economic and political organizations are significantly shaped by family ties.[16] These ties include not only the nuclear family of parents and offspring but also the near and distant relatives and friends. Successful persons are expected to help the members of their extended family in a wide range of matters like education, employment, and business. Those without family ties are hugely at a disadvantage and suffer from a lower status. In a collectivist culture, such as Iran, this kind of nepotism is morally accepted and appreciated.[17]

Hierarchical Distance

Historically, Iran's society was divided into tiers: the first tier was devoted to the upper classes, the second to the middle classes, and the third to the lower classes.[18] Herodotus in the fifth century BC reported that the relative rank of two Iranians meeting on the street could be determined simply by observing the greetings they exchanged.[19] The class culture is still quite prevalent. Many scholars and travelers have reported that Iran is a highly hierarchical society in which there are huge differences in the distribution of power, wealth, and resources.[20] The antecedents of high hierarchical distance are deeply rooted in many aspects of Iranian mythology, history, politics, religion, and family structure. For instance, associated with the hierarchical distance is a very strong sense of class and status. In the postrevolutionary era, the old order of society changed and many Islamists from lower classes ascended to important government positions, got education, and accumulated wealth; however, the class-based culture remained almost intact. The hierarchical distance has many bases and forms including income, professional status, place of birth, urban or village origin, education, title, family, kinship, and genealogy.[21] For instance, low income and high income families are visibly separated along cultural, linguistic, and spatial lines. In the Iranian families, the high degree of hierarchical distance is manifested as a patriarchic order as the head of the household is generally the husband or father who expects respect and obedience from the members of his family.[22] Hierarchical distance is important in marriage as many people view it as shameful marrying into classes lower than their own. In such a hierarchical culture, title, education, and ascription are widely used to enhance the influence and social status. In postrevolutionary Iran, a large number of government officials who had humble family origins, rushed to colleges and universities—and in some cases—obtained forged university diplomas and professional titles to enhance their status and recognition. In 2008, a public scandal over the fake doctorate degree of Iran's interior minister resulted in a political crisis and ultimately led to his resignation.

The high hierarchical distance is translated into authoritarianism in the Iranian political system. As Hoveyda[23] pointed out the Iranian leaders act paternally; they seem compassionate on the one hand and stern and cruel on the other. In his famous book *The Great Civilization,* former Shah of Iran maintained that "A king in Iran represents people … he is the teacher, the master, the father, in short he is everything."[24] Likewise, the collection of Iranian mythology *Shahnameh* (Book of Kings) is marked by exaggerations about miraculous achievements of powerful kings and superheroes such as Rostam, Jamshid, and Keykhosrow. Not surprisingly, for over

2500 years, monarchy and dynastic rule were the norms of political life in Iran. By one count, there have been 46 such dynasties and over 400 ruling Shahs (kings) in Iran.[25] This long and old monarchical tradition was interrupted in 1979 with proclamation of Islamic Republic and the adoption of a republican constitution. Nevertheless, shortly after a popular uprising, a similar hierarchical order of theocratic guardianship was restored.

Gaze at the Past

Traveling across Iran in the 1860s, the French novelist and anthropologist, Count de Gobineau, reported that the past was a favorite subject of conversation among people. This observation points to the past orientation of Iran's national culture. Iran represents one of the most traditional countries of the world that has always been haunted by the shadow of its long history. Many mythological beliefs both from pre-Islam and Islamic eras are still present in the collective psyche of Iranians and affect their behaviors.[26] Before revolution, ancient Persian Empire and its legends were considered as guiding principles for the Shah who was assuming the role of Cyrus the Great in leading the country toward the so-called *Great Civilization*. After the Islamic revolution, Islamic Shia tradition and its Imams were chosen as the role models for moving toward a utopia full of justice and perfection. Thus, it seems that both the Pahlavi monarchy and the Islamic Republic have overemphasized the past to push forward their respective agendas. The objective of Islamic Republic as stated by its founders was to create a society very similar to the Prophet Mohammad's era. Indeed, all religions, to some extent, are fueled by the past and rely on their historical myths. The Shia and Islamic religious ceremonies are associated with veneration of martyrs, pilgrimage to shrines, commemoration of the martyred Imams, and their passions, which all imply a constant gaze at the past.[27] While the Shah and the Islamic agendas might seem quite different, both are marked by a constant gaze at the past.

Short-Term Orientation and the Pick-Axe Society

Another trait of the Iranian culture is its remarkable short-term orientation. Future, and by extension, long-term planning and preparation do not receive enough attention in Iran and social arrangements are driven by short-termism. To better describe the short-term character of Iranian culture, Katouzian[28] refers to the short life cycle of buildings in Iran that is almost 20 to 30 years. The 30-year-old buildings may be sound in foundation and structure, but lose their market value due to their outdated exterior and interior designs. In other words, the common practice of constructing and demolishing a building within a 30-year period is an indication of the prevalence of short-termism in Iran's culture. Katouzian[29] labels it as the pick-axe society (*Jameheh-ye Kolangi*), the society where economic, political, and social arrangements are constantly receiving the *pick-axe* treatment by short-term caprices. Therefore, one may notice that many economic activities, business enterprises, and institutions operate on short-term basis and are regarded as personal privileges that seldom last more than one generation. For example, many businesses have a short life expectancy and are closed down after the demise of their founders and owners. By the same logic, architecture, urban development, strategic planning, and investment are often driven by short-term objectives.

An Evolving and Fading Religiosity

A glimpse at the Iranian society reveals the centrality of Islamic religion in all aspects of life including architecture, dress code, education, literature, art, and above-all political system. According to a study conducted by the World Values Survey in the 1990s, 82 percent of Iranian respondents considered themselves as religious, 99 percent believed in God, 90 percent considered God as important in life, and 87 percent sought comfort and strength from religion.[30] According to the same study, only 1.3 percent of the respondents were atheist. Based on these results, Iran is considered a highly religious society among some 56 countries included in the study.[31] No matter the ethnicity, education, age, or intellectual and philosophical orientation, almost all Iranians consider religion as something important in their lives.[32] This tendency toward religiosity or spirituality may lead to exaggerated, and even superstitious, beliefs. Obviously all the leaders of Islamic Republic are fervent religious Muslims or clerics, but even before the Islamic Revolution, Iranian leaders and politicians were mainly religious. For instance, despite his Western education and liberal ideas, the former Shah of Iran was a faithful Shia Muslim. In his interview with the Italian journalist, Oriana Fallaci, the former Shah expressed his religious convictions very frankly and claimed to be saved or protected by Shia Imams.[33] Even Iranian secular intellectuals, scientists, and physicians have a remarkable tendency toward religiosity and spirituality and see all world affairs as the manifestations of God's power. It is important to mention that while Iran scores high on religiosity, it is ranked less religious than many other Muslim countries such as Pakistan, Bangladesh, Indonesia, and Egypt. While the data for other countries is not available, it is plausible to suggest that Iran is possibly less religious than many other Muslim countries. While Iran is the world's only constitutional theocracy, it is one of the least religious countries in the Middle East.[34] The American author and television personality Rick Stevens reported how he was surprised by the general mellowness of the atmosphere in Iran compared to other Muslim countries.[35] Based on his experience, despite a highly theocratic political system, Iran ironically seems less religious than neighboring Muslim countries that he has visited. Rick Stevens reports that in Turkey, mosques spill over with people during prayer times, but in Iran one can hardly hear a call to prayer and minarets are not seen in the skyline.[36] Indeed, many observers suggest that the actual level of religiosity in Iran is much lower than what it was reported by the World Values Survey in the 1990s. Increasingly, there are signs and symbols in pop music, literature, and cinema indicating that the younger generations are becoming less religious. Part of the explanation may be attributed to the *adverse effects* of an aggressive theocratic political system over the past 35 years. A lower level of religiosity could be viewed as an antithesis to the state-supported and forceful Islamization campaign that started after the revolution. An alternative explanation is that according to Modernization theorists, secularity is an outcome of human development and as the standards of living, educational levels, and urbanization rates improve, the societies abandon their religiosity and instead move toward more rationality and secularity.[37] In the past three decades, Iran's Human Development Index and by extension, standards of living and educational levels have been constantly growing. Thus, one may speculate that the passage toward secularity will be accelerated in the coming years.

Mistrust and Conspiracy Theories

As mentioned in the previous chapters, the history of Iran is marked by many foreign brutal attacks and as a nation; Iranians have always felt under threat of foreign forces, their invasions, and particularly their plots. It is not surprising that the social life has been structured accordingly and this has resulted in a feeling of suspicion and a need for mistrust toward outsiders. Most of the conspiracy theories are directed to the foreign powers, notably Great Britain, the United States, Israel, and Russia for harming the nation's interests and exploiting its wealth. Iranian psyche is suspicious especially of Great Britain because of its meddling during the 19th century and of the United States because of its role in overthrowing the popular and democratically elected Prime Minister Mossadegh in 1953. Iranians, on the one hand, look at the ruins of Persepolis and remember their ancient glory. On the other hand, they remember their contemporary humiliations by the West. Due to their tragic history, they are still mourning, are pessimistic, and have good reasons to distrust foreigners. It is not uncommon to see ordinary Iranians putting the blame on foreigners for many social and even natural problems such as narcotic addiction, diseases, droughts, and earthquakes. Some Islamic and Shia religious notions and teachings such as the inherent contradiction between the appearance (*Zaher*) and the inner truth (*Baten*) provide support for mistrust and conspiracy theories. Iranians are the firm believers in the saying that the things are not always as they seem because appearances can be deceiving. The conspiracy theories offer quick reliefs from harsh realities that bother Iranian social consciousness, however they create some relief. The conspiracy theories provide a fatalistic outlook of a world in which people cannot change anything because everything is determined by the invisible hands of some evil powers. The prevalence of mistrust and conspiracy theories are well shown in a popular novel *My Uncle Napoleon* by Iraj Pezeshkzad.

The Dichotomy of Good Versus Evil

A very predominant theme in the Iranian culture is the dichotomy between good and evil and their mutually exclusive natures. To understand this dichotomous conflict, we should remember that the ancient religion of Iran is Zoroastrianism, which consists of a monotheistic worship of Ahura Mazda (the Lord of Wisdom) and an ethical dualism opposing good and evil spirits. This duality of good and evil is a central theme in Iran's culture. One of the most well-known forms of ethical dualism in the Iranian culture is the commemoration of Ashura tragedy in which Imam Hossien was martyred by Yazid. Shia Muslims recognize the symbolic importance of this tragedy by supposing that Imam Hossein scarified himself in order to clarify the path of good from evil. It is often believed that the incessant battle between good and evil is inevitable and it will continue until the coming of the 12th Imam who will restore justice and order in the world. Not surprisingly in order to enhance their success, in 1979, revolutionaries used this notion to label Ayatollah Khomeini as Imam or Angel and former Shah as Yazid or Evil. Similarly, they used the appellations of Yazid and the Great Satan respectively for former Iraqi president and the United States. The dichotomy of good and evil may explain the quest for the universal justice in the Iranian culture.

Attitude Toward the West

Iranians have an ambivalent attitude toward the West in general and the United States in particular. This attitude is a mixture of hate and admiration, like and dislike. First of all, they have good reasons to hate the West because they have unpleasant memories of their relationships with the Western powers during the 19th and 20th centuries and in the recent years. In the 19th century, after bloody wars, large parts of Iranian territory were annexed to the Russian Empire. In the 20th century, the national sovereignty of Iran was violated and the country was invaded by the British and Russians armies.[38] In the past decades, the West in general and the Americans in particular have not respected the Iranian Revolution and supported Saddam Hussein in a long and destructive war against Iran.[39] In the Iranians' view, the Western powers are hypocrite, because they talk about human rights, but wage wars and conflicts and plunder Iran's resources. Similarly, they believe that the Western powers have used and accumulated the most lethal and dangerous weapons, but continue to deny the Iranian national rights to develop a peaceful nuclear technology. The resentment of the West—and by extension of the Western culture—has received support from both religious and secular groups mainly from leftist intellectuals. Despite this resentment, many Iranians, chiefly the middle class urban population, have a high admiration of the Western, particularly American, culture.[40] They maladroitly apply the American styles in their urban development, architecture, education, literature, movies, and even food and clothing. They are fascinated by the American role models and send their children to American universities.[41] We may propose that even their anti-Western rhetoric, to some extent, is affected by the Western intellectuals.

Harmony, Subjugation, and Pernicious Fatalism

Generally speaking, the Eastern cultures are marked by harmony and subjugation toward natural forces.[42] Iran is no exception. Furthermore, Iran's culture is traditionally pervaded by beliefs in religion and God that imply maintaining a harmonious and even passive relationship with natural forces. In Islamic teachings, after a horrific natural disaster such as earthquake, flood, or thunder, people are invited to pray and remember God's superior might. In Iran and other Islamic countries, natural disasters are often seen as *divine examinations* or *punishments* for sinful behavior. For example, a few years ago, BBC reported that a top Iranian cleric blamed earthquakes on immodest women clothing. More recently in 2014, another leading ayatollah and politician has called on people to pray for rain.[43] This traditional cultural orientation by virtue of religiosity considers human beings as subjugated to their destiny or their God and implicitly prescribes a pernicious fatalism. Like many other Muslim countries, Iranians use the famous word *Inshallah* (God Willing) to justify their fatalistic laziness, their lack of planning, and their neglect of responsibilities. The manifestations of harmony and subjugation cultural traits are seen easily in the Persian music and literature, as they are pervaded by calm, passive, sad, and even pathetic sensations. Kassravi, an influential intellectual, has lambasted this fatalistic worldview as the main cause of Iranian backwardness.[44]

A Tendency Toward Rebellion

Some may suggest that Iranians have a propensity toward revolt against authority. This rebellion orientation, which is very distinctive in the Middle

Eastern countries, might be attributed to Iran's historical experience. A glance at the nation's history reveals some striking examples of social movements and civil unrest. For instance, despite the acceptance of Islam, Iranians revolted against the political supremacy of the Muslim Arabs at the very beginning in the seventh century. Later, they advocated relocation of the Islamic empire's capital from Damascus to Baghdad, where they could better influence the political decision making. Eventually, Persians were instrumental in undermining the Umiyad dynasty and replacing it by more friendly Abbasids. The social revolt continued in the 8th and 9th centuries with nationalistic, brave men such as Abu Muslim, Babak and Mazyar, Assassins (Hassan Sabbah) against Arab Muslims and in the 14th and 15th centuries with Sar-bedaaraan and Hurufiyya movements against Mongols. In the modern times, the revolt and social movements have been crystallized against the Western powers such as Russia, Great Britain, and the United States. The Constitutional Revolution from 1905 to 1911, Oil Nationalization Movement (1953), Qom Revolt (1963), and the Islamic Revolution (1979) are some salient examples of this tendency toward revolt. National pride, honor, Shia ideology, and social justice can be seen as the main reasons explaining this rebellion orientation.

The Iranian Chivalry and Zeal

Traditionally, Iranians have a substantial tendency toward chivalry and qualities such as courage, graciousness, loyalty, hospitality, and compassion. While these cultural traits are essentially rooted in the pre-Islamic Persian culture, they have been affected and enriched by Sufism and mysticism.[45] A chivalrous man is supposed to defend the weak, sacrifice his personal interests for the sake of others, and behave politely and graciously in his community. Among Persian characters, Rostam and Kaveh, and among Iranian-Islamic religious figures, Imam Ali and Imam Hossein are recognized as prime examples of chivalry and courage. Associated with the chivalry is a tendency toward spirituality, an appreciation of higher values, and a moderate contempt of world ephemeral vanities and enjoyments. While the new generations are gradually distancing from the old ethos of chivalry, it is possible to witness many manifestations of chivalry even among the Iranian youth.

Likewise, the Iranian zeal is regarded as an enormous passionate force that motivates people to protect moral matters such as honor, religion, homeland, and family. Iranians have relied on this cultural value to respond to personal and national affronts vigorously.[46] A good example of this passionate force is the incredible and spontaneous sacrifice of population during the imposed war from 1980 to 1988 to defend their home country against the aggression of Iraqi forces. During the war, the deployment of highly motivated and zealous volunteers helped Iranian military overcome Iraq's military and logistic superiority.

CHAPTER 14

Communication and Negotiation Styles

Communication, Negotiation, and Culture

During the communication process, information is encoded in a verbal or nonverbal message and is imparted by a sender to a receiver via some medium. Subsequently, the receiver decodes the message and gives the sender a feedback. In the same way, negotiation can be described as a back-and-forth communication process aimed at achieving an arrangement between two parties with some interests that might be shared or different.[1] Since communication and negotiation are forms of social relations, they are likely to be influenced by national culture. Culture impacts communication and negotiation through its effects on all important components including interests, commitments, compromises, meanings, relationships, and contacts between two parties. Edward T. Hall,[2] an American anthropologist, identified three elements that are essential in understanding the effects of culture on communication and negotiation processes, namely, context of communication, temporal orientation, and proxemics. In this section, we rely on Hall's three elements to analyze the communication and negotiation patterns in Iran.

A High Context Communication Culture

According to Hall,[3] a high-context communication is one in which most of the meaning is in the context while very little is in the transmitted message. On the other hand, "in low-context cultures, most of the information must be in the transmitted message in order to make up for what is missing in the context."[4] The Western cultures, notably Germany, Scandinavia, Great Britain, and the United States are classified as low-context because in such cultures the meaning is transmitted mainly through the message and it does not depend very much on the context of communication.[5] Like many other oriental nations, the Iranian culture is categorized as high-context, because a considerable portion of the meaning is transmitted through the context of communication. The high-context communication involves ambiguous and context-bound messages. The ambiguity is seen in many aspects of the Iranian society such as language, literature, history, religion, and politics. Farsi (Persian) language is rich in terms that involve tantalizing, ambiguous, and even contradictory meanings and connotations. In their daily communications, Iranians use a wide range of vague and contradictory metaphors, parabolas, allusions, images, and emblems that require interpretation. The Persian literary masterpieces such as Hafiz's poems are well known for implying a high degree of ambiguity and contradiction, so they can be interpreted very differently. For many centuries, the Persian literary masters have boasted of the art of ambiguous communication in their lyrics. The quality of any communication between Iranians and the Westerners may be impacted by their differences in high- and low-context dimension. While the Iranian high-context communication is partly attributed to the linguistic issues, it is also an efficient negotiation strategy. A common form of high-context communication in Iran's culture is *Taarof*, which can be literally translated as politeness, but has a much more profound significance. The Iranian *Taarof* has two important dimensions: chivalrous behavior and indirect communication. The chivalrous dimension of *Taarof* may include politeness, compliments, pleasant behavior, and offering help to others. The second dimension or indirect communication of *Taarof* involves verbal games and expressions to gain advantage in business and negotiation. Extreme degrees of *Taarof* can be viewed as promise, dissimulation, or even deception. In *Taatof*, the meanings of words may depend on the context of communication. For example, people may *verbally* tell that they are willing to do something for you while they are not really comfortable doing it. Similarly, they might offer you a precious gift while they expect that you reject it out of courtesy.[6] It is widely recognized that *Taarof* tactic gives Iranian negotiators a considerable advantage in their dealings.[7] Like many other Eastern countries, this kind of context-bound communication may be used as an effective strategy to outsmart the business partners. Exaggeration is another high-context communication technique that is frequently used in Iran to capture the audience's attention and pave the way for making a business deal. The exaggeration technique may involve the use of multiple metaphors, images, comparisons, and other verbal or nonverbal subtleties.

Temporal Orientation

Temporal orientation deals with the ways in which cultures perceive time and structure their activities accordingly. With this regard, Hall has distinguished monochronic and polychronic temporal orientations. Monochronic cultures perceive time as linear, sequential and focus on one thing at a time. People in northern Europe, the United States, Germany, Switzerland, and Scandinavia are mainly monochronic. By contrast, the polychronic cultures have a different perception, view time as circular and as a result get involved in different concurrent tasks. The polychronic orientation is common in Asia, Africa, the Middle East, Mediterranean, and to some extent in European countries including France, Italy, Greece, and also Mexico. The temporal orientation impacts the perception of future and planning activities. For instance, the monochronic cultures adhere religiously to plans, but the polychronic cultures tend to change plans more easily and quite frequently. In addition, ploychronic cultures attach more importance to interpersonal and human relationships rather than on the plans and regulations.

As members of a polychronic culture, Iranian negotiators try to build interpersonal relations with their counterparts before getting involved in business or professional discussions. That's why they may pay attention to their counterparts' appearance, attire, title, education, qualification, specialization, and personal background. They may conduct lengthy and circular discussions and use compliments to break the ice and get closer to their interlocutors. They put a good deal of emotion in their negotiations and try to change the course of negotiation by building amicable relations with other parties.[8] Their temporal cyclicality implies that in general they do not have detailed plans for what they want to say and consequently, they prefer to improvise during the negotiation and communication process. For example, Iran's clerics often deliver very long speeches of two to three hours and furnish huge amounts of information without referring to any notes or documentations. Since Iranians have a cyclical conception of time, they may change the topics very frequently during the negotiation process, or they may interrupt the communication abruptly and start a new topic. Sometimes they cunningly utilize irrelevant topics to gather information about the interlocutors and manipulate them more effectively. This communication style can be annoying for the monochronic Westerners who are characterized by temporal linearity, result-orientation, and well-thought plans and deadlines. Another important effect of the temporal cyclicality is that Iranians in general prefer oral and face-to-face communication over written and impersonal modes such as e-mail and letter. One may suggest that during an oral and face-to-face communication, Iranians can use the contextual factors more effectively to transmit their messages and affect the interlocutors. As a direct consequence of temporal cyclicality, punctuality is not a major concern in Iran. While they try to be punctual, their tardiness is customary. Iranian negotiators often operate under uncertainty and envisage a short time horizon assuming that in future everything might be different.[9] They are well known for their tendency toward procrastination, and therefore their negotiations become generally long and exhausting. Skillful negotiators may use procrastination as an effective strategy to defend their positions, distract the interlocutors, and eventually achieve their desired goals. Furthermore, most of Iranian negotiators want to take some time to establish a personal relationship before they decide whether they want to do business with their counterparts. This is in contrast with German and American styles viewing time as linear and measuring it in terms of economic value.

Proxemics

Space is another central element of Hall's theory, which may have different meanings and implications. Hall[10] maintained that intimate and public spaces are perceived differently across cultures. He suggested that each person has around him an invisible bubble of space that, depending on the national culture, may expand or contract.[11] While Iran, the Mediterranean, Arab, and Latin American cultures conceive space as public, the Westerners in general and the American and Scandinavian cultures in particular protect their personal space.[12] Like other Eastern cultures, Iranians tend to keep a close distance among each other during the communication and other social exchanges. For the same reason, they may convey their messages by touching the interlocutor. In Iran, holding hands, kissing on the cheek, and hugging are generally accepted between people of the same sex, however, males and females do not show these signs unless they are husband and wife or brother and sister. According to Iran's sociocultural norms, the place of seating in a gathering is highly meaningful. For instance, seating near the door may be an indication of one's low rank while seating at the head of the table may mean one's high rank and influence. In political or family gatherings, the distance between the host and guests is an indication of the degree of their seniority, status, or influence. Furthermore, being placed in the left or right side may convey different meanings. For instance, during official meetings, important and senior government officials are often seated close to the supreme leader. Generally, raising the head during negotiation means disagreement or dissatisfaction but lowering the head shows affirmation or satisfaction.[13] Likewise, keeping one's head down and putting one hand on the chest is an expression of sincerity and friendship toward others.

Linguistic Protocols and Haggling

The Persian language is highly important in Iran and is viewed as the essence of national identity. Persian is a flowery, euphonic, and literary language enriched by various proverbs, maxims, aphorisms, and poetic expressions. Poetry is often more important than prose in Persian culture and Iranians boast of their famous classical poets. Skillful communicators and negotiators can artfully use poetic expressions and metaphors to make their case more euphonic and convincing. It is common to seek endorsements from credible persons or start a conversation with some verses from the great Persian masters such as Saadi, Rumi, Hafiz, or Ferdowsi. Those who are more religious wrap their words in Koranic verses and make references to the Prophet or Imams. Some have a tendency to employ Arabic or English words and expressions to impress the interlocutor. Because of their proclivity toward shrewdness, Iranians consider negotiations as a game of chess where they can exert their smart tactics. In trading and business, negotiators are involved in tough haggling and verbal competition. They may use empty threats to strengthen their positions or to slash the prices. In business negotiations, it is customary to see significant discounts on initial prices. On some occasions, informal mechanisms seem more practical and the negotiators seek backchannels to attain their goals. Some observers believe that apart from financial gain, Iranians might have a tendency toward haggling and verbal competition.[14]

An Extraordinary Sense of Humor

Iranians are famous for having a sharp and refined sense of humor. They dexterously play with words and express their humor in various forms. Farsi (Persian) is especially a flexible and powerful language to transmit humor and satire in poem and prose. The topics of humor cover a wide range of individual, social, sexual, political, ethnic, and even religious matters. A famous satirical figure in Iran is Mullah Nasreddin who is well known for his funny and witty anecdotes. Mullah Nasreddin's stories have a subtle, educational, and philosophical nature.[15] With the advent of cellular phones, a growing number of Iranians have been using text messaging to communicate implicit or explicit satirist messages. Some newspapers and weeklies have special satirist columns where they can express their ideas more freely and even criticize the well-established social or political authorities without facing criminal charges. In a highly conservative and collectivistic society such as Iran, it seems that humor plays a major role in provoking open-minded and even controversial ideas. Moreover, Iranians view humor as a relief from some of their bitter realities such as corruption, inflation, oppression, nepotism, hypocrisy, and international sanctions.

Impacts of Cultural Collectivism and Hierarchical Distance on Communication and Negotiation

In collectivistic societies, loyalty toward group and family is extremely important and for that reason, the communication should be in conformity with the group's interests and conventions. That's why in collectivistic societies the freedom of speech is often low and the communicators cannot express their intentions freely or easily. As a collectivistic society, Iranians from an early age learn to be careful about what they say and are advised to use an indirect language for expressing their intentions.[16] This is in stark contrast with the Western societies that emphasize individualism, autonomy, and consequently freedom of speech. As we mentioned previously, the communication style in Iran is marked by ambiguity and therefore, intentions and messages are not necessarily identical.[17] A very frequently cited Iranian proverb emphasizes the importance of dissimulation and teaches people to be careful about what they say: *A long tongue shortens thy life*. The traditional Iranian houses consisted of two separate and different parts—outer (*birooni*) and inner (*andarooni*). The outer part was dedicated to receptions and meetings, but the inner part was occupied by wife and children. This architecture involved a duality of reality versus appearance, or inner versus outer. It is important to emphasize that Iranians appreciate honesty very much, but like other collectivist cultures, they are not comfortable to do or say something against the widely-accepted conventions of their communities. Since identity is based in the social system, keeping face is extremely important and the outcome of negotiation may be affected by how the negotiator can save his face and honor. Therefore, Iranian negotiators may concede some privileges in order to boost their honor or prestige.

In a hierarchical culture such as Iran, a good deal of attention is attached to the communicator and very often the messenger becomes more important than the message. That is why in any negotiation, it is important to find out about the rank and power of negotiators. Furthermore, devotion to a superior goes beyond the work relationship and affects all aspects of communication and negotiation process. Likewise, age, seniority, and experience determine the way interlocutors are involved in the communication process. Due to high hierarchical distance, the decision making is mainly centralized and the negotiators especially in the government agencies do not have much power; rather they consult with *the center* before making important decisions and accepting resolutions. This centralized decision making may result in tedious and even fruitless discussions, especially when the negotiators are not sufficiently empowered. In personal or business negotiations, negotiators are usually the owners or managers who are capable of making important decisions. In official dealings, the center of political decision making is the leader or a high ranking official.

Glossary

Aab: water

Aabad: a suffix used in place names meaning a habitable community, village, or city

Ahura Mazda: a deity of goodness and light in Zoroastrianism, literally the Wise God

Andarooni: inner

Ayatollah: a title for high-ranking Shia clerics

Basij: a paramilitary volunteer militia organization under the order of the Supreme Leader

Basiji: a member of the paramilitary volunteer militia organization

Baten: the inner truth

Bonyad: a revolutionary and religious foundation engaged in economic and business activities

Birooni: outer

Chelo: saffroned Persian rice

Chelo-Kabab: saffroned Persian rice and kabab

Faghih: a Shia jurist

Hijab: a veil that covers the head and chest

Hoseiniyeh (Huseiniyeh): a Shia congregation place serving as site for religious ceremonies especially during the anniversary of Imam Hossein's martyrdom

Imam: one of the 12 Shia religious leaders

Imamzadeh: a shrine-tomb of the descendants of Imams who are related to Prophet Mohammad

Iran-shahr: the Greater Iran, the regions of western, central and southern Asia that have been under Iranian rule

Jameheh-ye Kolangi: "pick-axe society," a society marked by short-termism

Koncour: a standardized test used as one of the means to gain admission to public universities

Majles Shoora Eslami: the Iranian Parliament

Marja: a high ranking Shia cleric

Mojahedin: (People's Mojahedin of Iran): a left-leaning Islamist-Marxist group opposing the Shah and the Islamic Republic regimes

Partibazi: benefiting from the advantages to which one is not entitled by establishing privileged interpersonal relationships

Pool-Chai: literally tea expenses, small bribes

Mojtahed: a high-ranking cleric who masters the religious jurisprudence and theology
Ostan: Iranian name for province
Ostandar: governor of a province
Qanat: a series of well-like vertical shafts, connected by sloping tunnels
Raante: rent
Ravabet: relationships
Taarof: a mixture of polite and friendly expressions and gestures
Tazieh: a theatrical passion play
Vali-Faghih: the Supreme Leader
Velayat Faghih: guardianship of the jurist
Zaher: the appearance

Notes

Chapter 1

1. Bonine (2003).
2. Library of Congress—Federal Research Division Country Profile: Iran, May 2008.
3. COI Service (2013).
4. http://www.ezilon.com/maps
5. COI Service (2013).
6. United Nations' Post Report for The Islamic Republic of Iran, Second Edition, December 2004—Update June 2008. http://www.un.org.ir/
7. Library of Congress—Federal Research Division Country Profile: Iran, May 2008.
8. http://www.who.int/en/
9. Bonine (2003).
10. Mostaghim and Sandels (2014).
11. Library of Congress—Federal Research Division. Country Profile: Iran, May 2008.
12. Bureau of Operation and Maintenance of Dams and Irrigation Networks (1995).
13. Deputy Ministry for Infrastructure Affairs (1991).
14. Bonine (2003); Beazley and Harverson (1982).
15. Cia.gov (2014).
16. Abbasi-Shavazi, McDonald, and Hosseini-Chavoshi (2009).
17. Abbasi-Shavazi and McDonald (2006).
18. Abbasi-Shavazi and McDonald (2006).
19. Abbasi-Shavazi, McDonald, and Hosseini-Chavoshi (2009).
20. Crane and Lal (2008).
21. Abbasi-Shavazi, Hosseini-Chavoshi, and McDonald (2007).
22. Abbasi-Shavazi, Hosseini-Chavoshi, and McDonald (2007); Farzanegan and Fereidouni (2014).
23. Farzanegan and Fereidouni (2014); BBC (2013).
24. Crane and Lal (2008).
25. OCHA (2003).
26. U.S. Census Bureau (2007).
27. Crane and Lal (2008).

28. Fingar (2009).
29. Bonine (2003).
30. Bonine (2003).
31. Kazemi and Wolfe (1997).
32. Post Report for the Islamic Republic of Iran, Second Edition, December 2004—Update June 2008.
33. Bonine (2003).
34. Post Report for the Islamic Republic of Iran, Second Edition, December 2004—Update June 2008.
35. Post Report for the Islamic Republic of Iran, Second Edition, December 2004—Update June 2008.
36. Kian-Thiebaut (2005).
37. Bonine (2003).
38. Post Report for the Islamic Republic of Iran, Second Edition, December 2004—Update June 2008.
39. Post Report for the Islamic Republic of Iran, Second Edition, December 2004—Update June 2008.
40. Bonine (2003).
41. Bonine (2003); Madanipour (1998).
42. Bonine (2003).
43. Post Report for the Islamic Republic of Iran, Second Edition, December 2004—Update June 2008.
44. Post Report for the Islamic Republic of Iran, Second Edition, December 2004—Update June 2008.
45. Zebardast (2006).
46. Statistical Center of Iran (2013).
47. Statistical Center of Iran (2013).
48. Douglass and Hays (2008).
49. Hassan (2007).
50. Richard (1991).
51. Kian-Thiebaut (2005).
52. Keddie (2003)
53. Bar (2004a).
54. Hassan (2007).
55. Dahlman (2002).
56. Bonine (2003); Richard (1991).
57. Hassan (2007).
58. United Kingdom: Home Office (2002).
59. United Kingdom: Home Office (2002).
60. United Kingdom: Home Office (2002).
61. BBC Monitoring Middle East (2006).

62. United Kingdom: Home Office (2002).
63. Crane and Lal (2008).
64. Crane and Lal (2008).
65. Higgins (1986).
66. Hassan (2007).
67. Bonine (2003); Hourcade et al. (1998).
68. U.S. Department of State (2007).
69. "Iranian Religious Groups" (2009).
70. Hassan (2007).
71. Hassan (2007); Blanchard (2010).
72. Blanchard (2010).
73. Blanchard (2010).
74. Keddie and Hooglund (1986).

Chapter 2

1. Daniel (2001).
2. Ladjevardian (1999).
3. Ladjevardian (1999).
4. Ladjevardian (1999
5. Ladjevardian (1999).
6. Abrahamian (2008).
7. Connell and McQuaid (2008).
8. Amanat (1997).
9. Latorre (2009).
10. Connell and McQuaid (2008).
11. Ghani (2001).
12. Connell and McQuaid (2008).
13. Abrahamian (2008).
14. Ladjevardian (1999).
15. Bayat (1998).
16. Connell and McQuaid (2008).
17. Bayat (1998).
18. Bayat (1998).
19. Connell and McQuaid (2008).
20. Skocpol (1982).
21. Skocpol (1982).
22. Keddie (2003).
23. Keddie (2003).
24. Douglass and Hays (2008).
25. Bayat (1998).

26. Skocpol (1982).
27. Ilias (2010).
28. Katzman (2010).
29. Douglass and Hays (2008).
30. Katzman (2010).
31. Connell and McQuaid (2008).
32. Keddie (2003).
33. Hoveyda (2003).
34. Keddie (2003).
35. Bar (2004a).
36. Bar (2004a).

Chapter 3

1. Malik (2013).
2. "Science, Technology and Innovation Policy Review: The Islamic Republic of Iran" (2005).
3. "Science, Technology and Innovation Policy Review: The Islamic Republic of Iran" (2005).
4. Malik (2013).
5. Malik (2013).
6. Malik (2013).
7. Malik (2013).
8. Malik (2013).
9. Inglehart (1997).
10. Tashakkori and Thompson (1988).
11. Ahmad ([1962] 1982).
12. Huntington (1996).
13. Khosrokhavar (2004).
14. Khosrokhavar (2004).
15. Khosrokhavar (2004).
16. Khosrokhavar (2004); Bakhtiari (1981).
17. Bakhtiari (1981).
18. Tashakkori and Thompson (1988); Bakhtiari (1981).
19. Juneau (2009).
20. Keddie (1993).
21. Moghadam (1988).
22. Moghadam (1988).
23. Kian-Thiébaut (1998).
24. Mernissi (1987).
25. Mehran (2003).

26. Mehran (2003); Baram-Tsabari et al. (2009).
27. Inglehart (1997); Yeganeh and May (2011).
28. Bahramitash and Kazemipour (2006).
29. Welzel, Inglehart, and Kligemann (2003).
30. Harrison (2006).
31. Mehran (2003).
32. Khosrokhavar (2004).
33. Abrahamian (1982).
34. Khosrokhavar (2004).
35. Khosrokhavar (2004).
36. Khosrokhavar (2004).
37. Fathi (1991); Metz (1989).
38. Torabi and Baschieri (2010).
39. Sadeghi (2008).
40. Moghadam (2003).
41. Sadeghi (2008).
42. Price (2005).
43. Naraghi (1992); Menashri (1992).
44. "Science, Technology and Innovation Policy Review: The Islamic Republic of Iran" (2005).
45. "Science, Technology and Innovation Policy Review: The Islamic Republic of Iran" (2005).
46. Harrison (2007).
47. The Economist (2014).
48. Juneau (2009).
49. Sadeghi (2008).

Chapter 4

1. Encyclopædia Iranica (2012).
2. Encyclopædia Iranica (2012).
3. Semati (2008).
4. Chehabi (1990).
5. Algar (1981)
6. Khosrokhavar (2004).
7. Skocpol (1982); Khosrokhavar (2004).
8. Khosrokhavar (2004).
9. Keddie (1998).
10. Gürbüz (2011); Bayat (1987); Kurzman (2004).
11. Gürbüz (2011).
12. Skocpol (1982).

13. Richard (1995).
14. Gürbüz (2011); Bayat (1987); Khosrokhavar (2004)
15. Kissinger (2014).
16. Bayat (1998).
17. Gürbüz (2011).
18. Abrahamian (2008).
19. Abrahamian (2008).
20. Amjad (1989).
21. Skocpol (1982).
22. Abrahamian (2008).
23. Zabih (1982); Ale-Ahmad (1984).
24. Amjad (1989).
25. Bayat (1998).
26. Bayat (1998).
27. Amuzegar (1991); Huntington (1996).
28. Skocpol (1982).
29. Skocpol (1982).
30. Skocpol (1982).
31. Keddie (1998).
32. Arjomand (1986).
33. Skocpol (1982).
34. Salehi (1988).
35. Bayat (1998).
36. Bayat (1998).
37. Bayat (1998).
38. Skocpol (1982).
39. Hunter (1992).
40. Kazemi (1980); Hooglund (1980).
41. Hunter (1992).
42. Najmabadi (1987).
43. Hunter (1992).
44. Najmabadi (1987).
45. Keddie (1966).
46. *International Socialist Review*, The Quarterly Journal of the International Socialist Organization, No. 57–62.
47. Bashiriyeh (1982).
48. Amineh and Eisenstadt (2007).
49. Jambet (1992); Khatami (2003).
50. Stauth (1994).
51. Foucault (1994); Foucault (1988).
52. Stevens (2014).

53. Amuzegar (1991).
54. Smith (1986).

Chapter 5

1. Keddie (1998).
2. Blanchard (2005).
3. Connell and McQuaid (2008).
4. Connell and McQuaid (2008).
5. Hunter (2015).
6. Blanchard (2005).
7. Munir (2003).
8. Munir (2003).
9. Husain (1995).
10. Munir (2003).
11. Blanchard (2005).
12. Ze'evi (2007).
13. Blanchard (2005).
14. Blanchard (2005).
15. "The Sunni-Shia Divide" (2015).
16. Hunter (2015).
17. Ze'evi (2007).
18. "The Sunni-Shia Divide" (2015).
19. Hunter (2015).
20. Ze'evi (2007).
21. Ze'evi (2007).
22. Terhalle (2007).
23. Ende, Steinbach, and Laut (2005).
24. Blanchard (2005).
25. Khosrokhavar (2004).
26. Khosrokhavar (2004).
27. Moghadam (2003).
28. Moghadam (2003).
29. Blanchard (2005).
30. "What is Ashura?" (2011).
31. "The Origins of the Shiite-Sunni Split" (2007).
32. Khalaji (2008).
33. Moghadam (2003).
34. Khalaji (2008).
35. Connell and McQuaid (2008).
36. Beehner (2006).

37. Schirazi (1997); Connell and McQuaid (2008).
38. Sreberny-Mohammadi (1990).
39. Khalaji (2011); Akhavi (1980).
40. Blanchard (2005).
41. Khalaji (2011)
42. Blanchard (2005).
43. Blanchard (2005).

Chapter 6

1. Connell and McQuaid (2008).
2. Bradley (2007).
3. Roy (1999); Zubaida (1988).
4. Voll and Esposito (1994).
5. Chehabi (2001).
6. Thaler (2010).
7. Hoveyda (2003).
8. Bar (2004b).
9. Thaler (2010).
10. Benab (2008).
11. Benab (2008).
12. Alexander and Hoenig (2008).
13. Ehteshami and Zweiri (2007).
14. Ramazani (1980).
15. Jones (2009).
16. Jones (2009).
17. Thaler (2010).
18. Keddie (2006).
19. Thaler (2010).
20. Roy (1999).
21. Alamdari (2005).
22. Moslem (2002); Rakel (2008).
23. Rakel (2008).
24. Hen-Tov (2007).
25. Moslem (2002).
26. Moslem (2002).
27. De Boer (2010).
28. Seifzadeh (2003).
29. Buchta (2000).
30. Buchta (2000).
31. Hoveyda (2003).

32. Zubaida (1988).
33. Kurzman (2004).
34. Gheissari and Nasr (2006).
35. Katzman (2010).
36. Thaler (2010).
37. Jones (2009).
38. Kurzman (2004).
39. Kurzman (2004).
40. Lowe and Spencer (2006).
41. Maleki (2008).
42. Thaler (2010).

Chapter 7

1. Bonine (2003).
2. Takeyh (2009).
3. Walt (1991).
4. Walt (1991).
5. Saghafi-Ameri (2012).
6. Ehteshami (2002).
7. Katzman (2010).
8. Maleki (2002).
9. Maleki (2002).
10. Walt (1991).
11. Canadian Security Intelligence Service (2009).
12. Ahmed (2008).
13. Canadian Security Intelligence Service (2009).
14. Ahmed (2008).
15. Melman and Javedanfar (2007).
16. Katzman (2010).
17. Canadian Security Intelligence Service (2009).
18. Bonine (2003); Melman and Javedanfar (2007).
19. Latorre (2009).
20. Redaelli (2009).
21. Katzman (2010).
22. Katzman (2010).
23. Fürtig (2009).
24. Cooper and Sanger (2007).
25. Katzman (2010).
26. Sadjadpour (2011).
27. Sadjadpour (2011).

28. Katzman (2010).
29. Katzman (2010).
30. Katzman (2010).
31. Canadian Security Intelligence Service (2009).
32. http://www.al-monitor.com/pulse/business/
33. Katzman (2010).
34. Razvi (1971).
35. Razvi (1971).
36. ECO Trade and Development Bank (2013).
37. Bonine (2003); Latorre (2009).
38. Kemp (1994).
39. Katzman (2010).
40. Bonine (2003).
41. Bonine (2003).
42. Bonine (2003).
43. Hinnebusch (2009).
44. Hinnebusch (2009).
45. Habibi (2012).
46. Habibi (2012).
47. Habibi (2012).
48. Habibi (2012).
49. Habibi (2012).
50. Latorre (2009).
51. Henry (2001).
52. Sariolghalam (2003).
53. Jones (2009); Katzman (2010).
54. Bill (2006).
55. Bill (2006); Sariolghalam (2003).
56. Ahmed (2008).
57. Cooper and Sanger (2007).
58. Shoup and Minter (1977).
59. State of the Union Address (1980).
60. Ahmed (2008).
61. Sariolghalam (2003).
62. Katzman (2010).
63. Bill (2006).
64. Inglehart and Abramson (1999).
65. Shayegan (2003); Huntington (1996); Keddie (2003).
66. Shayegan (2003); Huntington (1996).
67. Iranian Studies Group at MIT (2011).
68. Kull (2007).

69. Kull (2007).
70. Kull (2007).
71. Posch (2009).
72. Posch (2009).
73. Izadi (2009).
74. "EU Imposes New Sanctions on Iran" (2012).
75. Latorre (2009).
76. Nanda (2008).
77. Berlin (2004); Fair (2007).
78. Intelligence and Terrorism Information Center (2009).
79. Intelligence and Terrorism Information Center (2009).
80. Intelligence and Terrorism Information Center (2009).
81. Bonine (2003); Tarock (1999); Latorre (2009).
82. Latorre (2009).
83. Bonine (2003).

Chapter 8

1. Jbili, Kramarenko, and Bailen (2007).
2. Nomani and Behdad (2006).
3. Ilias (2010).
4. Katzman (2003)
5. Nomani and Behdad (2006).
6. Howell (1998); Behdad (2000).
7. Ilias (2008).
8. Central Intelligence Agency, The World Factbook.
9. Economic Intelligence Unit, 2013 (derived from World Bank, World Development Indicators).
10. Central Intelligence Agency, The World Factbook.
11. IMF (2007).
12. Sachs (2005).
13. Jbili, Kramarenko, and Bailén (2007).
14. Bozorgmehr and Khalaf (2008).
15. Crane and Lal (2008).
16. Gordon et al. (2009).
17. EIU (2007).
18. *Tehran Times*, Monday, April 21, 2014.
19. UNCTAD (2005).
20. *Tehran Times*, Monday, April 21, 2014.
21. IMF (2007).
22. Central Intelligence Agency, The World Factbook.

23. EIU (2007).
24. EIA (2007).
25. Global Insight (2008).
26. Sachs and Warner (2001).
27. Mehlum, Moene, and Torvik (2006).
28. Bjorvatn and Selvik (2008).
29. Bina (1989).
30. Yates (1996); Mahdavy (1970).
31. Karl (1997).
32. Ilias (2010).
33. EIU (2007).
34. "Iran Calls for Foreign Investments in Petrochemical Projects." (2008).
35. EIU (2007).
36. Ilias (2010).
37. Ilias (2010).
38. Central Intelligence Agency, The World Factbook.
39. EIU (2007).
40. Blas (2008).
41. Ilias (2010).
42. Ilias (2010).
43. IMF (2007).
44. IMF (2007).
45. Ilias (2010)
46. Global Insight (2008).
47. Sadjadpour (2011).
48. Sadjadpour (2011).
49. Ilias (2010).
50. United Arab Emirates (2012).
51. "The Constitution of Islamic Republic of Iran." (2015).
52. Khajehpour (2000).
53. UNCTAD (2005)
54. Index of Economic Freedom, see http://www.heritage.org/index/
55. Crane and Lal (2008).
56. Alizadeh (2003).
57. Thaler (2010).
58. Ilias (2010).
59. Bahaee and Pisani (2009); Thaler (2010).
60. Ilias (2010).
61. Thaler (2010).
62. Katzman (1993).
63. Alfoneh (2007).

64. Ilias (2010).
65. Yar-Shater (1990).
66. Algar (1969).
67. Parsa (1989).
68. Crane and Lal (2008).
69. Katzman (1993).
70. Ilias (2010).
71. Ilias (2010).
72. Gordon et al. (2009).
73. ECO Trade and Development Bank (2013).
74. ECO Trade and Development Bank (2013).

Chapter 9

1. Energy Information Administration (2012).
2. Ministry of Energy of Iran, http://news.moe.gov.ir/News/International.aspx
3. National Iranian Tanker Company, http://www.nitc.co.ir/iran-daily/1387/3267/html/economy.htm
4. News.tavanir.org.ir (2012).
5. EIA (2007).
6. EIU (2007).
7. Zawya.com (2010).
8. "Invest in Iran's Renewable Energy? Not So Crazy (2012).
9. Suna.org.ir (2012).
10. Domestic Economy (2012).
11. ECO Trade and Development Bank (2013).
12. The Iranian Institute for Research and Planning in Higher Education (2012).
13. Energy Information Administration (2012).
14. Energy Information Administration (2012).
15. ECO Trade and Development Bank (2013).
16. ECO Trade and Development Bank (2013).
17. Energy Information Administration (2012).
18. Cia.gov (2012).
19. Birol (2010).
20. Iran Sees Boom in Cross-Border Fuel and Goods Smuggling (2013).
21. *Financial Times*, http://www.ft.com/intl/cms/s/0/0bf026ec-c14b-11e2-9767-00144feab7de.html?siteedition=intl#axzz3Lg9wGeit (accessed 19 October 2014).
22. Yazdan, Behzad, and Shiva (2012).
23. Energy Information Administration (2012).

24. Energy Information Administration (2012).
25. Khajehpour (2013b).
26. Ilias (2010).
27. Energy Information Administration (2012).
28. Energy Information Administration (2012).
29. Khajehpour (2013b).
30. Energy Information Administration (2012).
31. Birol (2010).
32. Windrem (2007).
33. Energy Information Administration (2012).
34. Crane and Lal (2008).
35. Motevalli (2014).
36. Energy Information Administration (2012).
37. Energy Information Administration (2012).
38. Energy Information Administration (2012).
39. Energy Information Administration (2012).
40. Energy Information Administration (2012).
41. Natural Gas Exports from Iran (2012).
42. Natural Gas Exports from Iran (2012).
43. Kinnander (2010).
44. Energy Information Administration (2012).
45. Natural Gas Exports from Iran (2012).
46. Energy Information Administration (2012).
47. ECO Trade and Development Bank (2013).
48. ECO Trade and Development Bank (2013).
49. ECO Trade and Development Bank (2013).
50. "Iran Gas Pipeline: Saudi Offer" (2010).
51. Hussain (2013).
52. "Turkey Seeks to Build Iran Pipeline Amid Uncertain Environment" (2014).
53. Birol (2010).
54. Birol (2010).
55. Recknagel (2014).
56. Recknagel (2014).

Chapter 10

1. UNCTAD (2005).
2. Clawson (2013).
3. ECO Trade and Development Bank (2013).
4. Clawson (2013).
5. The Trade Promotion Organization of Iran (2014).

6. ECO Trade and Development Bank (2013).
7. ECO Trade and Development Bank (2013).
8. Rezaian (2013).
9. ECO Trade and Development Bank (2013).
10. "SAPCO: Iran Automotive Industry's Market Shares" (2001).
11. Iran Autos Report Q4 (2008).
12. Iran Autos Report Q1 (2013).
13. Abedini and Péridy (2009).
14. ECO Trade and Development Bank (2013).
15. U.S. Geological Survey, Mineral Commodity Summaries (2014).
16. Iran Exports Cement to 40 Countries (2010).
17. ECO Trade and Development Bank (2013).
18. "Business in Iran: Awaiting the Gold Rush" (2014).
19. Domestic Economy (2011); http://www.tehrantimes.com/economy-and-business/97519-technical-engineering-exports-surpass-20-billion-over-a-decade
20. http://www.tehrantimes.com/economy-and-business/97519-technical-engineering-exports-surpass-20-billion-over-a-decade
21. "Iran Ranks First in Mideast in Steel Production" (2014).
22. ECO Trade and Development Bank (2013).
23. Trend News Agency (2014).
24. ECO Trade and Development Bank (2013).
25. ECO Trade and Development Bank (2013).
26. ECO Trade and Development Bank (2013).
27. Trend News Agency (2014).
28. ECO Trade and Development Bank (2013).
29. *Financial Times*, http://www.ft.com/intl/cms/s/0/0bf026ec-c14b-11e2-9767-00144feab7de.html?siteedition=intl#axzz3Lg9wGeit (accessed 19 October 2014).
30. "Telecoms and Technology Forecast for Iran" (2008.)
31. "Iran Exports 400 Million Dollars of Software Products" (2014).
32. "Telecoms and Technology Forecast for Iran" (2008).
33. Zawya Business Iintelligence Report (2012).
34. ECO Trade and Development Bank (2013).
35. Cia.gov (2012).
36. ECO Trade and Development Bank (2013).
37. ECO Trade and Development Bank (2013).
38. ECO Trade and Development Bank (2013).
39. ECO Trade and Development Bank (2013).
40. Koshteh and Urutyan (2005).
41. ECO Trade and Development Bank (2013).

42. ECO Trade and Development Bank (2013).
43. ECO Trade and Development Bank (2013).
44. "Country profile – Iran" (2008).
45. ECO Trade and Development Bank (2013).
46. ECO Trade and Development Bank (2013).
47. "Country profile – Iran" (2008).
48. USGS (2003).
49. Mining & Development (2010).
50. ECO Trade and Development Bank (2013).
51. "Iran's Mineral Exports up 39 Percent" (2011).
52. ECO Trade and Development Bank (2013).
53. Domestic Economy (2008).
54. ECO Trade and Development Bank (2013).
55. ECO Trade and Development Bank (2013).
56. ECO Trade and Development Bank (2013).
57. "Iran Travel and Tourism Forecast" (2008).
58. ECO Trade and Development Bank (2013).
59. Presstv.com (2010).
60. http://www.bank-maskan.ir
61. Domestic Economy (2006).
62. Valentine, Nash, and Rice (2013).
63. ECO Trade and Development Bank (2013).
64. UNCTAD (2005).
65. ECO Trade and Development Bank (2013).
66. ECO Trade and Development Bank (2013).
67. UNCTAD (2005).
68. UNCTAD (2005).
69. UNCTAD (2005).

Chapter 11

1. IMF (2008b).
2. Ilias (2010).
3. Shoamanesh (2009).
4. Khajehpour (2013a).
5. Shoamanesh (2009).
6. Barden (2013).
7. Clark (2014).
8. "France Sees Iran Opportunity If Sanctions Are Lifted—oscovici" (2014).
9. The World Bank (2011).

10. The World Bank (2011).
11. Khajehpour (2013a).
12. Hanouz, Geiger, and Doherty (2014).
13. The Heritage Foundation Trade Freedom Report (2013).
14. Heritage Foundation (2014).
15. Alipour (2013).
16. Garro´n, Machicado, and Capra (2003); Alipour (2013).
17. Alipour (2013).
18. Imanirad (2003).
19. *PressTV* (2011).
20. "Bank Melli Iran, the Largest Islamic Bank" (2009).
21. Curtis and Hooglund (2008).
22. Turquoise Partners Report (2011).
23. Jahan-Parvar, Mohammadi, and Moshrefi (2011).
24. "Business in Iran: Awaiting the Gold Rush" (2014).
25. "Business in Iran: Awaiting the Gold Rush" (2014).
26. "What Is Behind Success of Tehran Stock Exchange?" (2013).
27. "What Is Behind Success of Tehran Stock Exchange?" (2013).
28. "In Iran, Stocks Are a Haven as Economy Hits the Skids" (2012).
29. Domestic Economy (2007).
30. Domestic Economy (2008).
31. Transparency International (2010).
32. Gwartney, Lawson, and Norton (2008).
33. IMF (2007).
34. IMF (2007).
35. Euromonitor International (2009).
36. Euromonitor International (2009).
37. Euromonitor International (2009).
38. Yeganeh and Su (2007).
39. Yeganeh and Su (2008).
40. Euromonitor International (2009).
41. Mehran (2003); Yeganeh and Su (2008).
42. Ghorbani and Tung (2007).
43. World Bank Group (2012).
44. Human Development Reports (2005).
45. Yeganeh and Su (2008).
46. Euromonitor International (2009).
47. Yeganeh and Su (2008).
48. Euromonitor International (2009).
49. Yeganeh and Su (2008).

50. Euromonitor International (2009).
51. Yeganeh and Su (2008).
52. Yeganeh and Su (2008).
53. Yeganeh and Su (2008).
54. Yeganeh and Su (2008).
55. Yeganeh and Su (2008); Dastmalchian, Javidan, and Alam (2001); House et al. (2004).
56. Yeganeh and Su (2008).
57. Yeganeh and Su (2008).
58. Dastmalchian, Javidan, and Alam (2001).
59. Yeganeh and Su (2008).

Chapter 12

1. Richards (1996).
2. Vazifedoost et al. (2013).
3. Han, Nunes, and Drèze (2010).
4. Yeganeh, Marcotte, and Bourdeau (2010); Kang and Park-Poaps (2010).
5. Behravan, Jamalzadeh, and Masoudi (2012).
6. IMF (2008a).
7. Statistical Center of Iran (2013).
8. Statistical Center of Iran (2013).
9. Euromonitor International (2009).
10. Euromonitor International (2009).
11. Euromonitor International (2009).
12. Barraclough (2001).
13. Richards (1996).
14. Euromonitor International (2009).
15. Euromonitor International (2009).
16. Atefi, Minooei, and Dargahi (2010).
17. Gholipour and Farzanegan (2015).
18. Zebardast (2006).
19. Thompson Reuters (2013).
20. Heslot (2014).
21. UNCTAD (2005).
22. Behravan, Jamalzadeh, and Masoudi (2012).
23. Thompson Reuters (2013).
24. Desebrock (2005).
25. "Iran's Healthcare Market on the Rise - Frost & Sullivan" (2013).
26. Euromonitor International (2009).
27. "Iran's Healthcare Market on the Rise - Frost & Sullivan" (2013).

28. "Iranian Ecommerce Thrives Despite Obstacles" (2014).
29. MVF Global Customer Acquisition (2014).
30. "Iranian Ecommerce Thrives Despite Obstacles" (2014).
31. MVF Global Customer Acquisition (2014).

Chapter 13

1. Lewis (2014).
2. Takeyh (2006).
3. Inglehart (2000).
4. Kasravi (1963).
5. Kasravi (1963).
6. Takeyh (2006).
7. Bar (2004b).
8. Bar (2004b).
9. Inglehart and Welzel (2005); Inglehart (1997).
10. Price (2005).
11. Torabi and Baschieri (2010).
12. Mernissi (1987).
13. Hofstede (2001); Toennies ([1887] 1963).
14. Triandis (1989).
15. Inglehart and Welzel (2005).
16. Chapin Metz (1989).
17. Chapin Metz (1989).
18. Chapin Metz (1989).
19. Daniel (2001).
20. Daniel (2001); Hofstede (2001); Yeganeh and Su (2007).
21. Abrahamian (1982).
22. Metz (1989).
23. Hoveyda (2003).
24. Pahlavi (1978).
25. Daniel (2001).
26. Hoveyda (2003).
27. Richard (1991).
28. Katouzian (2004).
29. Katouzian (2004).
30. Inglehart et al. (2004).
31. Inglehart (1997); Inglehart et al. (2004).
32. Inglehart (1997).
33. Fallaci (1976).
34. "Business in Iran: Awaiting the Gold Rush" (2014).

35. Stevens (2014).
36. Stevens (2014).
37. Inglehart (1997).
38. Stanley (2006).
39. Bar (2004b).
40. Bar (2004a).
41. Richard (1991).
42. Pattberg (2009).
43. BBC (2014).
44. Kasravi (1963).
45. Baldick (1990).
46. Bar (2004a).

Chapter 14

1. Carnevale and Pruitt (1992).
2. Hall (1960).
3. Hall (1960).
4. Hall (1976).
5. Hall (1960, 1976).
6. Abrahamian (1982).
7. Bar (2004a).
8. Beeman (1986).
9. Bar (2004a).
10. Hall (1976).
11. Hall (1976).
12. Hall (1960).
13. Bar (2004a).
14. Bar (2004a).
15. Javadi (2007).
16. Dastmalchian, Javidan, and Alam (2001).
17. Beeman (1986).

References

Abbasi-Shavazi, M.J., M. Hosseini-Chavoshi, and P. McDonald. 2007. "The Path to Below Replacement Fertility in the Islamic Republic of Iran." *Asia-Pacific Population Journal* 22, no. 2, pp. 91–112.

Abbasi-Shavazi, M.J., and P. McDonald. 2006. "Fertility Decline in the Islamic Republic of Iran: 1972–2000." *Asian Population Studies* 2, no. 3, pp. 217–37.

Abbasi-Shavazi, M.J., P. McDonald, and M. Hosseini-Chavoshi. 2009. *The Fertility Transition in Iran: Revolution and Reproduction*, 100–101. New York: Springer.

Abedini, J., and N. Péridy. 2009. "The Emergence of Iran in the World Car Industry: An Estimation of Its Export Potential." *The World Economy* 32, no. 5, pp. 790–818.

Abrahamian, E. 1982. *Iran Between Two Revolutions*. NJ: Princeton University Press.

Abrahamian, E. 2008. *A History of Modern Iran*, 67. New York: Cambridge University Press.

Ahmad, J.A.E. (1962) 1982. *Gharbzadegi* (*Weststruckness*). Translated by John Green and Ahmad Alizadeh. Lexington, KY: Mazda Publishers.

Ahmed, N.M. July 2008. "The Iran Threat: Why War Won't Work." *Paper prepared for the Nobel Peace Prize Laureates Conference*, Stavanger—European Capital of Culture, September 10–12.

Akhavi, S. 1980. *Religion and Politics in Contemporary Iran*. New York: SUNY Press.

Alamdari, K. 2005. "The Power Structure of the Islamic Republic of Iran: Transition from Populism to Clientelism, and Militarization of the Government." *Third World Quarterly* 26, no. 8, pp. 1285–301.

Ale-Ahmad, J. 1984. *Occidentosis: A Plague from the West*, 126. Berkeley, CA: Mizan Press.

Alexander, Y., and M.M. Hoenig. 2008. *The New Iranian Leadership: Ahmadinejad, Nuclear Ambition, and the Middle East*, 14–15. Westport, CT: Greenwood Publishing Group.

Alfoneh, A. October 22, 2007. "How Intertwined Are the Revolutionary Guards in Iran's Economy?" *American Enterprise Institute*.

Algar, H. 1969. *Religion and State in Iran, 1785-1906; The Role of the Ulama in the Qajar Period*. Berkeley, CA: University of California Press.

Algar, H. 1981. *Islam and Revolution: Writings and Declarations of Imam Khomeini*. Berkeley, CA: Mizan Press.

Alipour, M. 2013. "Has Privatization of State-Owned Enterprises in Iran Led to Improved Performance?" *International Journal of Commerce and Management* 23, no. 4, pp. 281–305.

Alizadeh, P. 2003. "Iran's Quandary: Economic Reforms and the Structural Trap." *The Brown Journal of World Affairs* 9, no. 2, p. 272.

Amanat, A. 1997. *Pivot of the Universe Nasir Al-Din Shah Qajar and the Iranian Monarchy, 1831-1896*. Berkeley, CA: University of California Press.

Amineh, M.P., and S.N. Eisenstadt. 2007 "The Iranian Revolution: The Multiple Contexts of the Iranian Revolution." *Perspectives on Global Development and Technology* 6, pp. 129–57.

Amjad, M. 1989. *Iran from Royal Dictatorship to Theocracy*. New York/London: Greenwood Press.

Amuzegar, J. 1991. *The Dynamics of the Iranian Revolution: The Pahlavis' Triumph and Tragedy*. New York: The State University of New York Press.

Arjomand, S.A. 1986. "Iran's Islamic Revolution in Comparative Perspective." *World Politics* 38, no. 3, pp. 383–414.

Atefi, Y., F. Minooei, and R. Dargahi. 2010. "Housing Affordability: A Study of Real Estate Market in Iran." *In Proceedings of the 28th International Conference of System Dynamics Society*.

Bahaee, M., and M.J. Pisani. 2009. "Iranian Consumer Animosity and US Products: A Witch's Brew or Elixir?" *International Business Review* 18, no. 2, pp. 199–210.

Bahramitash, R., and S. Kazemipour. 2006. "Myths and Realities of the Impact of Islam on Women: Changing Marital Status in Iran." *Critique: Critical Middle Eastern Studies* 15, no. 2, pp. 111–28.

Bakhtiari, B. 1981. *A Comparison of the Ideologies of Ali Shariati and the People's Mojahedin in Iran* [Thesis]. MA: University of Virginia.

Baldick, J. 1990. *The Iranian Origin of the Futuwwa,* Vol. 50, pp. 345–61. Istituto Universitario Orientale di Napoli.

"Bank Melli Iran, the Largest Islamic Bank." 2009. *PressTV*, August 28. http://edition.presstv.ir/detail/104662.html (accessed October 10, 2012).

Bar, S. 2004a. "Iran: Cultural Values, SelfImages and Negotiation Behavior." *Institute for Policy and Strategy, The Lauder School of Government, Diplomacy and Strategy IDC Herzliya,* Israel.

Bar, S. 2004b. "Iranian Defense Doctrine and Decision Making." *Institute for Policy and Strategy, The Lauder School of Government, Diplomacy and Strategy IDC Herzliya,* Israel.

Baram-Tsabari, A., R.J. Sethi, L. Bry, and A. Yarden. 2009. "Asking Scientists: a Decade of Questions Analyzed by Age, Gender, and Country." *Science Education* 93, no. 1, pp. 131–160.

Barden, S. June 20, 2013. "Iran's New Government and Australia's Opportunity." http://www.businessspectator.com.au/article/2013/6/20/global-news/irans-new-government-and-australias-opportunity

Barraclough, S. 2001. "Satellite Television in Iran: Prohibition, Imitation and Reform." *Middle Eastern Studies* 37, no. 3, pp. 25–48.

Bashiriyeh, H. 1982. *The State and Revolution in Iran 1962–1982.* New York: St. Martin's Press.

Bayat, A. 1987. *Workers and Revolution in Iran: A Third World Experience of Workers' Control.* New York/London: Zed Books.

Bayat, A. 1998. "Revolution Without Movement, Movement Without Revolution: Comparing Islamic Activism in Iran and Egypt." *Comparative Studies in Society and History* 40, no.1, pp. 136–69.

BBC. 2014. "Iran: Top Cleric Leads Prayers for Rain." http://www.bbc.com/news/blogs-news-from-elsewhere-29503624 (accessed July 10, 2014).

BBC. 2013. "11 Percent of Men Marry Women Older Than Themselves." BBC Persian. http://www.bbc.co.uk/persian/iran/2013/04/130408_l57_ir_marriage.shtml

Beazley, E., and M. Harverson. 1982. *Living with the Desert: Working Buildings of the Iranian Plateau.* Warminster, UK: Aris and Phillips.

Beehner, L. June 16, 2006. "Shia Muslims in the Mideast." Council on Foreign Relations. http://www.cfr.org/religion/shia-muslims-mideast/p10903 (accessed February 28, 2015).

Beeman, W.O. 1986. *Language, Status and Power in Iran.* Bloomington, IN: University Press.

Behdad, S. 2000. "From Populism to Economic Liberalism: The Iranian Predicament." *In The Economy of Iran: Dilemmas of an Islamic State,* 100–41. London, UK: I.B.Tauris & Co Ltd.

Behravan, N., M. Jamalzadeh, and R. Masoudi. 2012. "A Review Study of Developing an Advertising Strategy for Westerner's Companies among Middle East Countries: the Islamic Perspective." *Information Management & Business Review* 4, no. 3, pp. 107–13.

Benab, Y.P. June 11, 2008. "The Origin and Development of Imperialist Contention in Iran; 1884-1921." Iran Chamber Society.

Berlin, D.L. 2004. "India-Iran Relations: A Deepening Entente." Asia-Pacific Center for Security Studies Special Assessment. http://www.apcss.org/wp-content/uploads/2010/PDFs/SAS/AsiaBilateralRelations/India-IranRelationsBerlin.pdf

Bill, J.A. 2006. "The Cultural Underpinnings of Politics: Iran and the United States." *Mediterranean Quarterly* 17, no. 1, pp. 23–33.

Bina, C. 1989. "Some Controversies in the Development of Rent Theory: The Nature of Oil Rent." *Capital and Class* 39, pp. 82–112.

Birol, F. 2010. World Energy Outlook 2010. International Energy Agency. http://www.worldenergyoutlook.org/media/weo2010.pdf

Bjorvatn, K., and K. Selvik. 2008. "Destructive Competition: Factionalism and Rent-Seeking in Iran." *World Development* 36, no. 11, pp. 2314–324.

Blanchard, C.M. February 2005. Islam: Sunnis and Shiites. Congressional Research Service (CSR) Report for Congress.

Blanchard, C.M. November 9, 2010. *Islam: Sunnis and Shiites.* Washington, DC: Congressional Research Service.

Blas, J. 2008. "Mideast Reels as Hunger Outgrows Oil Earnings." *Financial Times*, May 7.

Bonine, M. 2003. "Iran: The pivotal state of Southwest Asia." *Eurasian Geography and Economics* 44, no. 1, pp. 1–39.

Bozorgmehr, N., and R. Khalaf. 2008. "World News—Iran: Bank Chief Takes a Realistic Tack." *Financial Times*, March 6.

Bradley, M. 2007. Political Islam, Political Institutions and Civil Society in Iran: A Literature Review. International Development Research Centre (IDRC), Ottowa.

Buchta, W. 2000. *Who Rules Iran?* 14. Washington, DC: Washington Institute for Near East Policy.

Bureau of Operation and Maintenance of Dams and Irrigation Networks. 1995. *Water Utilization in the Year 1993.* Deputy Ministry of Water Affairs, Ministry of Agriculture.

"Business in Iran: Awaiting the Gold Rush." 2014. *The Economist*, November 1.

Canadian Security Intelligence Service. 2009. Insights into the Future of Iran as a Regional Power. A Conference of the Canadian Security Intelligence Service Jointly Sponsored by Foreign Affairs and International Trade Canada, National Defence Canada and the Privy Council Office.

Carnevale, P. and D. Pruitt. 1992. "Negotiation and Mediation." *Annual Review of Psychology* 43, no. 1, pp. 531–82.

Chehabi, H.E. 1990. *Iranian Politics and Religious Modernism: The Liberation Movement of Iran Under the Shah and Khomeini.* London, UK: I.B.Tauris & Co Ltd.

Chehabi, H.E. January 2001. "The Political Regime of the Islamic Republic of Iran in Comparative Perspective." *Government and Opposition* 36, no. 1, pp. 48–70.

Cia.gov. 2012. The World Factbook. https://www.cia.gov/library/publications/the-world-factbook/docs/whatsnew.html (accessed on February 5, 2012).

Cia.gov. 2014. The World Factbook: Iran. https://www.cia.gov/library/publications/the-world-factbook/geos/ir.html

Clark, M. 2014. "Western Companies Eyeing Opportunities in Iran Should Sanctions Ease." *International Business Times,* July 02. http://www.ibtimes.

com/western-companies-eyeing-opportunities-iran-should-sanctions-ease-1617578

Clawson, P. April 3, 2013. *Iran Beyond Oil?* The Washington Institute. http://www.washingtoninstitute.org/policy-analysis/view/iran-beyond-oil

COI Service. September 26, 2013. Iran—Country of Origin Information (COI) Report, United Kingdom Border Agency.

Connell, M.E., and J.V. McQuaid. 2008. The Persian Complex: A Centuries-Old Quest for Respect: Political Cultural and Religious Antecedents of the Iranian Worldview, No. MISC D0019397. A1. Center for Naval Analyses Alexandria, VA.

Cooper, H., and D. Sanger. 2007. "Strategy on Iran Stirs New Debate at White House." *New York Times*, June 16.

"Country Profile – Iran." 2008. http://www.new-ag.info/en/country/profile.php?a=430

Crane, K., and R. Lal. 2008. *Iran's Political, Demographic, and Economic Vulnerabilities*. Santa Monica, CA: Rand Corporation.

Curtis, G.E., and E. Hooglund, eds. 2008. *Iran a Country Study*. http://lcweb2.loc.gov/frd/cs/pdf/CS_Iran.pdf

Dahlman, C. June 2002 "The Political Geography of Kurdistan." *Eurasian Geography and Economics* 43, no. 4, pp. 271–99.

Daniel, E. 2001. *The History of Iran*. Westport, CT: Greenwood Press.

Dastmalchian, A., M. Javidan, and K. Alam. 2001. "Effective Leadership and Culture in Iran: An Empirical Study." *Applied Psychology* 50, no. 4, pp. 532–58.

De Boer, L.R. 2010. *Analyzing Iran's Foreign Policy: The Prospects and Challenges of Sino-Iranian Relations*. London, UK: Lap Lambert Academic Publishing.

Deputy Ministry for Infrastructure Affairs. 1991. *Summary of the Social and Agricultural Economy of Iran*. Ministry of Agriculture.

Desebrock, N. 2005. "Iran—A Major Gold Market in Hiding." *The London Bullion Market Association*. http://www.lbma.org.uk/assets/alch42_iran.pdf (accessed May 2015)

Domestic Economy. December 2006. *Iran Daily*.

Domestic Economy. February 14, 2007. *Iran Daily*.

Domestic Economy. December 10, 2008. *Iran Daily*.

Domestic Economy. April 2011. *Iran Daily*.

Domestic Economy. February 2012. *Iran Daily*.

Douglass, C.A., and M.D. Hays. 2008. A US strategy for Iran (Walker paper no. 11). Maxwell Air Force Base, Alabama: Air University Press.

ECO Trade and Development Bank. 2013. Iran, Country Partnership Strategy – 2013-14. http://www.etdb.org/public_ftp/CPSReports/Country%20Partnership%20Strategy%20Report%20for%20I.R.%20of%20Iran%20-%202013-14.pdf

Ehteshami, A. 2002. "The Foreign Policy of Iran." In *The Foreign Policies of Middle East states*, eds. R. Hinnebusch and A. Ehteshami, 288. Boulder, CO: Lynne Rienner Publishers.

Ehteshami, A., and M. Zweiri. 2007. *Iran and the Rise of Its Neoconservatives: The Politics of Tehran's Silent Revolution*, xviii. New York: I.B. Tauris.

EIA (U.S. Energy Information Administration). January 9, 2007. "World Proved Reserves of Oil and Natural Gas, Most Recent Estimates."

EIU. 2007. Iran: Country Profile. http://www.eiu.com/home.aspx

Encyclopædia Iranica. 2004. "Industrialization ii. The Mohammad Reza Shah Period, 1953-79." Vol. XIII, Fasc. 1, 110–12 and Vol. XIII, Fasc. 2, pp. 113–19.

Ende, W., U. Steinbach, and R. Laut. 2005. *Der Islam in der Gegenwart.* Germany: C.H. Beck.

Energy Information Administration. 2012. "Country Analysis Briefs: Iran." http://www.eia.gov/

Euromonitor International. December 2009. "Consumer Lifestyles in Iran." http://www.researchandmarkets.com/reports/1203193/consumer_lifestyles_iran

"EU Imposes New Sanctions on Iran." October 15, 2012. BBC. http://www.bbc.com/news/world-middle-east-19947507 (accessed September 20, 2013).

Fair, C.C. 2007. "India and Iran: New Delhi's Balancing Act." *Washington Quarterly* 30, no. 3, pp. 145–59.

Fallaci, O. 1976. *Interview with History.* New York: Liveright.

Fathi, A., ed. 1991. *Iranian Refugees and Exiles Since Khomeini.* Costa Mesa, CA: Mazda Publishers.

Fingar, C.T., ed. 2009. *Global Trends 2025: A Transformed World.* DIANE Publishing.

Foucault, M. 1988. "The Spirit of the World Without Spirit." In *Politics, Philosophy, Culture*, ed. L.D. Kritzman, 218. London, UK: Routledge.

Foucault, M. 1994. "A quoi revent les Iraniens." *Le Nouvel Observateur* 727, pp. 48–49.

"France Sees Iran Opportunity If Sanctions Are Lifted—Moscovici." 2014. Reuters. http://www.reuters.com/article/2014/02/02/us-france-iran-sanctions-idUSBREA110KR20140202

Fürtig, H. 2009. "Iran and Saudi Arabia: Eternal "Gamecocks"?" The Middle East Institute. http://www.mei.edu/content/iran-and-saudi-arabia-eternal-gamecocks

Garro´n, B.S., C.G. Machicado, and K. Capra. 2003. *Privatization in Bolivia: The Impact on Firm Performance.* Washington, DC: The Latin-American and Caribbean Research Network Project, Inter-American Development Bank.

Ghani, C. 2001. *Iran and the Rise of Reza Shah: From Qajar Collapse to Pahlavi Rule.* London, UK: I.B. Tauris Publishers.

Gheissari, A., and S.V.R. Nasr. 2006. *Democracy in Iran: History and the Quest for Liberty.* New York: Oxford University Press.

Gholipour, H.F., and M.R. Farzanegan. 2015. "Marriage Crisis and Housing Costs:Empirical Evidence from Provinces of Iran." *Journal of Policy Modeling* 37, no. 1, pp. 107–23.

Ghorbani, M., and R.L. Tung. 2007. "Behind the Veil: An Exploratory Study of the Myths and Realities of Women in the Iranian Workforce." *Human Resource Management Journal* 17, no. 4, pp. 376–92.

Global Insight. April 1, 2008. "Iran: Global Risk Service."

Gordon, J., R. Button, K.J. Cunningham, T.I. Reid, I. Blickstein, P. Wilson, and A. Goldthau. 2009. *Domestic Trends in the United States, China, and Iran.* RAND Monograph.

Gürbüz, M.V. 2011. "The Iranian Revolution." *Kahramanmaraş Sütçü İmam Üniversitesi.*

Gwartney, J., R. Lawson, and S. Norton. 2008. Economic Freedom of the World 2008 Annual Report. The Fraser Institute.

Habibi, N. 2012. "Turkey and Iran: Growing Economic Relations Despite Western Sanctions." Middle East Brief, No. 62, Crown Centers for Middle East Studies, Brandies University. http://www.brandeis.edu/crown/publications/meb/MEB62.pdf

Hall, E.T. May–June 1960. "The Silent Language of Overseas Business." *Harvard Business Review*, pp. 87–95.

Hall, E.T. 1976. *Beyond Culture.* New York: Anchor Press.

Han, Y.J., J.C. Nunes, and X. Drèze. 2010. "Signaling Status with Luxury Goods: The Role of Brand Prominence." *Journal of Marketing* 74, no. 4, pp. 15–30.

Hanouz, M.D., T. Geiger, and S. Doherty. 2014. The Global Enabling Trade Report 2014. World Economic Forum (WEF) Geneva.

Harrison, F. 2006. "Women Graduates Challenge Iran." *BBC News*, September 19. http://news.bbc.co.uk/2/hi/middle_east/5359672.stm

Harrison, F. 2007. "Huge Cost of Iranian Brain Drain." *BBC News*, January 8. http://news.bbc.co.uk/2/hi/middle_east/6240287.stm

Hassan, H.D. May 2007. *Iran: Ethnic and Religious Minorities.* Washington, DC: Library of Congress, Congressional Research Service.

Henry, K. 2001. *Does America Need a Foreign Policy?* 196. New York: Simon and Schuster.

Hen-Tov, E. Winter 2007. "Understanding Iran's New Authoritarianism." *The Washington Quarterly* 30, no. 1, pp. 163–79.

Heritage Foundation. 2014. 2015 Index of Economic Freedom: Iran. http://www.heritage.org/index/

Heslot, S. 2014. "Global Food and Water Crises Research Programme." Future Directions International: Iran's Food Security. http://www.futuredirections.org.au/publications/food-and- water-crises/1858-iran-s-food-security.html

Higgins, P.J. 1986 "Minority-State Relations in Contemporary Iran." In *The State, Religion, and Ethnic Politics: Afghanistan, Iran, and Pakistan*, eds. A. Banuazizi and M. Weiner, 167–97. New York: Syracuse University Press.

Hinnebusch, R. 2009. "The Syrian-Iranian Alliance." The Middle East Institute. www.mideasti.org

Hofstede, G. 2001. *Culture's Consequences: Comparing Values, Behaviors, Institutions, and Organizations across Nations*. 2nd ed. Thousand Oaks, CA: Sage.

Hooglund, E. 1980. *Land and Revolution in Iran*. Austin, TX: Texas University Press.

Hourcade, B., H. Mazurek, M. Taleghani, and M.-H. Papoli-Yazdi. 1998. Atlas d'Iran. Montpellier-Paris, France: RECLUS et La Documentation Française.

House, R.J., P.J Hanges, M. Javidan, P.W. Dorfman, and V. Gupta, eds. 2004. *Culture, Leadership, and Organizations: The GLOBE Study of 62 Societies*. Thousand Oaks, CA: Sage publications.

Hoveyda, F. 2003. *The Shah and the Ayatollah: Iranian Mythology and Islamic Revolution*. Westport, CT: Praeger.

Howell, L.D. 1998. *The Handbook of Country and Political Risk Analysis*. New York: The PRS Group.

Human Development Reports. 2005. http://hdr.undp.org/en/reports/global/hdr2005

Hunter, S.T. 1992. *Iran After Khomeini*. New York: Praeger Publishers.

Hunter, S.T. 2015. "Is Iran the Leader of a Shia International?" LobeLog. http://www.lobelog.com/is-iran-the-leader-of-a-shia-international/ (accessed February 4, 2015).

Huntington, S.P. 1996. *The Clash of Civilizations and the Remaking of World Order*. New York: Simon & Schuster.

Husain, M.Z. 1995. *Global Islamic Politic*, 95. New York: HarperCollins College Publishers.

Hussain, I. 2013. "US Warns Pakistan of Sanctions Over Iran Gas Pipeline Deal." *The News International*, January 29.

"Iran Exports 400 Million Dollars of Software Products." 2014. *Press TV*. http://presstv.com/detail/2014/02/27/352546/iran-software-industry-communication-information-technology-it/

"Invest in Iran's Renewable Energy? Not So Crazy." September 12, 2012. The Christian Science Monitor. http://www.csmonitor.com/Environment/Energy-Voices/2012/0910/Invest-in-Iran-s-renewable-energy-Not-so-crazy

"Iran Ranks First in Mideast in Steel Production." January 26, 2014. *Press TV*, http://www.presstv.com/detail/2014/01/26/347828/iran-ranks-first-steel-producer-in-mideast/

Ilias, S. August 2008. *Iran's Economy*. Washington, DC: Congressional Research Service (Library of Congress).

Ilias, S. 2010. *Iran's Economic Conditions: US Policy Issues*. Darby, PA: Diane Publishing.

Imanirad, M. 2003. *The Role of Small and Medium Industries in Iran's Exports*. Ministry of Industry, Department of SMI, p. 272.

IMF (International Monetary Fund). March 2007. Islamic Republic of Iran: 2006 Article IV Consultation. IMF Country Report No.07/100, p. 6, 7.

IMF. August 2008a. Islamic Republic of Iran: 2006 Article IV Consultation. IMF Country Report No. 08/284.

IMF. June 2008b. Staff Report for the 2008 Article IV Consultation. Executive Summary

"In Iran, Stocks Are a Haven as Economy Hits the Skids." 2012. *The Wall Street Journal*, October 30.

Inglehart, R. 1997. *Modernization and Postmodernization: Cultural, Economic, and Political Change in 43 Societies*, Vol. 19. Princeton, NJ: Princeton University Press.

Inglehart, R. 2000. "Codebook for World Values Survey." *Ann Arbor: Institute for Social Research*.

Inglehart, R., and P.R. Abramson. 1999. "Measuring Postmaterialism." *American Political Science Review* 93, no. 3, pp. 665–77.

Inglehart, R., M. Basañez, J. Diez–Medrano, L. Halman, and R. Luijkx. 2004. Human Beliefs and Values: A Cross–Cultural Sourcebook Based on the 1999–2002 Values Surveys. Mexico City: Siglo XXI Editores.

Inglehart, R. and C. Welzel. 2005. *Modernization, Cultural Change, and Democracy: The Human Development Sequence*. Cambridge, MA: Cambridge University Press.

Intelligence and Terrorism Information Center. July 29, 2009. Iran's Activity in East Africa, the Gateway to the Middle East and the African Continent. http://www.terrorism-info.org.il/data/pdf/PDF_09_197_2.pdf

Iran Autos Report Q4. 2008. Market Report, Industry Analysis and Market Trends–02 October 2008. Companiesandmarkets.com (accessed November 28, 2010).

Iran Autos Report Q1. 2013. Business Monitor International. http://iaiic.com/my_doc/irankhodro/BMIQ1.pdf

"Iranian Ecommerce Thrives Despite Obstacles." 2014. *Financial Times*, October 1. http://www.ft.com/cms/s/0/e44136e6-3cdb-11e4-9733-00144feabdc0.html

"Iran Exports Cement to 40 Countries" 2010. *Tehran Times*. http://www.tehrantimes.com/index_View.asp?code=213927 (accessed 18 October 2011).

"Iran Gas Pipeline: Saudi Offer." 2010. Dawn News, April 15. http://www.dawn.com/news/710605/iran-gas-pipeline-saudi-offer

"Iran's Healthcare Market on the Rise - Frost & Sullivan." July 23, 2013. Drugs.com. http://www.drugs.com/news/iran-s-healthcare-market-rise-frost-sullivan-46506.html

"Iran's Mineral Exports up 39 Percent". 2011. *PressTV*, January 17. http://edition.presstv.ir/detail.fa/160504.html (accessed October 18, 2011).

"Iranian Religious Groups." 2009. Global Security.Org. http://www.globalsecurity.org/military/world/iran/religion.htm

"Iran Sees Boom in Cross-Border Fuel and Goods Smuggling." 2013. *The Financial Times*, May 8. http://www.ft.com/intl/cms/s/0/235e02e4-b7dd-11e2-9f1a-00144feabdc0.html#axzz3dUDLztlQ

Iranian Studies Group at MIT. 2011. http://isgmit.org (accessed June 11).

"Iran Travel and Tourism Forecast." August 18, 2008. Economist Intelligence Unit.

Izadi, P. 2009. "Iran and France: Shattered Dreams." The Middle East Institute. http://www.mei.edu/content/iran-and-france-shattered-dreams

Jahan-Parvar, M.R., H. Mohammadi, and G. Moshrefi. 2011. Efficiency, Risk, and Events in the Tehran Stock Exchange. http://iraneconomy.csames.illinois.edu/full%20papers/Jahan-Parvar%20-%20Efficiency,%20Events,%20Returns,%20and%20Risk%20in%20Tehran%20Stock%20Exchange.pdf

Jambet, C. 1992. "The Constitution of the Subject and Spiritual Practice." In *Michel Foucault: Philosopher*. Translated by T.J. Armestrang, 241. Hemel Hempstead, UK: Harvester Wheatsheaf.

Javadi, H. 2007. "Molla Nasreddin i. the Person." Encyclopaedia Iranica. http://www.iranicaonline.org/articles/molla-nasreddin-i-the-person (accessed July 5, 2011).

Jbili, A., V. Kramarenko, and J. Bailén. 2007. *Islamic Republic of Iran: Managing the Transition to a Market Economy*. IMF, pp.1–5

Jones, S. December 11, 2009. The Islamic Republic of Iran: An Introduction. United Kingdom: Parliament, House of Commons Library, Research Paper 09/92. http://www.refworld.org/docid/4b41bca92.html (accessed December 6, 2014).

Juneau, T. 2009. "Insights into the Future of Iran as a Regional Power." *Highlights from the conference 30–31 March 2009*, Ottawa. http://publications.gc.ca/collections/collection_2013/scrs-csis/PS73-1-2009-06-2-eng.pdf

Kang, J., and H. Park-Poaps. 2010. "Hedonic and Utilitarian Shopping Motivations of Fashion Leadership." *Journal of Fashion Marketing and Management: An International Journal* 14, no. 2, pp. 312–28.

Karl, T.L. 1997. *The Paradox of Plenty: Oil Booms and Petro-State*. Berkeley, CA: University of California Press.

Kasravi, A. 1963. *Hafez Che Migooyad?* [In Persian.] Tehran.

Katouzian, H. 2004. "The Short-Term Society: A Study in the Problems of Long-Term Political and Economic Development in Iran." *Middle Eastern Studies* 40, no. 1, pp. 1–22.

Katzman, K. 1993. *The Warriors of Islam: Iran's Revolutionary Guard*. UK: Westlaw Press.

Katzman, K. January 2003. *Iran: Current Developments and US Policy*. Washington, DC: Congressional Research Service (Library of Congress).

Katzman, K. 2010. *Iran: US Concerns and Policy Responses*. Darby, PA: Diane Publishing.

Kazemi, F. 1980. *Poverty and Revolution in Iran*. New York: New York University Press.

Kazemi, F., and L.R. Wolfe. 1997. "Urbanization, Migration, and Politics of Protest in Iran." In *Population, Poverty, and Politics in Middle East Cities*, ed. E.B. Michael, 256–84. Gainesville, FL: University Press of Florida.

Keddie N.R. 1966. *Religion and Rebellion in Iran: The Tobacco Protest of 1891–1892*. London, UK: Frank Cass.

Keddie, N. 1993. "Iranian Revolutions in Comparative Perspective." In *The Modern Middle East: A Reader*, eds. A. Hourani, P.S. Khoury, and M.C. Wilson. Berkeley, CA: University of California Press.

Keddie, N. 1998. "Iran: Understanding the Enigma: A Historian's View." *Middle East* 2, no. 3, p. 2.

Keddie, N. 2003. *Modern Iran: Roots and Results of Revolution*. New Haven, CT: Yale University Press.

Keddie, N., and E. Hooglund. 1986. *The Iranian Revolution and the Islamic Republic Syracuse*. New York: Syracuse University Press.

Keddie, N.R. 2006. *Modern Iran: Roots and Results of a Revolution*, 72. New Haven, CT: Yale University Press.

Kemp, G. 1994. *Forever Enemies? American Policy and the Islamic Republic of Iran*, 42. Washington, DC: The Carnegie Endowment for International Peace.

Khajehpour, B. 2000. "Domestic Political Reforms and Private Sector Activity in Iran." *Social Research* 67, no. 2, pp. 577–609

Khajehpour, B. 2013a."Economic Scorecard for Rouhani's First 100 days." Al- Monitor: The Pulse of the Middle East. http://www.al-monitor.com/pulse/originals/2013/12/rouhani-100-days-progress-scorecard.html

Khajehpour, B. September 2013b. "The Future of the Petroleum Sector in Iran." Legatum Institute.

Khalaji, M. 2008. "Apocalyptic Politics: On the Rationality of Iranian Policy." The Washington Institute for Near East Policy (WINEP): Policy Focus. http://

www.washingtoninstitute.org/policy-analysis/view/apocalyptic-politics-on-the-rationality-of-iranian-policy

Khalaji, M. 2011. "Iran's Regime of Religion." *Journal of International Affairs* 65, no. 1, p. 131.

Khatami, M. 2003. "Foucault on the Islamic Revolution of Iran." *Journal of Muslim Minority Affairs* 23, no. 1, pp. 121–25.

Khosrokhavar, F. 2004. "The Islamic Revolution in Iran: Retrospect after a Quarter of a Century." *Thesis Eleven* 76, no. 1, pp. 70–84.

Kian-Thiébaut, A. 1998. "Secularization of Iran: A Doomed Failure?: The New Middle Class and the Making of Modern Iran." *Travaux et mémoires de l'Institut d'Etudes Iraniennes.*, Vol. 3. Paris: Peeters.

Kian-Thiebaut, A. 2005. "From Motherhood to Equal Rights Advocates: The Weakening of Patriarchal Order." *Iranian Studies* 38, no. 1, pp. 45–66.

Kinnander, E. 2010. *The Turkish-Iranian Gas Relationship: Politically Successful, Commercially Problematic.* Oxford Institute for Engergy Studies.

Kissinger, H. 2014. *World Order.* New York: Penguin.

Koshteh, K., and V. Urutyan. 2005. "Global Pistachio Production and Marketing Challenges." *Indian Journal of Economics and Business* 4, no. 1.

Kull, S. 2007. "Public Opinion in Iran and America on Key International Issues." World Public Opinion.org. http://www.worldpublicopinion.org/pipa/pdf/jan07/Iran_Jan07_rpt.pdf

Kurzman, C. 2004. *The Unthinkable Revolution in Iran*, 121. Cambridge, MA: Harvard University Press.

Ladjevardian, R. 1999. *From Ancient Persia to Contemporary Iran: Selected Historical Milestones.* Washington, DC: Mage Publishers.

Latorre, A.M. 2009. *Role of Revolutionary Leadership in Iran on Its Foreign Policy* [Doctoral dissertation]. Orlando, FL: University of Central Florida.

Lewis, B. 2014. *The Jews of Islam.* Princeton, NJ: Princeton University Press.

Lowe, R., and C. Spencer, eds. 2006. *Iran, Its Neighbours and the Regional Crises: A Middle East Programme Report.* London, UK: Chatham House.

Madanipour, A. 1998. *Tehran: The Making of a Metropolis.* New York: John Wiley and Sons.

Mahdavy, H. 1970. "The Patterns and Problems of Economic Development in Rentier States: The Case of Iran." In *Studies in the Economic History of the Middle East*, ed. M.A Cook. London, UK: Oxford University Press.

Maleki, A. 2002. "Decision Making in Iran's Foreign Policy: A Heuristic Approach." *Journal of Social Affairs* 19, no. 73, pp. 39–59.

Maleki, A. 2008. *Iranian Foreign Policy: Past, Present and Future Scenarios.* London, UK: Routledge.

Malik, K. 2013. "Human development report 2013." *The rise of the South: Human progress in a diverse world.*

Mehlum, H., K. Moene, and R. Torvik. 2006. "Cursed by Resources or Institutions?" *The World Economy* 29, no. 8, pp. 1117–31.

Mehran, G. 2003. "The Paradox of Tradition and Modernity in Female Education in the Islamic Republic of Iran." *Comparative Education Review* 47, no. 3, pp. 269–86.

Melman, Y., and M. Javedanfar. 2007. *The Nuclear Sphinx of Tehran*, 81. New York: Carroll & Graf Publishers.

Menashri D. 1992. *Education and the Making of Modern Iran*. Ithaca/London: Cornell Universsity Press.

Mernissi, F. 1987. *Beyond the Veil: Male-Female Dynamics in Modern Muslim Society*, Vol. 423. Bloomington, IN: Indiana University Press.

Metz, H.C. 1989. *Iran; a Country Study*. Washington, DC: Federal Research Division (Library of Congress).

Mining & Development. November 24, 2010. "Mines, Biggest Advantage for Long-Term Goals: Iranian Mines and Mining Industries Development and Renovation." *Organization* 4, no. 39, p. 8.

Moghadam, A. 2003. "The Shi'i Perception of Jihad." *Al Nakjlah*.

Moghadam, V. 1988. "The Left and Revolution in Iran: A Critical Analysis." In *Post-Revolutionary* Iran, eds. H. Amirahmadi and M. Parvin. Boulder, CO: Westview Press.

Motevalli, G. August 5, 2014. "IMF Says Rouhani Has Stabilized Iran's Economy." Bloomberg Business. http://www.bloomberg.com/news/2014-08-05/imf-says-rouhanihas-stabilized-iran-s-economy.html

Moslem, M. 2002. *Factional Politics in Post-Khomeini Iran*. New York: Syracuse University Press.

Mostaghim, R., and A. Sandels. 2014. "Dying Lake Urmia reflects a broader problem in Iran." Los Angeles Times. http://www.latimes.com/world/middleeast/la-fg-iran-lake-20140321-story.html

Munir, L.Z. October 14, 2003. "Islam, Modernity and Justice for Women." A paper presented at the Islam and Human Rights Fellow Lecture.

MVF Global Customer Acquisition. 2014. http://www.mvfglobal.com/iran (accessed December 12, 2014).

Najmabadi, A. 1987. "Iran's Turn to Islam: From Modernism to a Moral Order." *The Middle East Journal*, pp. 202–17.

Nanda, P. 2008. *Rising India: Friends and Foes*, ISBN 9780979617416. India: Lancer Publishers.

Naraghi E. 1992. *Enseignement et Changements Sociaux en Iran du VII° au XX° Siècle*. Paris: MSH.

Natural Gas Exports from Iran. October 2012. Iran Threat Reduction and Syria Human Rights Act. Washington, DC: U.S. Department of Energy. http://www.eia.gov/analysis/requests/ngexports_iran/pdf/full.pdf

Nomani, F., and S. Behdad. 2006. *Class and Labor in Iran: Did the Revolution Matter?* New York: Syracuse University Press.

OCHA (United Nations Office for the Coordination of Humanitarian Affairs). 2003. "Iran: Focus on Family Planning." http://www.irinnews.org/report/19627/iran-iran-focus-on-family-planning

Pahlavi, M.R. 1978. *Toward the Great Civilization.* Tehran, Iran: Satrap Publishing.

Parsa, M. 1989. *Social Origins of the Iranian Revolution.* New Brunswick, NJ/London: Rutgers University Press.

Pattberg, T. 2009. *The East-West Dichotomy,* ISBN 978-0984209101. New York: LoD Press.

Posch, W. 2009. "The European Union and Iran." The Middle East Institute. www.mideasti.org

Price, M., ed. 2005. *Iran's Diverse Peoples: A Reference Sourcebook.* Santa Barbara, CA: ABC-CLIO.

Rakel, E.P. 2008. *The Iranian Political Elite, State and Society Relations, and Foreign Relations since the Islamic Revolution* [PhD thesis]. FMG: Amsterdam Institute for Social Science Research (AISSR).

Ramazani, R.K. 1980. "Constitution of the Islamic Republic of Iran." *The Middle East Journal* 34, no. 2, pp. 181–204.

Razvi, M. 1971. *The Frontiers of Pakistan; A Study of Frontier Problems in Pakistan's Foreign Policy.* Karachi, Pakistan: National Publishing House.

Recknagel, C. 2014. "Iran Says Ready To Supply Natural Gas To Europe." *Radio Free Europe,* May 15 http://www.rferl.org/content/iran-says-ready-to-supply-natural-gas-to-europe-/25386226.htm.

Redaelli, R. 2009. "The Dichotomist Antagonist Posture in the Persian Gulf." The Middle East Institute. www.mideasti.org

Rezaian, J. 2013. "Iran's Automakers Stalled by Sanctions." *Washington Post,* October 14. http://www.washingtonpost.com/world/irans-automakers-stalled-by-sanctions/2013/10/14/515725aa-3261-11e3-ad00-ec4c6b31cbed_story.html

Richard, Y. 1991. *L'islam chi'ite: croyances et idéologies.* Paris, France: Fayard

Richard, Y. 1995. *Shi'ite Islam: Polity, Ideology, and Creed.* Oxford: Blackwell.

Richards, A. 1996. *A Political Economy of the Middle East.* New York: Perseus Books Group.

Roy, O. 1999. "The Crisis of Religious Legitimacy in Iran." *The Middle East Journal* 53, no. 2, pp. 201–16.

Sachs, G. 2005. How solid are the BRICs? Global Economics Paper No. 134.

Sachs, J., and A.M. Warner. 2001. "The Curse of Natural Resources." *European Economic Review* 45, no. 4–6, pp. 827–38.

Sadeghi, F. 2008. "Negotiating with Modernity: Young Women and Sexuality in Iran." *Comparative Studies of South Asia, Africa and the Middle East* 28, no. 2, pp. 250–59.

Sadjadpour, K. 2011. *The Battle of Dubai: The United Arab Emirates and the U.S.-Iran Cold War*. Washington, DC: Carnegie Endowment for International Peace.

Saghafi-Ameri, N. 2012. Middle East Institute. "In This Series Analysis." Middle East Institute. http://www.mideasti.org/

Salehi, M.M. 1988. *Insurgency Through Culture and Religion: The Islamic Revolution of Iran*. New York/London: Praeger.

"SAPCO: Iran Automotive Industry's Market Shares." September 2001. Wayback Machine. https://web.archive.org/web/20080617154335/http://www.atiehbahar.com/Resources/Automotive.htm (accessed November 14, 2008).

Sariolghalam, M. 2003. "Understanding Iran: Getting Past Stereotypes and Mythology." *Washington Quarterly* 26, no. 4, pp. 69–82.

Schirazi, A. 1997. *The Constitution of Iran*. London, UK: I.B. Tauris.

"Science, Technology and Innovation Policy Review: The Islamic Republic of Iran." February 2005. *United Nations Conference on Trade and Development*, UNCTAD/ITE/IPC/2005/7.

Seifzadeh, H.S. 2003. "The Landscape of Factional Politics and Its Future in Iran." *The Middle East Journal* 57, no. 1, pp. 57–75.

Semati, M. 2008. *Media, Culture and Society in Iran: Living with Globalization and the Islamic State*. London, UK: Routledge.

Shayegan, D. 2003. *Le Regard Mutilé: Schizophrénie Culturelle: Pays Traditionnels Face à la Modernité*. France: de l'Aube, La Tour d'Aigues.

Shoamanesh, S.S. November 1, 2009. "Iran is a Riddle, Wrapped in a Mystery, Inside an Enigma. But What of the Over Three Million Iranians Outside Iran?" Global Brief. http://globalbrief.ca/blog/2009/11/01/on-the-iranian-diaspora/

Shoup, L.H., and W. Minter. 1977. *Imperial Brain Trust: The Council on Foreign Relations and US Foreign Policy*, 163–64. New York: Monthly Review Press.

Simmons, M. 2005. *Twilight in the Desert: The Coming Saudi Oil Shock and the World Economy*. London: Wiley & Sons. See for instance Jim Landers, "Skeptics doubt Saudi Arabia can boost oil supply", Dallas Morning News (24 June 2008)

Skocpol, T. 1982. "Rentier State and Shi'a Islam in the Iranian Revolution." *Theory and Society* 11, no.3, pp. 265–83.

Smith, G. 1986. *Morality, Reason and Power: American Diplomacy in the Carter Years*. New York: Hill and Wang.

Sreberny-Mohammadi, A. 1990. "Small Media for a Big Revolution: Iran." *International Journal of Politics, Culture, and Society* 3, no. 3, pp. 341–71.

Stanley, W. 2006. "The Strategic Culture of the Islamic Republic of Iran." *Science Applications International Corporation* 17.

State of the Union Address. January 23, 1980. Jimmy Carter. http://www.thisnation.com/library/sotu/1980jc.html

Statistical Center of Iran. 2013. http://www.amar.org.ir/ (accessed January–November 2013).

Stauth, G. 1994. "Revolution in Spiritless Times." In *Michel Foucault: Critical Assessments*, Vol. III, ed. H. Smart, 379–401. London, UK: Routledge.

Stevens, R. 2014. "Iran's 'Revolution of Values': Living in a Theocracy." Rick Steves Europe. https://www.ricksteves.com/watch-read-listen/video/tv-show/tv-specials/iran/irans-revolution-of-values-living-in-a-theocracy (accessed November 5, 2014).

Takeyh, R. 2006. *Hidden Iran: Paradox and Power in the Islamic Republic*, 61. New York: Times Books.

Takeyh, R. 2009. *Guardians of the Revolution: Iran and the World in the Age of the Ayatollahs*, 2. New York: Oxford University Press.

Tarock, A. 1999. *Iran's Foreign Policy Since 1990: Pragmatism Supersedes Islamic Ideology*. New York: Nova Science Publishers.

Tashakkori, A., and V.D. Tompson. 1988. "Cultural Change and Attitude Change: An Assessment of Postrevolutionary Marriage and Family Attitudes in Iran." *Population Research and Policy Review* 7, no. 1, pp. 3–27.

Terhalle, M. 2007. "Are the Shia rising?" *Middle East Policy* 14, no. 2, p. 69.

"Telecoms and Technology Forecast for Iran." August 18, 2008. Economist Intelligence Unit. http://www.eiu.com/landing/industry_analysis (accessed July 6, 2009).

Thaler, D.E. 2010. *Mullahs, Guards, and Bonyads: An Exploration of Iranian Leadership Dynamics*, Vol. 878. Arlington, VA: Rand Corporation.

"The Constitution of Islamic Republic of Iran." June 17, 2015. Iran Chamber Society. http://www.iranchamber.com/government/laws/constitution.php

The Economist. November 1, 2014. "Religion Take It or Leave It: Ordinary Iranians Are Losing Interest in the Mosque." The Global Competitiveness Report 2011–2012. http://www.weforum.org/reports/global-competitiveness-report-2011-2012

The Heritage Foundation Trade Freedom Report. 2013. http://www.heritage.org

The Iranian Institute for Research and Planning in Higher Education. 2012. http://www.irphe.ac.ir/

"The Origins of the Shiite-Sunni Split." February 12, 2007. National Public Radio (NPR). http://www.npr.org/blogs/parallels/2007/02/12/7332087/the-origins-of-the-shiite-sunni-split

The Trade Promotion Organization of Iran. May 2014. "Iran's Non- Oil Exports Statistics." http://en.tpo.ir

"The Sunni-Shia Divide." 2015. Council on Foreign Relations. http://www.cfr.org/peace-conflict-and-human-rights/sunni-shia-divide/p33176#!/ (accessed March 2).

The World Bank. 2011. *Doing Business 2012: Doing Business in a More Transparent World.* Washington, DC.

Thompson Reuters. 2013. "State of the Global Islamic Economy." http://auscif.com/2013/12/02/thomson-reuters-state-of-the-global-islamic-economy-report-2013/

Toennies, F. (1887) 1963. *Community and Society.* New York: Harper & Row.

Torabi, F., and A. Baschieri. 2010. "Ethnic Differences in Transition to First Marriage in Iran: The Role of Marriage Market, Women's Socio-economic Status, and Process of Development." *Max Planck Institute for Demographic Research* 22, pp. 29–62.

Transparency International. 2010. "Corruption Perceptions Index 2010." www.transparency.org/policy_research/surveys_indices/cpi/2010/results (accessed September 11, 2010).

Trend News Agency. February 26, 2014. "U.S. Pharmaceutical Giant in Iran." http://en.trend.az/iran/2246341.html

Triandis, H.C. 1989. "The Self and Social Behavior in Differing Cultural Contexts." *Psychological Review* 96, no. 3, p. 506.

"Turkey Seeks to Build Iran Pipeline Amid Uncertain Environment." 2014. *Today' Zaman Daily,* February 09. http://www.todayszaman.com/business_turkey-seeks-to-build-iran-pipeline-amid-uncertain-environment_338859.html Turquoise Partners Report. July 2011. Iran Investment, Vol. 5, no. 58. http://www.turquoisepartners.com/iraninvestment/IIM-Jul11.pdf

U.S. Census Bureau. January 25, 2007. International Database, 2006, 2007. http://www.census.gov/ipc/www/idbnew.html

U.S. Department of State. March 6, 2007. "Iran: Bureau of Democracy, Human Rights, and Labor." http://www.state.gov/j/drl/rls/hrrpt/2006/78852.htm

U.S. Geological Survey, Mineral Commodity Summaries. February 2014. http://minerals.usgs.gov/minerals/pubs/commodity/cement/mcs-2014-cemen.pdf

United Arab Emirates. 2012. Trade Exchange Statistics. http://tradeexchange.ae

UNCTAD. February 2005. "Science, Technology and Innovation Policy Review, the Islamic Republic of Iran." UNCTAD/ITE/IPC/2005/7.

United Kingdom: Home Office. 2002. "UK Home Office Immigration and Nationality Directorate Country Assessment - Iran." http://www.refworld.org/docid/3c2b4e116.html (accessed September 21, 2014).

USGS (United States Geological Survey). 2003. *Minerals and Materials Information.* , Washington: DC: United States Department of the Interior.

Valentine, A., J.J. Nash, and L. Rice. January 2013. *The Business Year 2013: Iran.* London, UK: The Business Year.

Vazifedoost, H., P. Charsetad, M. Akbari, and A. Kaveh. 2013. "The Role of Iranian Consumers' Demographic Traits in Their Shopping Behaviors." *Journal of Applied Business and Finance Researches* 2, no. 4, pp. 97–105.

Voll, J.O., and J.L. Esposito. 1994. "Islam's Democratic Essence." *Middle East Quarterly* 1, no. 3.

Walt, S.M. 1991. "The Renaissance of Security Studies." *International Studies Quarterly* 35, no. 2, pp. 211–39.

Welzel, C., R. Inglehart, and H.D. Kligemann. 2003. "The Theory of Human Development: A Cross-cultural Analysis." *European Journal of Political Research* 42, no. 3, pp. 341–79.

"What is Ashura?" December 6, 2011. British Broadcasting Corporation (BBC). http://www.bbc.com/news/world-middle-east-16047713

"What Is Behind Success of Tehran Stock Exchange?" September 3, 2013. Al-Monitor: The Pulse of the Middle East. http://www.al-monitor.com/pulse/originals/2013/09/what-is-behind-success-of-tehran-stock-exchange.html

Windrem, R. January 26, 2007. "Are Saudis Waging an Oil-Price War on Iran?" MSNBC,.

World Bank Group. 2012. *World Development Indicators 2012*. World Bank Publications.

Yar-Shater, E., ed. 1990. *Encyclopedia Iranica*, Vol. 4. New York: Routledge and Kegan Paul.

Yates, D.A. 1996. *The Rentier State in Africa*. Trenton, NJ: African World Press.

Yazdan, G.F., V. Behzad, and M. Shiva. 2012. "Energy Consumption in Iran: Past Trends and Future Directions. *Procedia-Social and Behavioral Sciences* 62, pp. 12–17.

Yeganeh, H. and Z. Su. 2007. "Comprehending Core Cultural Orientations of Iranian Managers." *Cross Cultural Management: An International Journal* 14, no. 4, pp. 336–53.

Yeganeh, H., and D. May. 2011. "Cultural Values and Gender Gap: A Cross-National Analysis." *Gender in Management: An International Journal* 26, no. 2, pp. 106–21.

Yeganeh, H., and Z. Su. 2008. "An Examination of Human Resource Management Practices in Iranian Public Sector." *Personnel Review* 37, no. 2, pp. 203–21.

Yeganeh, H., P. Marcotte, and L. Bourdeau. 2010. "Bridging Culture and Consumer Value: Towards an Integrative Framework." *International Journal of Business and Emerging Markets* 2, no. 2, pp. 147–62.

Zabih, S. 1982. *The Mossadegh Era: Roots of the Iranian Revolution*, 149. Chicago, IL: Lake View Press.

Zawya.com. December 12, 2010. "Solar Power Plants to Replace Fossil Fuel."

Zawya Business Iintelligence Report. 2012. http://www.zawya.com/story/Iran_reaches_100_telecommunications_penetration_BMI-ZAWYA20120412035355/

Ze'evi, D. 2007. "The Present Shia-Sunna Divide: Remaking Historical Memory." Crown Center for Middle East Studies, Nisan.

Zebardast, E. 2006. "Marginalization of the Urban Poor and the Expansion of the Spontaneous Settlements on the Tehran Metropolitan Fringe. *Cities* 23. no. 6, pp. 439–54.

Zubaida, S. 1988. An Islamic State? The Case of Iran. Middle East Report, no. 153, pp. 3–7.

Index

OTHER TITLES IN THE INTERNATIONAL BUSINESS COLLECTION

Tamer Cavusgil, Georgia State; Michael Czinkota, Georgetown; and Gary Knight, Willamette University, Editors

- *China: Doing Business in the Middle Kingdom* by Stuart Strother
- *Essential Concepts of Cross-Cultural Management: Building on What We All Share* by Lawrence A. Beer
- *As the World Turns...: Observations on International Business and Policy, Going International and Transitions* by Michael Czinkota
- *Assessing and Mitigating Business Risks in India* by Balbir Bhasin
- *The Emerging Markets of the Middle East: Strategies for Entry and Growth* by Tim Rogmans
- *Doing Business in China: Getting Ready for the Asian Century* by Jane Menzies and Mona Chung
- *Transfer Pricing in International Business: A Management Tool for Adding Value* by Geoff Turner
- *Management in Islamic Countries: Principles and Practice* by UmmeSalma Mujtaba Husein
- *Burma: Business and Investment Opportunities in Emerging Myanmar* by Balbir Bhasin
- *Global Business and Corporate Governance: Environment, Structure, and Challenges* by John Thanopoulos
- *The Intelligent International Negotiator* by Eliane Karsaklian
- *As I Was Thinking....: Observations and Thoughts on International Business and Trade* by Michael R. Czinkota
- *A Strategic and Tactical Approach to Global Business Ethics, Second Edition* by Lawrence A. Beer
- *Innovation in China: The Tail of the Dragon* by William H.A. Johnson
- *Dancing With The Dragon: Doing Business With China* by Mona Chung and Bruno Mascitelli

Lightning Source UK Ltd.
Milton Keynes UK
UKHW010218271118
332995UK00015B/1780/P